MULTICULTURAL EDUCATION SERIES

James A. Banks, Series Editor

Teaching and Learning in Two
Languages: Bilingualism and Schooling
in the United States
EUGENE E. GARCÍA

Improving Multicultural Education:
Lessons from the Intergroup Education
Movement
CHERRY A. MCGEE BANKS

Education Programs for Improving
Intergroup Relations: Theory,
Research, and Practice
WALTER G. STEPHAN AND
W. PAUL VOGT, EDITORS

Walking the Road: Race, Diversity,
and Social Justice in Teacher
Education
MARILYN COCHRAN-SMITH

City Schools and the American Dream:
Reclaiming the Promise of Public
Education
PEDRO A. NOGUERA

Thriving in the Multicultural Classroom:
Principles and Practices for Effective
Teaching
MARY DILG

Educating Teachers for Diversity:
Seeing with a Cultural Eye
JACQUELINE JORDAN IRVINE

Teaching Democracy: Unity and
Diversity in Public Life
WALTER C. PARKER

The Making—and Remaking—
of a Multiculturalist
CARLOS E. CORTÉS

Transforming the Multicultural Education
of Teachers: Theory, Research, and
Practice
MICHAEL VAVRUS

Learning to Teach for Social Justice
LINDA DARLING-HAMMOND, JENNIFER FRENCH,
AND SILVIA PALOMA GARCIA-LOPEZ, EDITORS

Culture, Difference, and Power
CHRISTINE E. SLEETER

Learning and Not Learning English:
Latino Students in American Schools
GUADALUPE VALDÉS

Culturally Responsive Teaching:
Theory, Research, and Practice
GENEVA GAY

The Children Are Watching: How the
Media Teach About Diversity
CARLOS E. CORTÉS

Race and Culture in the Classroom:
Teaching and Learning Through
Multicultural Education
MARY DILG

The Light in Their Eyes: Creating
Multicultural Learning Communities
SONIA NIETO

Reducing Prejudice and Stereotyping in
Schools
WALTER STEPHAN

We Can't Teach What We Don't Know:
White Teachers, Multiracial Schools
GARY R. HOWARD

Educating Citizens in a Multicultural
Society
JAMES A. BANKS

Multicultural Education, Transformative
Knowledge, and Action: Historical and
Contemporary Perspectives
JAMES A. BANKS, EDITOR

TEACHING AND LEARNING IN TWO LANGUAGES

Bilingualism & Schooling in the United States

EUGENE E. GARCÍA

TEACHERS
COLLEGE
PRESS

Teachers College, Columbia University
New York and London

Published by Teachers College Press, 1234 Amsterdam Avenue, New York, NY 10027

Library of Congress Cataloging-in-Publication Data

García, Eugene E., 1946–
    Teaching and learning in two languages : bilingualism & schooling in the United States / Eugene E. García.
        p. cm. — (Multicultural education series)
    Includes bibliographical references and index.
    ISBN 0-8077-4537-5 (cloth) — ISBN 0-8077-4536-7 (pbk.)
    1. Education, Bilingual—United States. 2. English language—Study and teaching—United States—Foreign speakers. 3. Limited English proficient students—Education—United States. I. Title. II. Multicultural education series (New York, N.Y.)

LC3731.G35 2004
370.117—dc22

    2004062042

ISBN 0-8077-4536-7 (paper)
ISBN 0-8077-4537-5 (cloth)

Printed on acid-free paper

Manufactured in the United States of America

12 11 10 09 08 07 06 05   8 7 6 5 4 3 2 1

Contents

Series *Foreword* by James A. Banks   vii

Preface   Why This Book?   xiii

1   Who Are These Children, Their Families, and Communities?   1

   U.S. Language Diversity   4
   Immigrant Students—U.S. Schools   16
   English Acquisition and Bilingualism in the U.S. Context   20
   Conclusion   21

2   Bilingualism Is Not the Arithmetic Sum of Two Languages   23

   Bilingual Development   23
   Linguistic Development   24
   Language Choice and Code-Switching   27
   Cognition, Language, and Culture   29
   Social/Communicative Aspects   34
   Language Development Considers Ways to Use It   35
   Conclusion   38

3   Education Comes in Diverse Shapes and Forms for U.S. Bilinguals   39

   Schooling Practices: The Debate   40
   What Works: Optimal Instruction and Learning Features   44
   Dual-Language Programs   47
   Beyond Language   50
   English-Language Development in a Bilingual Program   51
   Developing "Academic" English in U.S. Bilinguals   53
   Specially Designed Academic Instruction   61
   Conclusion   62

4   Bilinguals in the United States Speak
More Than a Foreign Language   64

   Dialects and Bilingualism   64
   U.S. Indigenous Bilingual Students   69
   Bilingual/Bicultural U.S. Deaf Students   71
   Conclusion   75

5   **The Policy Debate and Related Policies Regarding
    U.S. Bilinguals**   **77**

    The Federal Courts   77
    Rights of Language-Minority Students   81
    State and Local Policies   85
    English-Only State Policies   86
    Convergence of Other State and Local Policies   88
    Federal Policy   92
    Conclusion   99

6   **Educational Reform and Schooling U.S. Bilinguals**   **100**

    An Integrated Conceptual Framework for the Instruction of U.S. Bilinguals   100
    Responsive Learning Communities   103
    The Design Study—A Responsive Bilingual Learning Community:
       Sites, Teachers, and Intervention   106
    Analysis of Writing, Creating, and Revising Writing Rubrics   114
    Conclusion   122

7   **Bilingual Student Achievement in a Reform Context**   **123**

    Sierra Madre Findings   124
    Chang Ching Findings   127
    Standardized Test Achievement Measures   136
    Teachers' Perceptions of Their Work, ALAS, and Instruction   139
    Conclusion   143
    Appendix: Additional Data for Chang Ching and Sierra Madre   146

8   **Final Thoughts Regarding Theory, Practice, and
    Policy Relevant to U.S. Bilingual Students**   **157**

    Language as a Cultural System   158
    Culture, Language, and Schooling   159
    Policy Considerations   160
    Educational Practice Implications   162
    From the General to the Specific   168
    Conclusion   169

References   **171**
Index   **187**
About the Author   **199**

Series Foreword

The nation's deepening ethnic texture, interracial tension and conflict, and the increasing percentage of students who speak a first language other than English make multicultural education imperative in the 21st century. The U.S. Census Bureau (2000) estimated that people of color made up 28% of the nation's population in 2000 and predicted that they would make up 38% in 2025 and 47% in 2050. In March 2004, the Census revised its projections and predicted that by 2050 people of color and Whites would each make up 50% of the U.S. population (El Nasser, 2004).

American classrooms are experiencing the largest influx of immigrant students since the beginning of the 20th century. About a million immigrants are making the United States their home each year (Martin & Midgley, 1999). More than 7.5 million legal immigrants settled in the United States between 1991 and 1998, most of whom came from nations in Latin America and Asia (Riche, 2000). A large but undetermined number of undocumented immigrants also enter the United States each year. The influence of an increasingly ethnically diverse population on the nation's schools, colleges, and universities is and will continue to be enormous.

Forty percent of the students enrolled in the nation's schools in 2001 were students of color. This percentage is increasing each year, primarily because of the growth in the percentage of Latino students (Martinez & Curry, 1999). In some of the nation's largest cities and metropolitan areas, such as Chicago, Los Angeles, Washington, D.C., New York, Seattle, and San Francisco, half or more of the public school students are students of color. During the 1998–1999 school year, students of color made up 63.1% of the student population in the public schools of California, the nation's largest state (California State Department of Education, 2000).

Language and religious diversity is also increasing among the nation's student population. In 2000, about 20% of the school-age population spoke a language at home other than English (U.S. Census Bureau, 2000). Harvard professor Diana L. Eck (2001) calls the United States the "most religiously diverse nation on earth" (p. 4). Most teachers now in the classroom and in teacher education programs are likely to have students from diverse ethnic, racial, language, and religious groups in their classrooms during their careers. This is true for both inner-city and suburban teachers.

An important goal of multicultural education is to improve race relations and to help all students acquire the knowledge, attitudes, and skills needed to participate in cross-cultural interactions and in personal, social, and civic action that will help make our nation more democratic and just. Multicultural education is consequently as important for middle-class White suburban students as it is for students of color who live in the inner city. Multicultural education fosters the public good and the overarching goals of the commonwealth.

The major purpose of the *Multicultural Education Series* is to provide preservice educators, practicing educators, graduate students, scholars, and policy makers with an interrelated and comprehensive set of books that summarizes and analyzes important research, theory, and practice related to the education of ethnic, racial, cultural, and language groups in the United States and the education of mainstream students about diversity. The books in the *Series* provide research, theoretical, and practical knowledge about the behaviors and learning characteristics of students of color, language-minority students, and low-income students. They also provide knowledge about ways to improve academic achievement and race relations in educational settings.

The definition of multicultural education in the *Handbook of Research on Multicultural Education* (Banks & Banks, 2004) is used in the series: Multicultural education is *"a field of study designed to increase educational equity for all students that incorporates, for this purpose, content, concepts, principles, theories, and paradigms from history, the social and behavioral sciences, and particularly from ethnic studies and women's studies"* (p. xii). In the *Series*, as in the *Handbook*, multicultural education is considered a "metadiscipline."

The dimensions of multicultural education, developed by Banks (2004b) and described in the *Handbook of Research on Multicultural Education*, provide the conceptual framework for the development of the books in the *Series*. They are: *content integration, the knowledge construction process, prejudice reduction, an equity pedagogy,* and *an empowering school culture and social structure.* To implement multicultural education effectively, teachers and administrators must attend to each of the five dimensions of multicultural education. They should use content from diverse groups when teaching concepts and skills, help students to understand how knowledge in the various disciplines is constructed, help students to develop positive intergroup attitudes and behaviors, and modify their teaching strategies so that students from different racial, cultural, language, and social-class groups will experience equal educational opportunities. The total environment and culture of the school must also be transformed so that students from diverse groups will experience equal status in the culture and life of the school.

Although the five dimensions of multicultural education are highly interrelated, each requires deliberate attention and focus. Each book in the series focuses on one or more of the dimensions, although each book deals with all of them to some extent because of the highly interrelated characteristics of the dimensions.

Worldwide migration has increased significantly within the last three decades as groups from developing nations have sought economic, political, and educational opportunities in wealthier nations. Migrant groups have greatly diversified the populations of developed nations, been a catalyst for change and innovation, fulfilled important labor needs, and created acid debates about citizenship (Banks, 2004a), minority rights, and social justice.

The language rights of indigenous language minorities and immigrant groups—and the ways in which these groups should be taught the national language—is one of the most hotly debated issues in democratic multicultural nation-states, including the United States. The language debate is contentious because of the conflicting ideologies of assimilationists and pluralists and because Americans hold divergent views about the role of diversity within the nation and about which groups should shape its present and future. Much of the debate about bilingual education and minority rights are characterized by what Rivlin (1973) calls forensic social science, in which each side states briefs and then marshals evidence to support its position. These debates in the United States have also been characterized by intense politicization and by the efforts of well-funded and powerful interest groups that promote a strong assimilationist agenda that ignores or distorts the substantial body of theory and research that indicates the ways in which students can best acquire a second language.

This book is timely and significant because the author uses a research-based, nuanced, and complex analysis to describe the ways in which students learn a second language and how schools can best facilitate the acquisition of a second language by bilingual students. García provides a comprehensive description of the theory and research on second-language teaching and learning, identifies the characteristics of effective bilingual education programs, and presents examples of school programs that exemplify these characteristics.

García depicts the vast scope and complexity of the problem of educating English language learners and sets forth a philosophical position to guide educational policy and practice that reflects democratic ideals and values. Immigrant students are the fastest-growing population in the nation's public schools. The percentage of students is U.S. public schools who speak a language other than English is growing rapidly. It doubled between 1985 and 1995, increasing from 1.5 million to 3.2 million. In 2000 English language learners made up about 20% of the student population and students of color made up 40%.

The population of both English-language learners and students of color is expected to continue to increase in the future. Students of color are projected to be the majority of the school population in 2035 (Hodgkinson, 2001).

García explains the intricate relationship among language, culture, identity, and effective instruction. He points out that language is an integral part of culture and that students learn best when their culture as well as their language is respected, affirmed, and used in instruction when they are learning a second language. García's philosophical position on second-language teaching and learning, which is grounded in research and theory, gives students the right to learn in their own language. Theory and research indicate that instruction that reflects democratic values—which is culturally responsive—best facilitates the learning of a second language, including the national language (Valdés, 2001). García's vision of second-language teaching and learning gives bilingual students and their families cultural democracy and freedom, which are essential components of a political democracy. I hope his informed, reasoned, and compassionate voice will be heeded in these highly politicized and troubled times.

James A. Banks
Series Editor

REFERENCES

Banks, J. A. (Ed.). (2004a). *Diversity and citizenship education: Global perspectives.* San Francisco: Jossey-Bass.

Banks, J. A. (2004b). Multicultural education: Historical development, dimensions, and practice. In J. A. Banks & C. A. M. Banks (Eds.), *Handbook of research on multicultural education* (2nd ed., pp. 3–29). San Francisco: Jossey-Bass.

Banks, J. A., & Banks, C. A. M. (Eds.). (2004). *Handbook of research on multicultural education* (2nd ed.). San Francisco: Jossey-Bass.

California State Department of Education (2000). Retrieved July 15, 2004 from http://data1.cde.ca.gov/dataquest

Eck, D. L. (2001). *A new religious America: How a "Christian country" has become the world's most religiously diverse nation.* New York: Harper.

El Nasser, H. (2004, March 18). Census projects growing diversity: By 2050: Population burst, societal shifts. *USA Today*, p. 1A.

Hodgkinson, H. (2001). Educational demographics: What teachers should know. *Educational Leadership*, 58(4), 6–11.

Martin, P., & Midgley, E. (1999). Immigration to the United States. *Population Bulletin*, 54(2), 1–44. Washington, DC: Population Reference Bureau.

Martinez, G. M., & Curry, A. E. (1999, September). *Current population reports: School enrollment–social and economic characteristics of students* (update). Washington, DC: U.S. Census Bureau.

Riche, M. F. (2000). America's diversity and growth: Signposts for the 21st century. *Population Bulletin, 55*(2), 1–43. Washington, DC: Population Reference Bureau.

Rivlin, A. M. (1973). Forensic social science. *Harvard Educational Review, 43*, 61–75.

U.S. Census Bureau. (2000). *Statistical abstract of the United States* (120th edition). Washington, DC: U.S. Government Printing Office.

Valdés, G. (2001). *Learning and not learning English: Latino students in American schools*. New York: Teachers College Press.

Why This Book?

The book addresses an increasingly important challenge confronted by schools in the United States: educating to high standards students from diverse language, culture, and social-class groups. Unfortunately, U.S. schools have not had success in meeting this challenge while at the same time the absolute and relative number of students whose native language is not English has grown significantly. In California, for example, over 25% of the school-age population entering school is identified as limited English Proficient (LEP), as English Language learners (ELL), or as culturally and linguistically diverse (CLD) (U.S. Census Bureau, 2000). I refer to this population of students as "bilingual" because they acquire communicative skills in at least two languages in schools.

The book takes a distinct approach in addressing issues of cultural and linguistic diversity and schooling. It confronts the educational debate regarding effective instructional practices for bilingual students but does not avoid the political and ideological debates around issues like bilingual education, English First, immigration, and assimilation, particularly as they are framed by well-known contemporary writers such as Linda Chavez, Richard Rodriguez, Rosalie Porter, Christine Rossel, and Ron Unz. These individuals have argued forcefully against the use of a student's primary language during instruction, emphasizing English-only instruction. Unz is the major force behind state propositions in California (1998), Arizona (2000), and Massachusetts (2002) that prescribe educational treatment of CLD students. A similar effort by Unz failed in Colorado in 2002.

The ongoing debate regarding the education of bilingual students has centered on the relationship between the student's native language and how that language is treated in the process of learning English. New perspectives have warned that the successful and effective education of these students must attend to processes that address more than native language issues and the teaching of English (August & Hakuta, 1997; García, 2001a, 2001b). This broader argument concludes that it is the understanding of these varied processes that will lead us to more productive educational environments in contexts in which linguistic diversity is the norm, not the exception. Specific conceptual/theoretical, educational practice, and quantitative and qualitative research will buttress this thesis in the chapters of this book.

In my book that preceded this one (García, 2001b), I made the case that education aimed at Hispanic children in the United States needed to recognize both their linguistic and cultural roots (*raíces*) as well as the educational wings (*alas*). It is my intent in this book to extend that argument to other cultural and linguistic groups that find their languages and cultures either absent from or minimally represented in their schooling. I will continue to concentrate on how primary social, cultural, linguistic, and psychological processes produce differences that are relevant to effective education within and between these students. Implicit in this understanding is that effective educational environments are not the same for all students. Linguistic and cultural diversity in students require culturally responsive educational practices that are based on our recent understandings of the "roots" of diversity and how it is related to developing strong educational "wings" for all students.

Chapter 1 of this book describes the circumstances of bilingual children. It draws on present demographic indicators to more fully explore their circumstances in the United States. It sets the stage for understanding why a discussion of education and diversity is important today. Chapter 2 addresses the linguistic and cultural attributes of the bilingual student. This foundation is critical for understanding present American society and the meaning of diversity. Chapter 3 describes the long-standing attempts by U.S. educators to identify specific instructional interventions to promote academic achievement for linguistically and culturally diverse populations. Chapter 4 expands this discussion by attending to a knowledge base regarding bilingual students who have only recently been "uncovered" in the United States. Chapter 5 addresses policy issues of significance to U.S. bilingual students.

Chapter 6 introduces discussion of conceptual/theoretical issues of significance to the education of U.S. bilingual students. The chapter provides the foundation for a specific treatment of educational reform research addressed in Chapters 7 and 8. In these chapters, a specific analysis is provided. In the mode of a "Pasteur," applied research in the form of an intervention generating new data on teaching and learning of a diverse population of U.S. bilingual students are presented.

Chapters 6 and 7 shift the emphasis from the general to the specific. Specific analyses of teachers, classrooms, schools, and communities that are making educational success a reality for bilingual students are presented. Bilingual student success is specifically identified.

Chapter 8, the concluding chapter, articulates how we can learn from these success stories about the challenges awaiting us in tomorrow's America and in the global village. These conclusions incorporate a rationale and a set of guidelines for a new conceptual framework. That new framework is built on the notion that our educational future depends on the understanding that in a diverse linguistic and cultural context, respect for the uniqueness of the individual is not enough. Instead, what must be added is the need to be educationally responsive to the culture and language in which the individual student develops and resides.

At the core of this book, as in most of my previous publications, is the notion that diversity in the United States is a resource that must be considered if the broader goal of educational success coupled with social success is to be a reality for bilingual students. I conclude that successful education for culturally and linguistically diverse students and the future of the United States as a diverse nation rest on two presuppositions:

> To honor diversity is to honor the cultural and linguistic complexity in which we live—to honor that diversity requires responding affirmatively to that cultural and linguistic diversity.

It is the intent of this book to integrate the most substantive theoretical and empirical accounts and debates that directly inform the effective educational treatment of the growing bilingual student populations in the United States. These students are characterized by the absence of proficiency in English as they enter school. This population includes a mix of students from immigrant and native/indigenous communities, including a recently recognized group of students from the deaf and hard-of-hearing community. The book is organized around a varied set of reviews of the literature and is firmly grounded in the analysis of empirical work in multilingual schools and communities. The thesis is straightforward: The implications of "acting" on these specific and conceptual understandings of linguistic and cultural diversity has led to and can lead to more responsive educational practices of significance to all students. There is no reason why this population's linguistic and cultural diversity should place them at educational risk for failure in U.S. schools.

CHAPTER 1

Who Are These Children, Their Families, and Communities?

The United States has long been a nation of incredible cultural and linguistic diversity. This trend of ethnic and racial population diversification continues most rapidly among its young and school-age children. Nationwide, White, non-Hispanic student enrollment has decreased since 1976 by 13%, or a total of 5 million students (Ovando, Collier, & Combs, 2002). As the overall total of the U.S. student population has decreased from 43 million to 41 million students (pre-K to grade 12) since 1976, the following demographic student indicators have become educationally significant:

1. Minority enrollment as a proportion of total enrollment in elementary and secondary education rose from 24% in 1976 to 40% in 2000.
2. As a proportion of total enrollment, Hispanics increased from 6.4% in 1976 to 12% in 1996. The number of Hispanic students increased from almost 3 million in 1976 to more than 4.5 million in 2000, an increase of 52%.
3. During this same period, Asian/Pacific Islander students increased from 535,000 to 1,158,000, an increase of 116% (Kendler, 2002).

The demographic transformation that has become more evident in the last decade was easily foreseen at least 10 years ago. Our future student growth is as predictable: In a mere 35 years, White students will be a minority in every category of public education as we know it today.

Unfortunately, these students, who form an emerging ethnic and racial majority, continue to be "at risk" in today's social institutions. The National Center for Children in Poverty (1990) provided a clear and alarming demographic window on these "at-risk" students. Of the 21.9 million children under 6 years of age in 1998 (who will move slowly through society's institutions—family, schools, the workplace), 5 million (25%) were living in poverty. Although less than 30% of all children under 6 years of age were non-White, over 50% of the children in poverty were non-White. In addition, these children continue to live in racial/ethnic isolation. Some 56% lived in racially isolated neighborhoods in 1966; 72% resided in such neighborhoods in 1998; 61% of these children live in concentrations of poverty, where 20% of the population is poor.

High school completion rates are alarming for these student populations. In 1998, the high school completion rate for the U.S. population was 81.1% for 19-year-olds, 86.5% for 24-year-olds, and a very respectable 86% for 29-year-olds. For Blacks and Hispanics, the rate of completion in all age groups was close to 60% (U.S. Department of Education, 1998). In 2001, 30% of 13-year-old students were one grade level below the norm on standardized achievement tests. However, this differed significantly for emerging majority and White students: 27% for White students, 40% for Hispanic students, and 46% for Black students.

Much more eloquent than any quantitative analyses of this situation is a recent letter from a new high school English teacher in Los Angeles to a former colleague:

> Hi . . .
>
> Here's the report from the Western Front. Please pass it around.
>
> What I initially perceived to be innovative use of year-round scheduling seems to be more mechanization run amok. Although they apparently were able to split the kids into three separate tracks with different vacations with little or no problem, the track system has virtually NO academic benefit, at least the way it operates here. There are about 600 9th and 10th graders per track and about 200 11th and 12th graders per track. Look at the dropout rate (near 50% if not more). And the school just received a 3-year accreditation rather than 7-year so things are pretty bad.
>
> In short, this school and school district are nightmares.
>
> Reading and writing levels are grotesque. I have only four students who are operating above grade level who could function in an honors program. That's out of 150 on the rolls.
>
> The dress code is not enforced . . . gangster wear is the norm, not the exception . . . and the administration, besides making occasional announcements, does nothing . . . thus none of the teachers care to stir the pot by even trying to enforce dress codes. Tardies are not enforced. This is LA and despite that kids are wandering through the halls and all over the campus all the time. There is one computer lab for Math, four or five computers in the library and that's about it. The textbooks left for me to use were 1980 copyright 10th grade lit books, and there were only enough for a classroom set. And, of course, all except one of the short stories was about teenage white (male) characters, and these kids Just Don't Relate to that. Plus, despite this being a major ESL school, no

supplementary resources "enrichment" materials exist that I can find that contain black or brown or multi-national short stories or poems. . . . They do know the main players in the OJ drama, but one must be careful here when making allusions to that. The Maya Angelou books were in pieces. The book accountability procedures here are non-existent.

There is one counselor per 1,000 students, an ESL program for half the students that doesn't seem to be upticking tests scores or achievement. Half the kids don't bring ANYTHING to school let alone pens and paper; forget assigning homework. I have 21 students with perfect attendance and no discipline problems. Half of them turn in work that is perhaps 4th or 5th grade level; the others don't turn in anything at all. But they are all there every day. I asked other teachers what to do about grades. Well, if they make it every day, pass them with a D even if they don't do anything. Other kids I see one day and then don't see them again for two weeks. The sixth period English class has 37 students on the roll and I have an average of 14–17 in daily regular attendance.

There are few AP classes but few students pass the tests. Kids who miss school for field trips and football games are not listed on an excuse sheet nor is there any other official notification. They just tell you they were on a field trip and you mark the grade book accordingly. I guess.

Very few—perhaps 10%—of the kids are black and so far the only white kids are from Armenia or Russia with the occasional native white kids spotted here and there.

I asked the Union Steward if all the schools were as screwed up as this one. He said that he has taught only here but that he hears it is the same way—but the sad thing is that it doesn't have to be that way. Indeed. The English teachers here are solid, intelligent and superb. But they all tell me to forget everything I know and just do the best you can with what tools you have and forget how it could be. The faculty has rich experience, but I have never seen so many good ideas from attendance to technology disappear into such a black hole of central administrative and school administrative ennui.

These kids are sweet. What lives they have led. So many are from El Salvador, fleeing the government violence. The native speakers are incredibly poor, but sweet kids. One kid, who works harder than any kid I have ever seen, literally just got off the boat from Korea in August. Another kid, from El Salvador, is as bright as the brightest I ever had . . . I would give anything to get that kid out of here . . . I have had the weird experience of having collaborative group work on short stories conducted in spoken languages other than English and then each group reports back to the entire class in English. But kids are kids. It's too bad this system here just processes them through, like the Pink Floyd mechanized conveyor belt "We don't need no education" song, but on a bad drug trip. (J. L. Walters, personal communication, 2000)

U.S. LANGUAGE DIVERSITY

The United States is beginning to realize its "new diversity," as the total number of students officially identified as, in the nationally derived legislative term of 1966, limited English proficient (LEP) increases (Wiese & García, 2001). Here and elsewhere these same students are referred to as language minority (LM), linguistically and culturally diverse (LCD), culturally and linguistically diverse (CLD), and/or English-language learners (ELLs). I will also refer to these students as "bilingual," because they are learning at least two languages in U.S. schools. Throughout my research in U.S. schools related to students who begin school unable to speak English (García, 1994, 1999, 2001a), I have found that the one attribute of these students that distinguishes them from others is bilingualism. Admittedly, some of these students are more proficient/fluent than others in each language, but all attain the capability of utilizing two formally recognized language systems as a result of the education they are receiving. This is the case even if instruction in the student's native language is ignored or even discouraged in the schooling process.

The book discusses an increasingly important challenge confronted by U.S. schools: educating to high standards students from diverse language, culture, and social class groups—these bilingual students. Unfortunately, our schools have not had success in meeting this challenge, while at the same time the absolute and relative numbers of students whose native language is not English have grown significantly. However, at the core of this book is the notion that linguistic and cultural diversity in the United States is a resource, not a problem.

The recent debate regarding the future education of bilingual students has centered on the relationship between the student's native language and how that language is treated in the process of learning English. New perspectives have warned that the successful and effective education of bilingual students must attend to processes that address more than native-language issues and the teaching of English. It is the understanding of these processes that will lead to more productive educational environments in contexts where diversity is the norm, not the exception. Specific concepts, practices, and research will buttress this thesis in this book.

Who Are These Bilingual Students?

What is surprising is that the 2000 U.S. Census reports that close to 10 million (9,774,099—see Table 1.1) 5- to 17-year-olds in the United States, about 20% of the school-age population, speak a language other than En-

Table 1.1. Population Speaking a Language Other Than English

	50 States and Washington D.C.
Speak only English	43,316,237
Speak Spanish	6,830,100
Speak other Indo-European languages	1,445,063
Speak Asian and Pacific Island languages	1,158,936
Speak other languages	345,667
Total 5 to 17 years	53,096,003

Source: U.S. Dept. of the Census, Brief Report/01. January 2001.

glish at home. This is a significant increase of about 40% from the 1990 U.S. Census (U.S. Census Bureau, 2001). As Table 1.1 indicates, this population is heavily Spanish-speaking, followed by speakers of other Indo-European (German, French, Italian, etc.) and Asian and Pacific Island language. This linguistic diversity will likely continue into the foreseeable future (Crawford, 1999; Garcia, 2001b).

Since 1990–1991, yearly increases in the number of bilingual students have averaged 8%. Based on U.S. Department of Education data (which are not exhaustive, since not all states are required to report such data), the number of these students over the past 10 years is as shown in Table 1.2.

Bilingual students are not distributed equally across the states. States with the largest numbers of enrollments for 2000–2001 are shown in Table 1.3.

The challenge of educating students learning English is widespread throughout the nation, with 46.3% of the schools reporting having bilingual students. For some school districts, the enrollment of bilinguals has

Table 1.2. Total Number of Bilingual Students Enrolled in U.S. Schools

School Year	Enrollment	% Increase from Prior Years
2000–01	4,584,946	32.2%
1998–99	3,038,000	15.9%
1994–96	2,735,000	7.9%
1992–93	2,430,000	10.5%
1990–91	2,199,000	2.0%

Source: U.S. Department of Education, 2002. Survey of the States' Limited English Proficient students and available Programs and Services: 2001 Survey Report.

Table 1.3. Distribution of Bilingual Enrollment Nationally in Selected States

State	Enrollment	% of Total
California	1,511,646	25.0%
Texas	570,022	14.0%
New York	239,097	8.3%
Florida	254,517	10.7%
Illinois	140,528	6.9%
Arizona	135,248	15.0%
New Mexico	63,755	19.9%
Washington	58,455	5.8%
New Jersey	52,890	4.3%
Colorado	59,018	8.1%
SUBTOTAL	3,085,176	

Source: U.S. Department of Education, 2002. Survey of the states' Limited English Proficient student and available Programs and Services. 2001 summary Report.

had a particularly strong impact. For these districts, the challenge to address the needs of students learning English is particularly urgent. Although it is generally known that many schools in the southwestern states have high levels of bilingual student enrollments, a surprising percentage of schools in southern states as well as parts of New England are also serving large populations of bilingual students. The regional distribution of schools with bilingual students indicates that ensuring a high-quality education for all children cannot be a concern of only a few states with particular ethnic groups.

These data indicate the reality that school districts in all regions of the nation are confronting the challenge of educating bilingual students. Providing students with a quality education is a national issue to which critical resources and attention are devoted. Moreover, according to data from the National Center for Educational Statistics (2000) on school size, poverty, and bilingual student enrollments, the most difficult conditions converge on a set of schools with specific characteristics. The 100 districts with the largest number of poor children house over 40% more children per school building than the nation's average. The nation's average number of students per school in public elementary and secondary schools was approximately 511; the average was 713 for these 100 districts. In addition, schools where 20% or more of the students receive free or reduced-price lunches are twice as likely to have bilingual students as those that have less than 20% eligible for such lunches. Seven out of 10 schools with minority enrollments of 20% or more have bilingual students, while only 3 in 10 schools with less than 20% minority enrollment have bilingual students.

The Council of Great City Schools (CGCS) (2000), a national organization of large urban districts, also reports high levels of bilingual student populations. This CGCS report indicates that large absolute and relative numbers of ELL students are found throughout the nation's urban schools. However, over half of these urban districts are in California. Districts in Texas are a distant second with regard to this demographic reality (see Table 1.3). As with high levels of students in poverty, large concentrations of bilingual students present a particular challenge for urban school.

A closer look is warranted for the most impacted state, California, which continues to lead the nation in absolute and relative numbers of bilingual students. Table 1.4 provides a summary of this demographic reality, with special attention to the overall distribution of bilingual students generally and Spanish-speaking bilingual students in particular. The table reflects the state's identification of bilingual students as limited English proficient or fluent English Proficient (FEP), based on a yearly state English language examination (California English Language Development Test—CELDT) required of each student in the state. As the table indicates, close to 1.2 million K–5 bilingual students attend the state's schools, reflecting 41% of the total state student population. The clear majority of these bilingual students, some 1 million, are classified as limited in their English proficiency. Surprisingly, 35% of the students in grades 6–12 are also bilingual, with an even distribution between LEP and FEP classifications. As in other states, Spanish-speaking students make up the majority of this sector of the student population. Over 80% of California bilingual students are Spanish-speaking.

California has not ignored this large and growing population of students in its schooling efforts and related policies. The state leads the nation in identifying and implementing curricula and instruction that are specific to this student group. Table 1.5 briefly outlines the types of programs in place. Moreover, the preparation of teachers to serve in California schools has attempted to address the educational needs of these students. In later chapters, I will discuss these efforts. I raise them here to reiterate the larger conclusion that as bilingual students grow within a state and nation, educational attention is drawn to their significant presence.

Immigration as a Variable in Understanding Bilingual Students

The experience of immigration is not new to generations of Americans. However, for bilingual students, it has and continues to be an ongoing

Table 1.4. California Bilingual and Spanish-Speaking Enrollment by Grade Level, 2001

	Limited English Proficient (EL)		Fluent English Proficient (FEP)		Bilingual Total		Total Enrollment
	Number	Percent of Total Enrollment	Number	Percent of Total Enrollment	Number	Percent of Total Enrollment	Number
ALL STUDENTS							
Grade K–5	907,379	32%	257,409	9%	1,164,788	41%	2,836,042
Grade 6–12	515,529	18%	498,363	17%	1,013,892	35%	2,916,775
Ungraded	19,784	22%	2,591	3%	22,375	25%	91,294
Total	1,442,692	25%	758,363	13%	2,201,055	38%	5,844,111
SPANISH-SPEAKING BILINGUAL STUDENTS							
Grade K–5	759,845	60%	160,115	13%	919,960	73%	1,262,243
Grade 6–12	403,531	36%	316,883	29%	720,414	65%	1,107,629
Ungraded	18,177	43%	2,104	5%	20,281	48%	42,187
Total	1,181,553	49%	479,102	20%	1,660,655	69%	2,412,059
(% of all students)	*(82%)*		*(63%)*		*(75%)*		*(41%)*

Source: California State Department of Education. (2001). *Language Census Summary Statistic, 1998–99* (Sacramento: Author).

Table 1.5. Descriptive Summary of Instructional/Program Alternatives

	Sheltered Instruction in English	Newcomer Program	Transitional Bilingual	Developmental Bilingual	Dual Language
Language goals	Academic English proficiency	English proficiency	Transition to all-English instruction	Bilingualism	Bilingualism
Cultural goals	Understanding of and integration into mainstream American culture	Understanding of and integration into mainstream American culture	Understanding of and integration into mainstream American culture	Integration into mainstream American culture and maintenance of home/heritage culture	Maintenance/integration into mainstream American culture and appreciation of other culture
Academic goals	Same as district/program goals for all students	Varied	Same as district/program goals for all students	Same as district/program goals for all students	Same as district/program goals for all students
Student characteristics	Limited or no English; some programs mix native and non-native English speakers	Limited or no English; low level literacy; recent arrival; variety of language/cultural backgrounds	Limited or no English; all students have same L1; variety of cultural backgrounds	Limited or no English; all students have same L1; variety of cultural backgrounds	Native English speakers and students with limited or no English; variety of cultural backgrounds
Grades served	All grades (during transition to English)	K–12; most prevalent at middle/high school levels	Primary and elementary grades	Elementary grades	K–8, preferably K–12
Entry grades	Any grade	Most students enter in middle or high school	K, 1, 2	K, 1, 2	K, 1
Length of student participation	Varied: 1–3 years or as needed	Usually 1 to 3 semesters	2–4 years	Usually 6 years (+K), preferably 12 years (+K)	Usually 6 years (+K), preferably 12 years (+K)
Participation of mainstream teachers	Yes; preferable if mainstream teachers have training in SI	Yes; mainstream teachers must have training in SI	Yes; mainstream teachers must have training in SI	No; stand-alone program with its own specially trained teachers	Yes; mainstream teachers with special training
Teacher qualifications	Often certified ESL or bi-lingual teachers and content teachers with SI training; preferably bilingual	Regular certification; training in SI; preferably bilingual	Bilingual certificate	Bilingual-multicultural certificate; bilingual proficiency	Bilingual/immersion certification; bilingual proficiency; multicultural training
Instructional materials, texts, visual aids	In English with adaptations; visuals; realia; culturally appropriate	In L1 or in English with adaptations	In L1 and English; English materials adapted to students' proficiency levels	In L1 and English; English materials adapted to students' proficiency levels	In minority language and English, as required by curriculum of study

Adapted from: Boyson, B., Ceppi, A., Christian, D., Collier, V., Echevarria, J., Goldenberg, C., et al. (1999). *Program Alternatives for Linguistically Diverse Students.* In F. Genesee (Ed.), *Center for Research on Education, Diversity, & Excellence.* EPR1, 3. Santa Cruz: University of California, Santa Cruz.

experience with particular attributes that influence present generations of immigrants as well as important lingering effects for second and third generations. Educationally, Eddie Ruth Hutton described the essence of such an experience for first-generation Mexican immigrants back in 1942:

> Manuel Segovia, Esperanza Guadarrama, Cheepe Ochoa, Tibursio Torres, Mariá Carrión. Strange names these and a hundred others representing the hundreds of strange boys and girls—first-generation Mexicans whom [sic] each year enter the high schools of the Southwest not speaking English. Most of these children come from the poorer homes in which diet and health are given little consideration. They are torn between the conflicting social customs instilled in them by their Mexican parents and those imposed upon them by a new society. They are apologetic for the peculiarities of their families, yet fearful of the alien social order in which they find themselves. (Hutton, 1942, p. 3)

This experience has changed very little for today's generation of Mexican immigrants and for many other immigrants. Lucas (1997) characterizes the experience of these first-generation immigrants, particularly school-age children, as manifested in confronting a set of critical transitions. Most U.S. students undergo a set of important and critical transitions: from home to school and from childhood to adolescence. Immigrant children move through these same critical transitions as well as those associated with transitioning to a new culture and language. How the individual confronts and moves through these transitions, individually and collectively, is the focus of the following discussion.

The U.S. Census Bureau conducts the Current Population Survey (CPS), the primary purpose of which is to collect employment data on a continuous basis. The March 2000 CPS includes an extra-large sample of Hispanics and is considered the best source for information on persons born outside of the United States—referred to as *foreign-born* by the Census Bureau, though, in the text that follows, *foreign-born* and *immigrant* are used synonymously. Analysis of the March 2000 CPS done by the Center for Immigration Studies (Camarota, 2001) indicates that 28.4 million immigrants now live in the United States, the largest number ever recorded in U.S. history and a 43 percent increase since 1990. As a percentage of the population, immigrants now account for close to 11% of U.S. residents, the highest percentage in 70 years (Garcia, 2001a).

In his summary of findings from the CPS report, Camarota (2001) concludes:

- More than 1.2 million legal and illegal immigrants combined now settle in the United States each year.
- The number of immigrants living in the United States has more than tripled since 1970, from 9.6 million to 28.4 million. As a percentage of the U.S.

population, immigrants have more than doubled, from 4.7 percent in 1970 to 10.4 percent in 2000.

- By historical standards, the number of immigrants living in the United States is unprecedented. Even at the peak of the great wave of the early 20th century immigration, the number of immigrants living in the United States was less than half what it is today (13.5 million in 1910).
- Immigration has become the determinate factor in population growth. The 11.2 million immigrants who indicated they arrived between 1990 and 2000 plus the 6.4 million children born to immigrants in the United States during the 1990s are equal to almost 70 percent of U.S. population growth over the last 10 years.
- The percentage of immigrants without a high school diploma is 30 percent, more than three times the rate for natives. Also, of all persons without a high school education, one-third are now immigrants.
- The poverty rate for immigrants is 50 percent higher than that of natives, with immigrants and their U.S.-born children (under age 21) accounting for 22 percent of all persons living in poverty.
- Immigration accounts for virtually all of the national increase in public school enrollment over the last two decades. In 2000, there were 8.6 million school-age children from immigrant families in the United States. (Camarota, 2001, p. 5)

Historical Comparisons. While immigration has played an important role in American history and schooling, the level of immigration and the size of the immigrant student population has varied considerably. The 28.4 million immigrants residing in the United States in 2000 are the most ever recorded. After growing in the early part of the 20th century, the immigrant population stabilized at around 10 or 11 million for about four decades. From the mid-1960s to the 1990s, a sudden wave of increases occurred, about 300,000 yearly in the 1960s and 800,000 yearly in the 1990s. As a result, between 1970 and 1980 the number of immigrants living in the United States grew by a record 4.5 million (U.S. Census Bureau, 2000).

The foreign-born population's growth rate since 1970 is higher than at any other time in U.S. history, far surpassing growth at the beginning of the 20th century. Between 1900 and 1910, the immigrant population grew by 31%, less than the 47% increase in the 1970s, the 40% increase in the 1980s, and the 43% growth in the 1990s (U.S. Census, 2000). Additionally, immigrants now account for a much larger share of the increase in the total U.S. population (Camarota, 2001). For most of the last century, the growth in the immigrant population accounted for little or none of the increase in the size of the U.S. population. Even during the first decade of the last century, when immigration was an important part of population growth, the immigrant contribution to U.S. population growth was much less than it is today.

The 3.2 million increase in the size of the immigrant population between 1900 and 1910 accounted for only 20% of the total increase in the U.S. population. In contrast, the 8.6 million increase in the immigrant population from 1990 to 2000 accounted for 34% of U.S. population growth in the 1990s (U.S. Census, 2000). Immigration accounts for such a large percentage of the population because the fertility of nonimmigrants was much higher in the early 1900s. As a result, the population grew regardless of immigration. Today, the nonimmigrant populations have only about two children on average, with the result that immigration now accounts for a very large share of population growth. Also in contrast to the past, a much higher percentage of today's immigrants remain in the United States rather than returning home. Because so many immigrants in the early 20th century eventually returned to their home countries, immigration at that time did not add permanently to the overall size of U.S. population in the way that it does today.

Significantly, the increase in immigration was an important factor in the overall U.S. population growth between 1990 and 2000 (Garcia, 2002). The 8.6 million increase in the size of the immigrant population between 1990 and 2000 is equal to approximately one-third of total U.S. population growth over this period. The impact of immigration on population growth is even larger (40%) if births to immigrants who arrived in the 1990s are added to the growth of the foreign-born population. If births to all immigrant women during the 1990s, including those who arrived prior to 1990, are added to the growth in the immigrant population, then immigration is equal to almost 59% of population growth.

Therefore, in terms of the impact of immigrants on the United States, both the percentage of the population made up of immigrants and the number of immigrants are clearly important. Moreover, 28.4 million immigrants, including a large percentage of school-age children, are having an enormous effect on the socioeconomic life of the United States.

State Data. California has the largest immigrant population; New York, the state with the next-largest number of immigrants, has fewer than half as many. Only a few states represented the vast majority of the foreign-born population. The nearly 8.8 million immigrants in California account for 30.9% of the nation's total immigrant population, followed by New York (12.8%), Florida (9.8%), Texas (8.6%), New Jersey (4.3%), and Illinois (4.1%). Despite having only 39.3% of the nation's total population, these six states account for 70.5% of the nation's immigrant population (Garcia, 2001a). A comparison of the 1990 Census counts of the immigrant population with the 2000 CPS indicates that the states that had large immigrant populations in 1990 continue to account for most of the growth in the immigrant population, but with substantial growth in the foreign-born populations in such states as Arizona, Colorado, North Carolina, and Nevada (Camarota, 2001). In New York, New Jersey, Massachusetts, Illinois, and California, it appears that absent immigration, these states might have declined in population or experienced little population growth. This is because there is a significant out-migration of nonimmigrants from these states.

Region and Country of Origin. Mexico accounts for 27.7% of all immigrants to the United States (7.9 million people), more than the number of immigrants from any other part of the world. Immigrants from Mexico, Central and South America, the Caribbean, and East Asia make up the majority of immigrants, with 69% of the foreign-born coming from these areas. For immigrants who arrived in the 1990s, these regions account for 71.2% of the foreign-born. Sub-Saharan Africa and Europe make up a relatively small portion of the immigrant population, accounting for only 17.1% of all immigrants and 13.8% of immigrants who arrived in the 1990s (Camarota, 2001).

Since 1970, Mexico has sent five times as many immigrants as the combined total for China, Taiwan, and Hong Kong. Latin American, Caribbean, and East Asian countries dominate the list of immigrant-sending countries, accounting for 14 of the top 20 since 1970.

Characteristics of Immigrants

While there is some variation, the percentage of immigrants in most states who are citizens falls near the national average of 40%. As a share of all eligible voters in each state, immigrants vary significantly: in California, immigrants account for 15.7% of eligible voters; in New York, 11.8%; in Florida, 10.8%; in Texas, 5.6%; in New Jersey, 9%; in Illinois, 5.2%; in Massachusetts, 6.5%; and in Arizona, 6%. Research indicates that some immigrants, primarily those from Mexico and Central America, tend to report that they are naturalized citizens when in fact they are resident aliens. Thus, the actual citizenship rate of immigrants is likely to be somewhat overstated in the CPS (Camarota, 2001).

The percentage of immigrants and their U.S.-born children (under age 21) who live in or near poverty, with "near poverty" defined as income less than 200 percent of the poverty threshold, differs significantly by state. However, immigrants and their U.S.-born children have much higher rates of poverty and near poverty than nonimmigrants, with the exception of those in Illinois. As a share of all persons in or near poverty, immigrants and their children account for more than one-half of the poor and near poor in California; roughly one-third in New York, Florida, and Arizona; 27% in Texas; and 29.3% in New Jersey.

With the exception of Illinois, immigrant household participation in federal or state welfare programs is higher than that of nonimmigrants in every state, accounting for a very significant percentage of welfare caseloads. In California, immigrant households account for 42.2% of all households using at least one major welfare program; in New York, 31.8%; in Florida, 26.4%; in Texas, 21.8 %; in New Jersey, 23.7%; in Illinois, 10.2%; and in Arizona, 26.6% (Garcia, 2001a). While higher than the rate of natives in almost every state, it is important to note that there is no state in which a majority of immigrant households are on welfare (Camarota, 2001).

While Los Angeles and New York have the largest immigrant populations, Miami ranks first in terms of the percentage of immigrants. Joined by Washington–Baltimore, Dallas, and Chicago, these six metropolitan areas account for nearly 53% of all immigrants living in the United States but only 23.1% of the nation's entire population (Camarota, 2001). These six cities continue to attract a large share of new immigrants. Of immigrants who arrived in the 1990s, 48.7% settled in these six metropolitan areas.

All six metro areas grew significantly in population during the 1990s. If we compare the population growth figures to the number of immigrants who arrived in the 1990s, it is clear that immigration played a very large role in the population growth of all six metro areas. Even in the Washington–Baltimore corridor, the number of immigrants who arrived in the 1990s (348,000) was equal to almost half of the 701,000-person increase in the area's total population (Camarota, 2001). If the 175,000 children born to immigrant parents in the Washington–Baltimore metropolitan area during the 1990s are added to the number of immigrants who arrived in the 1990s, then immigration is equal to almost 75% of this area's population growth.

Immigrants are much more likely than nonimmigrants to live in central cities. In 2000, 44.8% of immigrants lived in the nation's central cities compared to 26.2% of nonimmigrants (Garcia, 2001b). But contrary to the general impression, most immigrants do not live in the nation's central cities. In fact, immigrants are just as likely as nonimmigrants to live in the suburbs. The primary difference between the two groups is that nonimmigrants are much more likely to live in rural areas while immigrants are more likely to live in central cities. (Camarota, 2001).

Immigration today is part of an increasingly transnational phenomenon based on borderless economies, new communication technologies, and new systems of mass transportation. In recent years anthropologists, not always with robust data or analytical rigor, have been arguing that the "new immigrants" are key actors in a new transnational stage (Portes, 1996; Suarez-Orozco, 1997). Today, there is much more massive back-and-forth movement between nations—not only of people but also of goods, information, and symbols—than ever before. Compared to many Hispanic immigrants today, the European immigrants of the last century simply could not maintain the level and intensity of contact with the "old country" that is now possible. Furthermore, the ongoing characteristics of Hispanic immigration to the United States constantly "replenishes" social practices and cultural models that would otherwise tend to ossify. In certain areas of the Southwest and Southeast, Hispanic immigration is generating a powerful infrastructure dominated by a growing Spanish-speaking mass media, new market dynamics, and new cultural identities.

Culturally, immigrants significantly reshape the ethos of their new communities. This is perhaps the hardest aspect of immigration for nonimmigrant citizens. For various psychosocial reasons, immigrants are, inevitably, active agents of change. We know much more—empirically and theoretically—about how the process of immigration changes immigrants than about how immigrants change their host communities. But there is little doubt that they do so. In large cities like Los Angeles and small communities like Watsonville, California, a Sunday afternoon walk through some local parks resembles the same walk (sights, sounds, food, play, etc.) in Mexico City or Guadalajara.

Another feature of the new immigration to the United States is that immigrants today are entering a nation that is economically, socially, and culturally unlike the country which absorbed—however ambivalently—previous waves of immigrants. Economically, the previous waves of immigrants arrived on the eve of the great industrial expansion in which immigrant workers and consumers played a key role. Immigrants today are part of a thoroughly globalized economy. Some theorists have argued that an important feature of the new economic landscape is its increasing "pyramid" shape (Portes, 1996). High-skilled immigrants are moving into well-paid, knowledge-intensive industries at an unprecedented rate (Waldinger & Bozorgmehr, 1996). Meanwhile low-skilled immigrants may be locking themselves into the low-wage sector in large numbers. More than one scholar, including Suarez-Orozco, has argued that, unlike the low-skilled industry jobs of yesterday, the kind of jobs typically available to low-skilled new immigrants today do not offer prospects of upward mobility (Portes, 1996). This may have important implications for the long-term social mobility of large numbers of immigrants and their children.

Another feature of immigration today is the increasingly segregated concentration of large numbers of immigrants in a handful of regions. Waldinger and Bozorgmehr (1996) have argued that as a result of the increasing segmentation of the economy and society, many low-skilled new immigrants "have become more, not less, likely to live and work in environments that have grown increasingly segregated from whites" (p. 20).

Yet another way the new immigrant experience seems incommensurable with earlier patterns relates to the cultural ethos today's immigrants encounter. New immigrants are entering U.S. society at a time when what we might term a "culture of multiculturalism" permeates the public space. Certainly, a century ago there were no major cultural models celebrating "ethnic pride." Nathan Glazer said it all in the wonderfully sarcastic title of his latest book, *We Are All Multiculturalists Now*. Some observers are afraid that these new cultural models and social practices tend to undermine "old-fashioned" assimilation, American style (Chavez, 1995).

It is, however, far from clear how the new "culture of multiculturalism" will affect, if at all, the long-term adaptations of immigrants and, especially, their children. Employers in Miami, with its large concentration of Spanish speakers, have trouble finding competent office workers with the ability to function in professional Spanish (Fradd, 1997). The issue of course is that immigrant children today are likely to rapidly learn English—or a version of it anyway—*while* they lose their mother tongue (Snow, 1997).

IMMIGRANT STUDENTS—U.S. SCHOOLS

In 2001 the U.S. Department of Education reported that the number of children in public schools had grown by nearly 8 million in the last two decades (García, 2001b). While it has been suggested that this increase is the result of the children of baby boomers reaching school age, it is clear from the CPS that immigration policy explains the growth in the number of children in public schools (García, 2001b). The same data indicate that 8.6 million school-age children (ages 5 to 17) are first-generation immigrants. While fewer than one-third of the 8.6 million children are immigrants themselves, the children of immigrants account for such a large percentage of the school-age population because a higher proportion of immigrant women are in their childbearing years and immigrants tend to have more children than nonimmigrants. In addition, the effect of immigration on public schools will be even larger in the coming years because 17.6% of children approaching school age have immigrant mothers.

An increasingly diverse student population is entering the schools at the same time as a record number of students in general (the baby-boom echo, a term used by demographers referring to children of the original baby boomers) are entering school. In the fall of 1996, over 51 million children entered school—a new national record (García, 1999). The Department of Education predicts that the numbers of students enrolled in school will not level off until 2006, when they reach 54.6 million, almost 3 million more than in 1996. The greatest increase over the next decade will be in high school enrollments, projected to increase by 15%. Thus, schools already struggling with the influx of immigrant students are also facing the strains of high overall enrollments.

The term *immigrant* includes only those students (including refugees) born outside the United States. Because of restrictive immigration laws, most new arrivals in the nineteenth century through the first half of the twentieth were from Europe. Following important changes in America's immigration laws in the mid-1960s, however, this pattern changed dramatically, contributing to a new period of large-scale immigration that shows no signs of abating soon. Immigrants to the United States now come from all over the globe, with the nations of Asia and Latin America supplanting those of Europe as primary sources of new arrivals.

Ruiz-de-Velasco and Mix (2000) report that in 1997 20% of school-age children in U.S. schools were children of at least one immigrant parent, a share that tripled between 1970 and 1997. Of these students, 40% are bilingual. This same analysis confirms that there is a decline in bilingual students across generations, with some 10% of them falling in the third-generation category (Ruiz-de-Velasco & Mix, 2000). However, bilingual status among second- and third-generation students varies across immigrant group. For example, Mexican immigrant students are twice as likely to be bilingual as Asian immigrant students. In general, the continued extensive presence of bilingual students in the United States is driven primarily by ongoing immigration and bilingual status among some groups that extends beyond the first generation.

There are two very important dimensions to this new pattern of immigration that are related to educational issues. First, recent immigrants are simultaneously more educated and less educated than native-born Americans—a higher percentage of immigrants than native-born Americans have a bachelor's or graduate degree, while a higher percentage of immigrants also have not completed high school (Ruiz-de-Velasco & Mix, 2000). Second, recent immigrants with high levels of education are disproportionately from several nations in East and South Asia, while those with little schooling are largely from a number of Latin American countries. This is of great significance educationally. Children from families in which the parents have a great deal of education tend to achieve at much higher levels in school than children from families in which the parents have little formal schooling (Rumbaut, 1997). Low levels of educational attainment are especially consequential for Mexican immigrants. They represent our largest immigrant group and one of the least well educated.

The large differences in education levels among immigrant groups are clearly illustrated in 2000 census data (Ruiz-de-Velasco & Mix, 2000). Among 25- to 29-year-old immigrants (a segment that includes many families with preschool or school-age children), 43% of the Asians had a bachelor's degree or more, while only 12% had less than a high school diploma. In contrast, just 4% of the young adult immigrants from Mexico had a college degree, while 62% had not completed high school. These percentages were 12% and 33%, respectively, for other Hispanic young adult immigrants (Garcia, 2001a).

Valdes (1996, 1998) studied Hispanic immigrant families and the schooling of their children. In the larger study, Valdes (1996) focused on two males and two females. Her study took place during a 2-year period and involved three middle schools, four newly arrived Latino focal children and their classmates, four different English-language teaching specialists (ESL teachers), and numerous subject-matter teachers who had the focal children in class. The study also involved interviews with school personnel, the students themselves, and their parents. Part of the study's purpose was to examine how immigrant children who arrive in this country with "zero" English acquire English in schools. To address this issue, Valdes (1998) selected a middle school undergoing rapid population shift and students aged 12–14. Two immigrant Hispanic students—one of Mexican origin and one of Honduran origin—participated in this research over a 7-year period.

Lilian, the student of Mexican origin, was 12 years old when she first arrived at her California school. Previously a student in Mexico, she had considerable reading ability in Spanish but almost no English-language or reading skills. Elisa, a 13-year-old Honduran immigrant, had completed sixth grade in her native country and also had considerable reading and writing experience in Spanish. Both Lilian and Elisa were eager to go to school and to learn English.

For each of these students, mastery of English became the predominant theme in their schooling experience. Valdes (1998) concludes that both students had difficulty escaping "the ESL ghetto." This phenomenon is a common one for many Hispanic immigrant students: They are placed repeatedly in courses that emphasize English-language acquisition at the expense of grade-level instruction in subject-matter domains. The result for both Lilian and Elisa was predictable, although Lilian dropped out of school at the age of 15 while Elisa finished high school but has only recently begun to attend a community college, where her measured lack of English on a required placement test has forced her to enroll in more ESL courses. Valdes (1998) was led to conclude that "the students who had looked forward to schooling in the United States were disappointed" (p. 11).

Olsen (1997), in a study similar to those of Valdes (1996, 1998), followed a cohort of immigrant Hispanic and Asian students through their high school experience at Madison High, an urban school in northern California. This study attempted to address the issues of becoming "American" in the world of immigrant students and their instructors and curricula. In the words of Olsen (1997), "The study illustrates efforts and heartbreaks of those engaged in activity to provide more educational opportunity and equal access to schooling for immigrants, as well as the confusion, blindness, and concerns of those who resist changing their ways for them" (p. 239).

The study of Madison High offered a hard look at the ways in which schools still track and determine very different futures based on race, class, and language. Immigrant students seemed to spend their educational time relegated to classes taught entirely in English in which they were unlikely to thrive or in separate "sheltered" English classes where the emphasis was on English-language development with little or no emphasis on grade-level curricula. Immigrant students themselves reported that the key to becoming American was simply to learn English. At the same time, teachers emphasized that the key to educational success was the mastery of basic skills and subject-matter content. These teachers reported "seeing" students divided into academic levels that were a result of a student's individual choice and effort. In essence, any student can be successful—achieve at high levels—if they choose to do so and work hard. These teachers' view of achievement contrasted drastically with immigrant students' experiences: "Pick your race and take your place" (Olsen, 1997, p. 241).

More specifically, Olsen concludes that the immigrant student experience is yet another important reflection of race and class negotiations and stratification in U. S. high schools that serve a diverse socioeconomic, racial, ethnic, and immigrant student body. Yet, particularly for immigrant students, taking one's place in the racial and socioeconomic hierarchy seemed coupled with:

1. The exclusion and separation of immigrants academically
2. The extreme pressure to give up national identity and language

Olsen (1997) is quick to point out that these phenomena are not uncontested. Students do try to rise to and overcome this challenge. And as Rumbaut (1997) indicates, some do. At Madison High, Hispanic immigrants were not likely to do so (Olsen, 1997).

While immigration's influence on social, economic, health, and education issues continues to be the subject of intense national debate, there can be no doubt that the large number of immigrants now living in the United States represents an enormous challenge. With more than half of post-1970 immigrants and their U.S.-born children living in or near poverty and one-third having no health insurance, the situation for immigrant families is clearly precarious. Without major changes in present immigration patterns, the Census Bureau projects that 11 to 12 million immigrants will arrive in the next decade alone (Camarota, 2001). Thus, the influence of immigrant students in U.S. schools will continue to grow.

ENGLISH ACQUISITION AND BILINGUALISM
IN THE U.S. CONTEXT

The increase in immigration to the United States in the 1970s and 1980s raised concerns about how well immigrants were being integrated into the social and economic fabric of the nation. The U.S. Department of Education conducted a national study that attempted to address this issue in depth by looking at adult residents of the United States who were either born in other countries or were born here but spoke a language other than English as young children. The 1992 National Adult Literacy Survey provides the most detailed portrait ever of the English-literacy abilities of adults living in the United States (Greenberg, Macias, Rhodes, & Chan, 2001). The survey sought to profile the literacy abilities of adults based on their performance on a wide array of tasks that reflect the types of materials and demands they encounter in their daily lives (e.g., understanding instructions in a warranty, reading maps, balancing a checkbook, or figuring out a tip). Survey data were gathered in 1992 by trained staff who interviewed more than 13,600 adults residing in U.S. households. The adults were randomly selected to represent the adult population of the nation as a whole. In addition, 1,000 adults were interviewed in each of 11 states that chose to participate in a concurrent survey designed to provide results comparable to the national data. Finally, 1,150 inmates in 80 state and federal prisons were surveyed.

Greenberg and colleagues' (2001) analysis of this survey indicates the following:

- The age at which an individual learned to speak English was related to his or her English-literacy proficiency as an adult. On average, individuals who entered the United States before age 12 had English-literacy skills as adults comparable to members of racial and ethnic groups who were born in the United States. Virtually everyone who was born in the United States or who immigrated to the United States before age 12 was fluent in English as an adult.

- There were racial and ethnic group differences in fluency and literacy in languages other than English among adults raised in homes where a language other than English was spoken. Individuals who grew up in homes where Spanish or an Asian language was spoken were more likely to report that they spoke that language as adults and considered themselves bilingual than were respondents who grew up in a home where a European language other than Spanish was spoken.

- Formal education played a fundamental role in the acquisition of English-language fluency and literacy for individuals who were raised in non-English-speaking homes, regardless of whether they were immigrants or native born. In particular, among immigrants who arrived in the United States at age 12 or older, level of formal education was related to English-language fluency and literacy. Immigrants who arrived in the United States at age 12 or older, without the benefit of a substantial amount of formal education in their native country, were the least likely to develop English-language skills. Immigrants who arrived at age 12 or older with a substantial level of formal education were likely to be biliterate and bilingual in English and their native language.

• Adults living in the United States who were not fluent in English, primarily immigrants who arrived at age 12 or older with low levels of formal education, were less likely to be employed and more likely to earn lower wages when they were employed, than individuals who were fluent and literate in English. However, fluency and literacy in English at the level of a native speaker was not necessary for successful integration into the American economy. Although individuals who learned English as their second language had lower English literacy—as measured by the National Adult Literacy Survey—than individuals who were raised in English-speaking homes, their average income and continuity of employment did not differ from that of native English speakers.

Contrary to the general impression among most native English-speaking residents, only non-native English speakers with low levels of formal education were truly disadvantaged in the labor market by their lack of English-language skills. Most members of this group were not being reached by existing educational opportunities. Educational participation makes a significant difference to these non-English speakers. Keep in mind that other non-native English speakers and immigrants, even those with low levels of English literacy as measured by the 1992 National Adult Literacy Survey, were generally able to learn enough English to exhibit employment patterns and earnings comparable to those of native English speakers. Most reported that English was learned in some form of formal educational setting.

CONCLUSION

This chapter set forth the demographic realities of an ever-increasing population of culturally and linguistically diverse, bilingual students in the United States. Of course, statistical summaries and the discussion of them paint only part of the picture.

In the chapters to come, it is recognized that infants are born into socially constructed environments. Young children are very directly socialized by family traditions. Moreover, at an early age, these same children enter school. In each of these settings, they assume certain roles, construct new roles, and behave in ways consistent with the expectations generated by themselves and others. Where diversity exists, schools work hard through various processes to directly or indirectly mold the individual into a prescribed but often incompatible set of roles. However, as the next chapter shows, this distinction between home and school culture is important in effectively addressing the educational needs of bilingual students.

Chapter 2

Bilingualism Is Not the Arithmetic Sum of Two Languages

No language develops externally from its physical and social context. What was once considered the study of habits and innate structures (Chomsky, 1959; Skinner, 1957) has become, today, an interlocking study of linguistic, psychological, and social domains, each independently significant but converging in a singular attempt to reconstruct the nature of the communicative experience. It is this multifaceted phenomenon that confronts a parent and educator when addressing the tasks of "teaching" language in homes and classrooms. For the educator of bilingual students, the issues related to languages of communication become particularly important.

Within the last few decades, research on language acquisition has incorporated studies of children acquiring one language (Brown, 1973; Ervin-Tripp, 1974), the comparative study of children from diverse linguistic societies (Bowerman, 1975; Fantini, 1985), and the study of children acquiring more than one language (Diaz & Klinger, 1991; García, 1983; Hakuta, 1986; Reyes, 2001). In addition, the recent study of this phenomenon has broadened to include aspects of language forms and functions (Hymes, 1974). The following discussion introduces the empirical knowledge bases related to an understanding of bilingualism and second-language acquisition and dialects as well as a broadened understanding of the communicative act as it relates to schooling contexts. Teaching/learning will be addressed as it relates to linguistic, cognitive, and social research and theory that has developed over the last two decades. Such contributions have reshaped in a dramatic way our view of bilingualism and language variation.

BILINGUAL DEVELOPMENT

Relative to native monolingual acquisition research, little systematic investigation has been available regarding children who are acquiring more than one language, simultaneously, during the early part of their lives. However, related work in this area, particularly in schooling contexts, has centered on the linguistic, cognitive, and social/communicative aspects of language acquisition. That is, research with young multilingual populations has concentrated independently in three areas: (1) the developmental nature of phonology, morphology, and syntax; (2) related cognitive attributes; and (3) the social/discourse characteristics of communication. This section reviews research in these areas in order to highlight similar and disparate theoretical conceptualizations and empirical findings generated by these research endeavors.

LINGUISTIC DEVELOPMENT

It seems clear from research that a child can learn more than one linguistic form in many societies throughout the world (DeHouwer, 1995; Grosjean, 1982). Sorenson (1967) describes the acquisition of three to four languages by young children who live in the Northwest Brazil region. The Tukano tribal language serves as the *lingua franca*, but there continue to exist some 25 clearly distinguishable linguistic groups. European colleagues Skutnabb-Kangas (1997) and Baetens Beardsmore (1982) have provided expanded discussions regarding the international proliferation of multilingualism. Skrabanek (1970), Waggoner (1984), Hakuta (1986), Veltman (1988), Zentella (1997), and Laosa (1998) report that school-age children in the United States continue to be bilingual. However, as Veltman (1988) and Hakuta and D'Andrea (1992) empirically demonstrate, bilingualism in the United States is largely transitional and results in shifts toward English within a few generations. This is particularly the case for new immigrants to the country (Ruiz-de-Velasco & Mix, 2000).

Regarding bilingual development in U.S. children, Padilla and Liebman (1975) reported a longitudinal linguistic analysis of Spanish/English acquisition in two 3-year-old children. By conducting an analysis of several dependent linguistic variables (phonological, morphological, and syntactic characteristics) over time, they observed gains in both languages, although several English forms were in evidence while similar Spanish forms were not. They also report the differentiation of linguistic systems at phonological, lexical, and syntactic levels. They concluded:

> The appropriate use of both languages in mixed utterances was evident; that is, correct word order was preserved. For example, there were no occurrences of "raining esta" or "a es baby," note there was evidence for such utterances as "esta raining" and "es a baby." There was also an absence of the redundancy of unnecessary words, which might tend to confuse meaning. (Padilla & Liebman, 1975, p. 51)

García (1983) reports developmental data related to the acquisition of Spanish and English by Chicano preschoolers (3 to 4 years old) and the acquisition of English by a group of matched English-only speakers. The results of that study can be summarized as follows: (1) Acquisition of both Spanish and English was evident at complex morphological levels for Spanish/English 4-year-old children; (2) for the bilingual children studied, English was more advanced based on the quantity and quality of obtained morphological instances of language productions; and (3) there was no quantitative or qualitative difference between Spanish/English bilingual children and matched English-only controls on English-language morphological productions.

Huerta (1977) conducted a longitudinal analysis of a Spanish/English 2-year-old child. She reported that similar identifiable stages appeared in which one language forged ahead of the other. Moreover, she reported the occurrence of mixed-language utterances making use of both Spanish and English vocabulary and morphology that were well formed and communicative.

García, Maez, and Gonzalez (1983), in a study of Spanish/English bilingual children 4 to 6 years old in the United States, found regional differences in the relative occurrence of switched-language utterances. Bilingual Spanish/English children from Texas, Arizona, Colorado, and New Mexico showed higher absolute (15% to 20%) incidences of switched-language utterances than children from California or Illinois, especially at prekindergarten levels. These findings suggest that some children may well pass through an intermediate developmental stage in which the two languages can merge, then move to the development of two independent language systems.

Learners' errors have been considered significant in providing an understanding of the strategies and processes the learner is using during second-language acquisition (Corder, 1976). Dulay and Burt (1974) studied the errors in the natural speech of 179 children 5 to 8 years old (including a sample of Chicano children in California) learning English as a second language. They classified errors as related either to first-language (interference errors) or to normal language development (developmental errors). Their analysis indicated that interference accounted for only 4.7% of the errors, whereas 87.1% of the errors were similar to those made by children learning English as a first language. They postulated that a universal "creative construction process" accounts for second-language acquisition.

The process was creative because no one had modeled the types of sentences that children produce when acquiring a second language, and the authors suggested that innate mechanisms caused children to use certain strategies to organize linguistic input. Dulay and Burt (1974) did not claim that they could define the specific nature of the innate mechanisms. They did claim, however, that these mechanisms have certain definable characteristics that cause children to use a limited set of hypotheses to deal with the knowledge they are acquiring. The strategies parallel those identified for first-language acquisition.

Krashen (1981, 1985, 1996) has developed a conceptualization of second language-acquisition that considers this innate creative construction process as fundamental. His "natural order" hypothesis indicates that the acquisition of grammatical structures by the second-language learner proceeds in a predictable "natural" order independent of first-language experiences and/or proficiency. Such acquisition occurs unconsciously, without the learner's concern for recognizing or using structural rules. However, Krashen's "monitor" hypothesis suggests that conscious learning of a second language can occur when the learner has achieved a significant knowledge of structural rules and has the time to apply those rules in a second-language learning situation.

Therefore, Krashen extends Dulay and Burt's creative construction and natural order conceptualizations by introducing the notion of the monitor hypothesis: learning a second language by first understanding the grammatical structure and having the time to apply that grammatical knowledge. He concludes, however, that conscious learning of a second language is not as efficient or functional as the natural acquisition of a second language.

Other research has documented a distinct relationship between first-language and second-language acquisition. Ervin-Tripp (1974) conducted a study of 31 English-speaking children between the ages of 4 and 9 who were living in Geneva and attending French schools. She found that the errors these children made in French, their second language, were a result of their application of the same strategies that they had used in acquiring a first language. Such strategies as overgeneralization, production simplification, and loss of sentence medial items predicted the kinds of errors that appeared. In overgeneralization, the American children acquiring French applied subject–verb–object strategy to all sentences in French, thus systematically misunderstanding French passives. In production simplification, they resisted using two forms if they felt that two forms had the same meaning. Also, medial pronouns were less often imitated than initial or final pronouns.

Ervin-Tripp (1974) believed that interference errors occur only when the second-language learner is forced to generate sentences about semantically difficult material or concepts unfamiliar in the new culture. Moreover, the strategies children use in acquiring a second language may change as they become more proficient in that language. At the beginning of second-language acquisition, imitation plays an important role in language learning. As children acquire more of the target language, they begin to use first-language acquisition strategies to analyze this input.

Hakuta (1974) demonstrated that children, through rote memorization, acquire segments of speech called prefabricated patterns. Examples include the segment "do you" as used in questions and the segment "how to" as embedded in *how* questions. These patterns are very useful but complex, and children use them without first understanding their structure but with knowledge of which particular situations call for which patterns.

Wong Fillmore (1976) spent a year observing five Spanish-speaking Chicano children acquiring English naturally, and she noticed the same phenomena. The first thing the children did was to figure out what was being said by observing the relationship between certain expressions and the situational context. They inferred the meaning of certain words, which they began to use as "formulaic expressions." (These expressions were acquired and used as analyzed wholes.) The formulaic expressions became the raw material used by the children to figure out the structure of the language. Wong Fillmore provided two examples of how children use first-language acquisition strategies to begin to analyze these expressions: (1) Children notice how parts of expressions used by others vary in accordance with changes in the speech situation in which they occur, and (2) children notice which parts of the formulaic expressions are like other utterances in the speech of others. As the children figured out which formulas in their speech could be varied, they were able to "free" the constituents they contained and use them in productive speech.

As McLaughlin (1985) has summarized, children acquiring a second language may depend initially on transfer from the first language and on imitation and rote memorization of the second language. In more practical terms, the less interaction a second-language learner has with native speakers, the more likely they are to transfer from the first to the second language. Many of the strategies that children use to acquire this second language seem to be the same as those used in first-language acquisition.

LANGUAGE CHOICE AND CODE-SWITCHING

Factors such as participant, situation, context, and function of discourse help the bilingual child decide which language to use. Fantini (1985) noticed that his son Mario was able to switch easily between languages according to the addressee. If Mario knew that the person was a Spanish-dominant or English-dominant speaker, he spoke Spanish or English, respectively. There was an exception when both of his children became close to and felt comfortable with an English-speaking person: They had an inclination to switch to Spanish, the language they spoke intimately and comfortably with loved ones. Bilinguals also report a tendency to switch to the more comfortable language when talking about a specific topic (Zentella, 1997); for some this might be L1, but not necessarily, since some bilinguals become dominant in L2.

Among themselves, bilinguals have the option of mixing their languages, referred to as code-switching (CS). There is an ongoing debate about whether borrowings, the switch at the one-word level, should be considered true code-switches. However, I will not make a distinction between these two types of language mixing and will discuss the general CS phenomenon in children regardless of the length of the switch.

Most of the studies of CS have focused on adults (Garcia, 1994). Studies of children's CS report the frequent use of one-word switches (Genishi, 1984; Reyes, 1998; Zentella, 1997). One explanation for this is that they lack the vocabulary in one language, so they switch to the other. There are, however, cases in which the child does seem to have the equivalents in both languages. Reyes (1998) observed cases in which children code-switched for one word but later, during the same conversation, used the same word in the other language. It might be more accurate to say that a CS is used mainly for a word that is not immediately accessible in the other language. Moreover, CS seems to be a way in which young learners of a second language begin playing with language, by which I mean exploring their two languages by imitating the sounds of new words learned in their second language. In this way, children start practicing their skills in L2.

The evidence to date concerning the development of CS behavior in young bilingual children consistently shows that both knowledge of the grammatical capabilities and sensitivity to the norms of code choice are major factors determining language choice. Grosjean (1982) and Fantini (1985) stress the importance of the child's social role. A child who is taking care of younger siblings will tend to switch to the language with which the youngest child feels most comfortable. In addition, older children tend to use CS as a clarification device when other children do not seem to understand. Similarly, Garcia (1983) observed that mothers used mixed utterances in Spanish and English when speaking to their young children "as a teaching aid" to clarify from one language to the other.

The other person's level of fluency is another important factor when making a language choice (Poplack, 1981). Fantini noticed that as early as age 4, his children could determine the ability of their audience to understand mixed-language utterances. Reyes (1998) also observed this phenomenon among immigrant children who were Spanish/English speakers. When children were paired with a friend, the older children, 10-year-olds, seemed to monitor their partners' level of understanding and to accommodate by code-switching to the language in which the other child was most proficient. The relative fluency of the speaker will also be a determining factor. When children are competent in both languages, CS is used as a verbal or communicative strategy and as a marker of group membership (Zentella, 1997).

Zentella (1997) reports that Puerto Rican children in New York switched freely when talking to members of their home community. However, they spoke the appropriate language when talking to monolinguals or those dominant in one of their languages. For these children, a complete separation of languages seemed almost impossible not because they could not linguistically achieve language separation but because in their everyday communication continuous mixing of their two languages was the norm. For them, code-switching was seen as an acceptable and natural conversational strategy. Therefore, code-switching is a very complex skill, not a deficiency.

The fact that children use two languages seems to make them more aware of the available possibilities for multiple-language use with community members who speak their two languages than with those who do not, referred to as meta-linguistic awareness. With time, children achieve and maintain a level of fluency in each language skill that in general reflects the need for that skill in a particular language (Grosjean, 1982).

In summary, current research suggests that natural communication situations must be provided for children to acquire two languages. Regardless of the differences in emphasis of the theories discussed above, recent theoretical propositions regarding bilingual acquisition suggest that through natural conversations the learner receive the necessary input and structures that promote second-language acquisition.

The above linguistic findings can be summarized as follows:

- The acquisition of two languages can be parallel but need not be. That is, the qualitative character of one language may lag behind, surge ahead of, or develop equally with the other language.
- The acquisition of two languages may result in an intermediate phase of language convergence that incorporates the attributes (lexicon, morphology, and syntax) of both languages. This need not be the case, however. Languages may develop independently.
- The acquisition of two languages need not structurally hamper the acquisition of either language.

COGNITION, LANGUAGE, AND CULTURE

A separate research approach to the understanding of bilingualism and its effects has focused on the cognitive (intellectual) character of the student. Based on correlation studies indicating a negative relationship between childhood bilingualism and performance on standardized tests of intelligence, a causal statement linking bilingualism to "depressed" intelligence was tempting, and this negative conclusion characterized much early work (Darcy, 1953). Because of the many methodological problems of studies investigating this type of relationship, any conclusions concerning bilingualism and intellectual functioning (as measured by standardized individual or group intelligence tests) are extremely tentative in nature (Darcy, 1963; Diaz, 1983).

With the general shift away from standardized measures of intelligence, the cognitive character of multilingual children has received attention. Leopold (1939), in one of the first investigations of bilingual acquisition, reported a general cognitive plasticity for his young bilingual daughter. He suggested that linguistic flexibility (in the form of bilingualism) is related to a number of nonlinguistic, cognitive tasks such as categorization, verbal signal discrimination, and creativity. Peal and Lambert (1962), in a summarization of their work with French/English bilinguals and English monolinguals, suggested that the intellectual experience of acquiring two languages contributed to advantageous mental flexibility, superior concept formation, and a generally diversified set of mental abilities.

Goncz and Kodzepeljic (1991) and Swain and Lapkin (1991) provide excellent overviews of international work in this arena. Research with Chicano bilingual children reported by Kessler and Quinn (1985, 1987) provides empirical support for the emerging understanding that other things being equal, bilingual children outperform monolingual children on specific measures of cognitive and meta-linguistic awareness. Kessler and Quinn (1987) had bilingual and monolingual children engage in a variety of symbolic categorization tasks that required their attention to abstract, verbal features of concrete objects. Spanish/English Chicano bilingual children of low socioeconomic status (SES) outperformed both low- and high-SES English monolinguals on these tasks. Such findings are particularly significant given the criticism by MacNab (1997) that many bilingual "cognitive advantage" studies have used only high-SES subjects of non-U.S. minority backgrounds. (It is important to note that findings of meta-linguistic advantages have been reported for low-SES Puerto Rican students as well [Galambos & Hakuta, 1988]).

Theoretical attempts linking bilingualism to cognitive attributes have emerged. In an effort to identify more specifically the relationship between cognition and bilingualism, Cummins (1979, 1981, 1984) has proposed an interactive theoretical proposition: that children who do not achieve balanced proficiency in two languages (but who are immersed in a bilingual environment) may be cognitively "different" and possibly "disadvantaged." Interestingly, Diaz (1985) has proposed an alternative hypothesis and supportive data suggesting that the cognitive "flexibility" of the multilingual individual is at its maximum during early stages of multilingual development, before balanced proficiency is attained.

Early theories of teaching and learning focused on the individual learner and were influenced most directly by findings in the field of psychology. Within the last 20 to 30 years, however, scholars trained in such fields as anthropology, sociology, cognitive science, and sociolinguistics have begun to explore the question of how thinking processes, language, and cultural experiences interact in schooling situations. The extent of fit or mismatch between home and school cultures provide a dynamic understanding of a wide variety of variables that affect student learning. Researchers in developmental and educational psychology are now devoting increased attention to the social context of learning and to the role of family, peer group, and community in children's school achievement.

During the last decade, many educational theorists have become interested in sociocultural theory, an international intellectual movement that brings together the disciplines of psychology, semiotics, education, sociology, and anthropology. This movement draws on work done earlier in the 20th century by the Russian theorists L. S. Vygotsky and Mikhail Bakhtin (Cole & Cole, 2001) and relates it to the thought of such theoreticians and philosophers of education as William James, John Dewey, C. S. Pierce, and Jean Piaget (Garcia, 2002). The aim is to find a unified way of understanding issues of language, cognition, culture, human development, and teaching and learning.

The importance of sociocultural theory for education is its proposal that individual learning and social interaction are inextricably connected. Sociocultural theorists argue that the psychology of the individual learner is deeply shaped by social interaction—in essence, that both student and teacher are engaged in the process of constructing their minds through social activity. In this view, knowledge is not a given set of fixed ideas that are passed from teacher to student. Rather, knowledge is created in the interaction between teacher and student. Higher-order mental processes, the tendency to look at things in certain ways, and values themselves are produced by shared activity and dialogue (Rogoff, 1990).

Our social lives, often considered to be the major products of culture and language, are instead for sociocultural theorists the major ingredients of cognition. Social experience is inseparable from thought. Moment by moment we construct reality. That process of construction and the understanding it generates depend on our previous understandings and our social experiences. Sociocultural theory considers education to be particularly important, partly because education has been a major interest of many of its founders but mostly because educational practice and theory need a unifying theory of teaching and learning. Educators of culturally diverse students will find this theoretical framework helpful because it conceives of learning as an interaction between individual learners and an embedding context. That embedding context may be as immediate as the social environment of the classroom or as indirect as the traditions and institutions that constitute the history of education. Both contexts and many other factors come into play whenever teachers and students interact. Important contexts for teaching and learning range from (1) close detailed instruction of individual learners and (2) concern for the social organization of classrooms to (3) a consideration of the cultural and linguistic attributes of teachers, students, and peers. These contexts interweave, and we can follow their strands to gain a new understanding of the relationship among language, culture, and cognition.

How do language and culture relate to cognitive development? Recall that human cognition—how and what we know—is a process of mental representation shaped by experience and the structural aspects of our minds. According to Vygotsky (Cole & Cole, 2001), language acquisition is the momentous occasion when internal mental representation and external reality converge. For him, "external reality" is first and foremost cultural: Through the development of language in interpersonal experiences, children begin to construct meaning. In this view, language functions significantly as a tool of thought. According to Hamers and Blanc (1989), the shared representations and scripts, which are basic to language proficiency, arise in the interaction between children and the significant others around them. The representations children construct are highly dependent on the shared social representations in their environment. Children will internalize those language functions that are valorized and used with them; it is through the socialization process that they become cognizant of functions and representations.

Thus, as children develop their ability to use language, they absorb more and more understanding of social situations and improve their thinking skills. This in turn allows them to learn how to control their own actions and thoughts. It is through a culturally bound and socially mediated process of language development that children construct mental frameworks (or schemas) for perceiving the world around them. If language is a tool of thought, it follows that as children develop more complex thinking skills, the mental representations through which language and culture embody the child's world play a significant role.

If, as Vygotsky (Cole & Cole, 2001) proposed, a child's cognitive schema for operating in the world is culturally bound, what are the effects of trying to learn in an environment where the culture of the classroom differs from the culture of the home? Linguistically and culturally diverse students face the challenge of either accommodating their existing schema or constructing a new schema. When the educational focus is on transitioning culturally diverse students to a mainstream culture rather than building on what they already know, the students are forced to change in order to meet the needs of the classroom. As Georges Duquette (1991) concludes, children need to be understood and to express themselves (in the same positive light experienced by other children) in their own first language, home context, and culture. Their minority background brings out the limitations not of the children but of the professionals who are asked to respond to those needs.

Bilingual students face a far greater challenge. It is through a child's first language that he or she creates mechanisms for functioning in and perceiving the world. If the culture of the classroom negates a child's first language and accompanying representations of the child's world, it negates the tools the child has used to construct a basic cognitive framework. Diaz and Klinger (1991) outline how language as a tool of thought has major consequences for a child's cognitive development. As language skills develop, a child's cognitive processes become more independent from the directly perceived environment. Through the use of language, children can organize and reconstruct their perceptions in terms of their own goals and intentions. Language development allows the child to act reflectively, according to a plan, rather than impulsively. As their language abilities mature, children can ultimately gain control over their own cognitive processes.

From the perspective of sociocultural theory, cognitive development is reflected in the increasing ability to use language in abstract ways. If the relationship between language and cognitive development operates as Vygotsky and later theorists claim, educational practices that ignore or negatively regard a student's native language and culture could have negative effects on the student's cognitive development. If a student's first language and culture are used only as a means to learn English and mainstream school culture and not to build on previous experiences and representations, then the student's cognitive development could be hindered or interrupted. In essence, children utilize native-language abilities as a tool to construct higher-order thinking processes. Limiting their opportunities to learn in their first language will limit their cognitive growth and related academic achievement.

From this theoretical perspective, policy and practice regarding the education of bilingual students is overly simplistic. Such an approach does not take into consideration the complex interweaving of students' cultural, linguistic, and cognitive development. In their study of the possible effects of language on cognitive development, Hakuta (1986) recognize the importance of acknowledging these three important strands in children's development and addressing them in our schools. They conclude that most of the variance in cognitive growth directly relates to the way in which society affects and manipulates cognitive capacities. Therefore, cultural and contextual sensitivity theories that examine the social and cultural aspects of cognitive development will best serve diverse students.

Any detailed conclusions concerning the relationship between the bilingual character of children and cognitive functioning must remain tentative (Garcia, 1991). However, bilingual children have been found to score higher on specific Piagetian, meta-linguistic, concept-formation, and creative cognitive tasks, and "balanced" and "unbalanced" bilinguals have outperformed monolinguals on specific cognitive and meta-linguistic tasks (August & Hakuta, 1997). More generally, recent sociocultural conceptualizations of cognition have placed language and culture in the center of cognitive development (Cole & Cole, 2001).

SOCIAL/COMMUNICATIVE ASPECTS

As previously noted, language is a critical social repertoire. The discourse component of any social interaction most often determines the general quality of that interaction (Canale, 1983; Cazden, 1988; Halliday, 1975; Heath, 1983; Hymes, 1974; Ramirez, 1985). In doing so, it carries special importance for culturally and linguistically diverse students in instances in which social tasks include language choice. Moreover, like other children who acquire the ability to differentially use linguistic codes determined by social attributes of the speaking context (Phillips, 1972), these children face the task of multiple code differentiation. Implicit in this discussion is the general notion that languages must not only be mastered in a structural sense and operate in conjunction with cognitive processes; they must be used as social instruments.

There are sociocultural variables that contribute to a child's motivation to communicate in the target language. The attitude that the learner has toward members of the cultural group whose language he or she is learning influences language acquisition. Gardner and Lambert (1972) found that the positive attitude of English-speaking Canadians toward French-speaking Canadians led to high integrative motivation to learn French. Ramirez (1985) reported a series of studies that investigated the relationship between Chinese, Japanese, and Chicano students' achievement in English and their attitude toward the foreign-language group. Positive attitudes toward the target-language group corresponded to higher language proficiency.

In addition, the relationship between the two cultures influences second-language acquisition. Schumann (1976) hypothesized that the greater the social distance between the two cultures, the greater the difficulty the second-language learner will have in learning the target language, and vice versa. Social distance is determined in part by the relative status of two cultures. Two cultures that are politically, culturally, and technically equal in status have less social distance than two cultures whose relationship is characterized by dominance and subordination. In addition, there is less social distance if the cultures of the two groups are congruent.

A child motivated to learn a second language still needs certain social skills to facilitate his or her ability to establish and maintain contact with speakers of the target language. Wong Fillmore (1976) and Wong Fillmore and Valadez (1986) suggest that individual differences in the social skills of the child influence the rate of second-language acquisition. Second-language learners who seem most successful use specific social strategies:

1. *Join a group and act as if you understand what is going on even if you do not.* The learner must initiate interactions and pretend to know what is going on. As a result, he or she will be included in the conversations and activities.
2. *Give the impression with a few well-chosen words that you can speak the language.* Children must be willing to use whatever language they have; as a result, other children will keep trying to communicate with them.
3. *Count on your friends for help.* The acquisition of language depends on the participation of both the learner and someone who already speaks the language—the friend. The child's friends can help in several ways (e.g., by showing faith in the learner's ability to learn the language and by including the learner in their activities) and can also provide natural linguistic input that he or she can understand.

Seliger (1977) has also demonstrated that high-input generators are the most successful second-language learners. High-input generators are learners who place themselves in situations in which they are exposed to the target language and are willing to use it for communication. Therefore they receive the necessary input as well as the opportunity for practice.

LANGUAGE DEVELOPMENT CONSIDERS WAYS TO USE IT

Another focus of research has been to investigate ways in which language is used and the rules that govern discourse. Language development considers both the explicit rules (grammar) of language and the explicit/implicit rules (grammar) for using it. In an early effort, a series of studies explored varieties of communicative strategies in different linguistic communities, contrasting these with the kinds of language used in classrooms. Phillips's (1972) research at Warm Springs Indian Reservation, now a classic study of discourse rule and cultural mismatching, compared the conditions for speech use in the Native American community and in the government school. She identified a basic distinction in participant structures, rules that govern who speaks when. Native American students were reluctant to speak when called on in class, which she attributed to differences in the ways in which authority is exercised in the

Indian community and the minimal role of verbalization in the teaching styles of Indian families. She compared the students' lack of verbal responsiveness in teacher-directed situations with their participation in peer-learning situations, which are more culturally congruent. Boggs (1972) addressed a similar reluctance among native Hawaiian children to respond to direct questioning by teachers. He documented the low frequency of adult questioning directed at a specific child in native Hawaiian homes. Boggs found that when students were invited to participate in the classroom in ways that were culturally congruent, they did, in fact, produce long narratives.

Heath's (1983) study of ways of talking in middle-class White and working-class African American families in a southern community extended this line of research. Heath described how working-class African American children were reluctant to answer teachers' questions because of differences in communicative patterns. Working-class African American parents rarely used the "known-answer" question. Heath (1986) later explored "ways with words" in Asian and Latino communities, searching for similar clues in the discontinuities between how language is used at home and at school. She introduced the construct of the oral genre, the type of organizing unit into which smaller segments of units of language fit. Genres, such as stories, accounts, and recounts, exist among all linguistic communities. However, their frequency varies among groups, as does the kind of language associated with each. Heath's research posited that discrepancies between sociolinguistic conventions are the source of confusion and misunderstanding between children from language-minority families and their mainstream teachers. She argued that the discontinuity between home and school languages is not as disconcerting and detrimental as is the discontinuity between ways of using language in the community and at school. This finding addresses Dolson's (1984) report that children from homes in which the first language is used achieve better in school than those whose parents and older siblings try to use English. Children whose limited-English-proficient (LEP) parents and siblings insist on using their weaker language for communication at home may be exposed to a far more restricted array of genres.

In a similar mode, Nine Curt (1984) identified areas that can cause particular confusion for Puerto Rican students: proxemics (personal space), occulisics (eye contact), haptics (touching), and kinesics (body movements). In a study exploring verbal and nonverbal forms of communication, Nine Curt (1984) found that Puerto Rican students born and raised on the mainland retained a high rate of Puerto Rican gestures. Students may be retaining more of the nonverbal than the verbal patterns of their parents' native Spanish. Nine Curt's observations about Puerto Rican culture have been further summarized by Irujo (1988). That work details the research that has documented the cultural variation in eye contact and gaze behavior among

African Americans and White North Americans, Arabs, Latin Americans, Southern Europeans, East Asians, Greeks, and Northern Europeans.

Garcia (1983) reports an investigation of mother–child interaction, including the description of Spanish/English used by children and adults (the children's mothers) in three different contexts: (1) preschool instruction periods, (2) preschool free-play periods, and (3) the home. These descriptions indicated that children were "choosing" to initiate an interaction in either Spanish or English as a function of the language the mother was using to initiate that interaction. A closer qualitative examination of the same mothers and children interacting is reported by Garcia and Carrasco (1981). Their analysis suggested that almost 90% of mother–child interactions were initiated by the mother, most often in Spanish (i.e., mothers most often did not allow children to initiate). For those small numbers of instances in which children did initiate, the topic determined language choice. That is, what the child spoke about was highly correlated with the language in which he or she chose to speak.

The richest data on bilingual children dealing with topic initiation come from child–child interactions. Genishi (1984), while investigating the use of Spanish and English among first graders, concluded that the general language initiation rule for these students was "Speak to the listener in his or her best language" (p. 133). Her analysis suggests that, when speaking with other children, these children were making distinctions about whether to initiate a conversation in Spanish or English based on their history of language use with specific fellow students. Therefore, use of Spanish or English was based on a very specific knowledge base. Zentella (1981) agrees that bilingual students make these decisions. However, she found another discourse rule operating: "You can speak to me in either English or Spanish." Although Genishi's (1984) and Zentella's (1981) discourse rules differ, each observation suggests that bilingual students make use of their social and language-use history to construct guidelines related to discourse initiation. These studies suggest that particular sociolinguistic environments lead bilingual students to be aware of language-choice issues related to discourse initiation.

While there is much that is encouraging in research that addresses the awareness of classroom discourse, it is not appropriate to conclude that all is well in those classrooms that serve culturally and linguistically diverse students. The one feature of the learning environments studied in detail by Ramirez and Merino (1990) and Ramirez, Yuen, Ramey, and Pasta (1991) was the quality of teacher and student language, whether in English or Spanish, in several language-minority education programs. From analyses of tape recordings of classroom interaction, they concluded that teachers in all programs offer a passive language environment, limiting student opportunities to produce language and develop more complex language and thinking skills.

This finding parallels similar results for "regular" classrooms in the United States (Cazden, 1988). Yet it might be quite important for language use to be a higher priority in classrooms with bilingual students. Ramirez and colleagues (1991) concluded:

> Direct observations reveal that teachers do most of the talking in classrooms making about twice as many utterances as do students. Students produce language only when they are working directly with a teacher, and then only in response to teacher initiations. Of major concern is that in over half of the interactions that teachers have with students, students do not produce any language as they are only listening or responding with non-verbal gestures or actions. Of equal concern is that when students do respond, typically they provide only simple information recall statements. Rather than being provided with the opportunity to generate original statements, students are asked to provide simple discrete close-ended or patterned (i.e., expected) responses. This pattern of teacher-student interaction not only limits a student's opportunity to create and manipulate language freely, but also limits the student's ability to engage in more complex learning (i.e., higher order thinking skills). (p. 8)

A comprehensive understanding of bilingual students must, therefore, take into consideration more than the linguistic nature of students' cognitive attributes. It must consider their complex and active communicative environment. Recent data best exemplified by Zentella (1997) tentatively suggest that social context will determine, in very complex ways, the specific social-language rules for each language and the roles assigned to each language.

CONCLUSION

The linguistic, cognitive, and social domains of a student's experience have been demonstrated as important in understanding the bilingual child. However, the integration of these domains seems to more clearly describe the ongoing developmental quality of this phenomenon:

1. The linguistic, cognitive, and social character of the child are developing simultaneously.
2. Linguistic, cognitive, and social development are interrelated. That is, cognitive-processing factors may influence linguistic and social development, linguistic development (the ability to operate within the structural aspects of languages) may influence social and potential cognitive functioning, and the development of social competence may directly influence the acquisition of linguistic and cognitive repertoires.

CHAPTER 3

Education Comes in Diverse Shapes and Forms for U.S. Bilinguals

For a school district staff with bilingual students, there are many program options: Transitional bilingual education, maintenance bilingual education, English as a second language, immersion, sheltered English, and submersion were developed as program types by the U.S. Government Accounting Office in 1987. Ultimately, staff should reject program and model labels and instead answer the following questions:

1. What are the native-language and English-language characteristics of the students, families, and communities we serve?
2. What model of instruction is desired?
   (a) How do we choose to use the native language and English as *mediums of instruction?*
   (b) How do we choose to handle the instruction in the native language and English?
3. What is the nature of staff and resources necessary to implement the desired instruction? (Garcia, 2001a)

These program initiatives can be differentiated by the way they use the native language and English during instruction (Ovando & Collier, 1998; Ovando et al., 2002). In the most recent yet highly outdated (no new national survey has been conducted since 1993) national survey, Development Associates (1993) surveyed 333 school districts in the 19 states that serve over 80% of language-minority students in the United States. For grades K–5, they report the following salient features about the use of language(s) during the instruction of language minority students:

1. Ninety-three percent of the schools reported that the use of English predominated in their programs; 7% indicated that the use of the native language predominated.
2. Sixty percent of the sampled schools reported that both the native language and English were used during instruction.

3. Thirty percent of the sampled schools reported minimal or no use of the native language during instruction.

Programs serving these students have been characterized primarily as bilingual transitional education (Ovando & Collier, 1998). These programs transition students from early-grade, native-language-emphasis instruction to later-grade, English-emphasis instruction and, eventually, to English-only instruction. Other programs that use the primary language, discussed later in this book, emphasize maintaining proficiency in the native language while adding English proficiency—these will be referred to as Dual-language programs.

For the one-third of the students receiving little or no instruction in their native language, two alternative types of instructional approaches likely predominate: English-language development/English as a second language (ELD/ESL) and sheltered English immersion (SEI). Each type depends on the primary use of English during instruction but does not ignore the fact that the students are limited in English proficiency. However, these programs do not require instructional personnel who speak the native language of the student. Moreover, they are suited to classrooms in which non-English-speaking students come not from one native-language background but from many.

School district staffs have been creative in developing a wide range of programs for language-minority students. They have answered the above questions differently for (1) different language groups, (2) different grade levels, (3) different subgroups within a classroom, and (4) different levels of language proficiency. The result has been a broad and at times perplexing variety of instructional arrangements (August & Hakuta, 1997; Garcia, 2001a; Ovando & Collier, 1998). This chapter addresses the theoretical and related goals of these diverse instructional arrangements.

SCHOOLING PRACTICES: THE DEBATE

The United States has been characterized by a long-lasting debate about the education of its bilingual students, particularly those of Spanish-language backgrounds. Linda Chavez, a journalist, TV commentator, and author of *Out of the Barrio* (1991), suggests:

> Every previous group—Germans, Irish, Italians, Greeks, Jews, and Poles—struggled to be accepted fully into the social, political and economic mainstream, sometimes against the opposition of a hostile majority. They learned the language, acquired education and skills, and adapted their own customs and traditions to fit an American context. (p. 2)

The key to success in the United States, Chavez argues, is minimizing the public and governmental recognition of students' native languages while promoting the assimilation into "mainstream" English-speaking society. She chides the government, particularly federal bilingual education programs during the 1960s through the 1990s, for promoting a permanent victim status and entitling people to government grants that promote bilingualism. Educational support, she believes, encourages students to maintain their language and culture—their specific identity—in return for rewards handed out through federal, state, and local educational policies that thwart assimilation.

Richard Rodriguez (1985) eloquently describes how his upbringing in a "Mexican" home and a Catholic school influenced his learning. His book, *Hunger of Memory* (1985), describes how this forced assimilation, painful as it was, propelled him to new heights of educational achievement. In his story, the English-speaking nuns literally beat the Spanish out of him. Hakuta (1986), Cummins (1997), Garcia (2001b), and others reach a very different conclusion. They argue that bilingualism is a positive linguistic, social, and education characteristic that should be developed in those children who come to school not speaking English. Crawford has (1998, 1999) articulated a set of misunderstandings or myths that are useful in beginning to sort through this debate (adapted from Crawford, 1998):

MYTH: English is losing ground to other languages in the United States.

More languages are spoken in the United States today than ever before. However, this is a quantitative, not a qualitative, change from earlier periods. Concentrations of non-English speakers were common in the 19th century, as reflected by laws authorizing native-language instruction in a dozen states and territories. In big cities as well as rural areas, children attended bilingual and non-English schools, learning in languages as diverse as French, Norwegian, Czech, and Cherokee. Yet English survived without any help from government, such as official-language legislation.

MYTH: Newcomers to the United States are learning English more slowly now than in previous generations.

To the contrary, today's immigrants appear to be acquiring English more rapidly than ever before. While the number of minority-language speakers is projected to grow well into the next century, the number of bilinguals fluent in both English and another language is growing even faster. Between 1980 and 1990, the number of immigrants who spoke non-English languages at home increased by 59%, while the portion of this population that spoke

English very well rose by 93% (Waggoner, 1995). In 1990, only 3% of U.S. residents reported speaking English less than *well* or *very well*. Only 0.8% spoke no English at all. About three in four Hispanic immigrants, after 15 years in this country, speak English on a daily basis, while 70% of their children become dominant or monolingual in English.

MYTH: The best way to learn a language is through "total immersion."

There is no credible evidence to support the "time-on-task" theory of language learning—the claim that the more children are exposed to English, the more English they will learn. Learning English in school is a complex process (August & Hakuta, 1997).

MYTH: School districts provide bilingual instruction in scores of native languages.

Where children speak a number of different languages, rarely are there sufficient numbers from each language group to make bilingual instruction practical for everyone. In any case, the shortage of qualified teachers usually makes it impossible. For example, in 1994 California enrolled recently arrived immigrants from 136 different countries, but bilingual teachers were certified in only 17 languages, 96% of them in Spanish.

MYTH: Bilingual education means instruction mainly in students' native languages, with little instruction in English.

Before 1994, the vast majority of U.S. bilingual education programs were designed to encourage an early exit to mainstream English-language classrooms, while only a tiny fraction were designed to maintain the native tongues of students.

Today, a majority of bilingual programs continue to deliver a substantial portion of the curriculum in English. For example, Garcia (1999) found that a randomly selected cohort of school districts in California reported that 28% of limited-English-proficient (LEP) elementary school students receive no native-language instruction. Among those who do, about a third receive more than 75% of their instruction in English; a third receive from 40% to 75% in English; and one-third of these receive less that 40% in English. Secondary school students are less likely to be instructed in their native language than elementary school students are.

MYTH: Bilingual education is far more costly than English language instruction.

All programs serving LEP students—regardless of the language of instruction—require additional staff training, instructional materials, and administration. So they all cost a little more than regular programs for native English speakers. But in most cases the differential is modest. A study commissioned by the California legislature examined a variety of well-implemented program models and found no budgetary advantage for English-only approaches. The incremental cost was about the same each year ($175–$214) for bilingual and English immersion programs, as compared with $1,198 for ESL pull-out programs. The reason was simple: The pull-out approach requires supplemental teachers but in-class approaches do not (Chambers & Parrish, 1992). Nevertheless, ESL pull-out remains the method of choice for many school districts, especially where LEP students are diverse, bilingual teachers are in short supply, or expertise is lacking in bilingual methodologies.

MYTH: Disproportionate dropout rates for Hispanic students demonstrate the failure of bilingual education.

Hispanic dropout rates remain unacceptably high. Research has identified multiple factors associate with this problem, including recent arrival in the United States, family poverty, limited English proficiency, low academic achievement, and being retained in grade (Lockwood, 1996). No credible studies, however, have identified bilingual education among the risk factors, because only a small minority of Hispanic children are in bilingual programs.

MYTH: Language-minority parents do not support bilingual education because they feel it is more important for their children to learn English than to maintain the native language.

Naturally, when pollsters place these goals in opposition, immigrant parents will opt for English by wide margins. Who knows better the need to learn English than those who struggle with language barriers on a daily basis? But the premise of such surveys is false. Truly bilingual programs seek to cultivate proficiency in both languages, and research has shown that students' native language can be maintained and developed at no cost to English (Christian, 1994). When polled on the principles underlying bilingual education—for example, that developing literacy in the first language facilitates literacy development in English or that bilingualism offers cognitive and career-related advantages—a majority of parents are strongly in favor of such approaches (Lindholm, 1999).

Allow me to shift away from this debate, although later it will surface in my discussion of national, state, and local policies that influence the education of bilingual students. Instead, I turn now to educational research that has attempted to determine what instruction and learning features serve bilingual students well.

WHAT WORKS: OPTIMAL INSTRUCTION AND LEARNING FEATURES

August and Hakuta (1997) provide a comprehensive review of optimal learning conditions for linguistically and culturally diverse populations that lead to high academic performance. Their reviews of 33 case studies identify the following attributes:

> A supportive school-wide climate, school leadership, a customized learning environment, articulation and coordination within and between schools, use of native language and culture in instruction, a balanced curriculum that includes both basic and higher-order skills, explicit skill instruction, opportunities for student-directed instruction, use of instructional strategies that enhance understanding, opportunities for practice, systematic student assessment, staff development, and home and parent involvement. (p. 171)

These features resonate with other recent studies of effectiveness for programs specifically designed for linguistically and culturally diverse populations. California Tomorrow (1995), in a study of early childhood care in California, concluded that a set of principles guided quality child care across a variety of care settings that serve a growing community of linguistically and culturally diverse families:

1. Support the development of ethnic identity and antiracist attitudes among children.
2. Build upon the cultures of families and promote cross-cultural understanding among children.
3. Foster the preservation of children's home language and encourage bilingualism among all children.
4. Engage in on-going reflection and dialogue. (p. 8)

In a state-mandated study of exemplary schools serving the state's linguistically and culturally diverse students, several key attributes were common (Berman, 1992). These features included: (1) *flexibility*—adapting to the diversity of languages, mobility, and special nonschool needs of these students and their families; (2) *coordination*—utilizing sometimes scarce and diverse resources, such as federal and state moneys and local community organizations, in highly coordinated ways to achieve academic goals; (3) *cultural validation*—schools validated their students' cultures by incorporating materials and discussions that built on the linguistic and cultural aspects of the community; and (4) *a shared vision*—a coherent sense of who the students were and what they hoped to accomplish led by a school's principal, staff, instructional aides, parents, and community (Berman, 1992).

Three more recent "effective-exemplary" analyses of schools that serve high percentages of linguistically and culturally diverse students nationally are worthy of mention (Thomas & Collier, 1995). Three key factors are reported as significant in producing academic success for students in studies of five urban and suburban school districts in various regions of the United States. The studies focus on the length of time needed to be academically successful in English and consider factors influencing academic success, such as the student, program, and instructional variables. These studies include about 42,000 student records per schoolyear and from 8 to 12 years of data from each school district.

1. Cognitively complex academic instruction through students' home language for as long as possible and through second language for part of the schoolday.
2. Use of current approaches to teaching academic curriculum using both students' home language and English through active, discovery, and cognitively complex learning.
3. Changes in the sociocultural context of schooling, such as integrating English speakers, implementation of additive bilingual instructional goals, and transformation of minority/majority relations to a positive plane (Thomas & Collier, 1995).

A series of case studies of exemplary schools throughout the United States serving highly diverse and poor student populations also illustrates what can be done to promote academic excellence (McLeod, 1996). In these studies, selected schools with demonstrated records of academic success were subjected to intensive site-by-site study with the goal of identifying specific attributes at each site related to the functioning of the school as well as a more ambitious effort to identify common attributes across the sites. Schools in four states (Texas, Illinois, California, and Massachusetts) were particularly successful in achieving high academic outcomes with a diverse set of students and used these common goals for ensuring high-quality teaching.

Foster English acquisition and the development of mature literacy. Schools used native-language abilities to develop literacy that promoted English-literacy development. Programs in these schools were more interested in this mature development than transitioning students quickly into English-language instruction. This approach paid off in English-language development at levels that allowed students to be successful in English instruction.

Deliver grade-level content. Challenging work in the academic disciplines was pursued simultaneously with the goals of English-language learning. Teachers organized lessons to deliver grade-level instruction through a variety of native-language, sheltered English, and ESL activities.

Organize instruction in innovative ways. Examples of innovations included: (1) "schools-within-schools" to more responsively deal with diverse language needs of the students; (2) "families" of students who stayed together for major parts of the schoolday; (3) "continuum classes" in which teachers remained with their students for 2 to 3 years, helping teachers become more familiar with and responsive to student diversity; and (4) grouping of students more flexibly on a continuous basis so as to respond to the developmental differences between their native and second language.

Protect and extend instructional time. Schools used after-school programs, supportive computer-based instruction, and voluntary Saturday schools and summer academies, activities that multiplied the opportunities for students to engage in academic learning. Regular teachers or trained tutors were used to extend this learning time. Not surprisingly, a majority of students took advantage of these voluntary extensions. Care was taken not to erode the daily instructional time that was available—erosion often related to auxiliary responsibilities for teachers that take valuable time away from instruction.

Expand the roles and responsibilities of teachers. Teachers were given much greater roles in curricular and instructional decision making. This decision making was much more collective in nature to ensure cross-grade articulation and coordination. Teachers in these schools became full co-partners, devising more "authentic" assessments that could inform instruction and developing assessment tools and scoring rubrics in reading and mathematics.

Address students' social and emotional needs. Because schools were located in low-income neighborhoods, a proactive stance with regard to issues in these communities was adopted. An after-school activity that was aimed at families—particularly dealing with issues of alcohol and drug abuse, family violence, health care, and related social service needs—brought the school staff together with social service agencies at one school site. Similar examples of actual family counseling and direct medical care were arranged at other sites.

Involve parents in their children's education. Some of the schools were magnet schools to which parents had chosen to send their children and where parental involvement was part of the school contract. Areas of parental involvement included participation in school committees, school festivals and celebrations, and student field trips. In nonmagnet schools, parent outreach services were an integral part of the school operation. In all cases, communication was accomplished on a regular basis in various home languages. Parental participation in governance of the school was a common attribute, although participation levels were highly variable (adapted from McLeod, 1996, pp. 13–33).

DUAL-LANGUAGE PROGRAMS

Dual-language (DL) programs are relatively new in the United States. These programs aim to create bilingual, bicultural students without sacrificing these students' success in school or beyond. The goals of DL are to provide high-quality instruction for language-minority students and to provide instruction in a second language for English-speaking students. Schools teach children language through content, with teachers adapting their instruction to ensure children's comprehension and using content lessons to convey vocabulary and language structure. Striving for half language-minority students and half English-speaking students in each classroom, DL programs also aim to teach cross-cultural awareness. Programs vary in terms of the amount of time they devote to each language, which grade levels they serve, how much structure they impose for the division of language and curriculum, and what populations they serve.

There are two main models of language division. In the 50:50 model, instruction is given half the day in English and half the day in Spanish throughout the grades. In the 90:10 model, children spend 90% of their kindergarten schooldays in the minority language, with the percentage gradually dropping to 50% by fourth or fifth grade. Currently, there are more than 225 DL programs in the United States, and the number is growing rapidly (Christian, 1999). While the vast majority offer instruction in Spanish and English, there are also programs that target Korean, Cantonese, Arabic, French, Japanese, Navajo, Portuguese, and Russian (Christian, 1997).

Two-way immersion programs have three major goals: to help language-minority children learn English and succeed in U.S. schools; to help language-majority children learn a foreign language without sacrificing their own success in school; and to promote linguistic and ethnic equity among the children, encouraging children to bridge the gaps between cultures and languages which divide our society. These goals are naturally interdependent. English-speaking children who understand that another language and culture are as important as their own will be more interested in learning about that culture and acquiring that language. Minority-language children who acquire higher school status due to their knowledge of their home language will have more confidence in their ability to learn English. Children who learn the language of their peers are more likely to want to become friends with them, regardless of racial or ethnic background.

Lambert (1990) suggests that DL programs are a perfect resolution to the dichotomy between foreign-language education and bilingual education in U.S. schools. He further suggests that the purpose of second-language pedagogy is bringing "language minority families into the American mold, to teach them our national language, to help them wash out as quickly as possible old country ways" (p. 323). On the other hand, "the foreign language approach aims to add refinement and international class to the down-to-earth, eminently practical American character" (p. 324). His clear conclusion: Two-way immersion will improve language teaching for everyone, both second-language learners and foreign-language. However, Valdes (1998) warns practitioners and researchers to be cautious. The attempt to meet the needs of two such different populations in one program is difficult and brings to the fore many questions of power distribution in the classroom and in society. She warns practitioners that when they modify the target language so that majority-language students can comprehend it, they may be watering down the language for minority-language students. There is a difference, Valdes (1998) asserts, between the acquisition of English for minority children and the acquisition of a foreign language for majority children: For minority children, the acquisition of English is expected. For mainstream children, the acquisition of a non-English language is enthusiastically applauded.

As these set of issues continue to receive attention, there is evidence to suggest that DL is an excellent model for academic achievement for language-minority children. It appears to promote English-language learning as well or better than other special programs designed for language-minority children. One hundred percent of Spanish-dominant children in the Key School, a 50:50 DL school in Arlington County, Virginia, demonstrated oral English fluency by third grade, as shown by the LAS-O Oral English Proficiency measure and classroom observations (Christian, 1997). Further, English writing samples collected from native Spanish speakers in fifth and sixth grade were indistinguishable from those of native English speakers, and all were of high quality (Christian, 1997). In a separate study of four DL schools following the 90:10 model in California, it was found that by fifth grade most students were clearly fluent in English and had made good gains in English reading at most schools (although they did not attain grade-level performance in reading) (Lindholm, 1999).

DL also appears to aid achievement in academic subjects in both English and the minority languages. In a study comparing DL students to a control population, Christian (1994) found that third graders from the Amigos Dual Immersion Program in Cambridge, Massachusetts, outperformed a Spanish-speaking cohort in a more conventional bilingual education program in reading and mathematics in both Spanish and English. In fact, these children performed consistently at or slightly below grade-level for children their age, including English-speaking children. DL provided these children with the tools they needed to perform well in school assessments in English, even though the majority of their school time had been spent in Spanish instruction. This was also shown in a study conducted several years later at the Amigos school. Here, children from fourth through eighth grade consistently performed at least as well as and often significantly better than control populations on standardized tests in both English and Spanish (Cazabon, Lambert, & Hall 1999). In Lindholm's (1999) study of four 90:10 schools in California, Spanish bilingual students scored at grade level in mathematics in Spanish and at or below grade level in mathematics in English. Performance in science and social studies was average to very high. Lindholm notes that these scores should be compared to California's scores in general, which are the lowest of all 50 states; thus to report that DL students "were scoring at or above grade level in reading and mathematics means that these students were scoring better than most students in California" (p. 16).

Spanish-speaking children in DL programs seem to maintain or improve their oral Spanish proficiency as well. At the Key School, while only 88% of first-grade Spanish-speaking children tested as fluent in Spanish, in grades 2 and above Spanish-speaking children all tested as fluent in Spanish. Christian (1997) asserts that this finding is similar to findings from previous years; even Spanish-dominant students seem to make oral gains in Spanish in these programs. California Spanish bilingual students in 90:10 programs also "maintained high levels of proficiency in their first language"(Lindholm, 1999, p. 15). This provides evidence to allay Valdez's fear that DL programs may water down Spanish-language instruction for minority children.

The evidence for English-speaking children is more mixed. It is clear that these students' English skills do not suffer at all from their time spent learning content in another language. English-speaking students in the Amigos program in Cambridge perform comparably to English controls in English reading and English-based mathematics at all grade levels (Christian, 1994). English bilingual students from DL programs in California "maintained high levels of proficiency in their first language" throughout their years in the program, and performed at or above grade level in English reading, mathematics, social studies, and science as measured by a nationwide norm standardized test (Lindholm, 1999, p. 31).

While it does appear that English-speaking children gain strong skills in their second language through their schooling alone, there are gaps in their language knowledge, probably attributable to the fact that English, not the target language, is the dominant language in our society. It is also difficult to determine whether their language acquisition is up to par, because there is no comparison of children learning a second language with which to compare them; comparing them to Spanish-speaking children learning English, as Valdes (1998) pointed out, can be confounding. In general, English speakers are not found to gain strong Spanish oral fluency in DL programs. Christian's (1994) findings at the Key School indicated that only 50% of English-dominant fourth and fifth graders demonstrated Spanish fluency (by the SOPR measure and classroom observations), in contrast to 100% of Spanish-dominant third graders in English. Lindholm (1999) found in her examination of 90:10 programs in California that "while most Spanish bilingual students were clearly fluent in English, many English bilingual students lacked the fluency, vocabulary and grammar to converse entirely in Spanish about a variety of topics" (Lindholm, 1999, p. 15).

Freeman (1998) describes in detail the dual immersion approach at Oyster School in Washington, D.C., acknowledged for its leadership in bilingual, multicultural education. Goals for the Oyster School include bilingualism for both native learners and bilinguals, a high expectation of academic achievement for all, and "a culturally pluralistic atmosphere" in which mutual acceptance is emphasized (p. 242). Freeman's study shows that at Oyster, while academic achievement is more emphasized in English than in Spanish, the school is largely successful. The researcher also emphasizes that all knowledge—linguistic, social, and cultural—that students bring to the school is valued; all students also experience the esteem and concern of all the teachers. Hornberger (1989) has stressed the importance of valuing what students from different sociolinguistic, educational, and social-class backgrounds bring to school with them.

BEYOND LANGUAGE

Duff and Early (1999) demonstrate what can happen when children's sociocultural knowledge base is not taken into consideration. They report that students who transition into mainstream classes may have difficulty both academically and socially because they don't share the cultural knowledge of the mainstream students in their school. The dual-immersion model addresses this issue through its inclusive approach to all cultures represented. Write Duff and Early, "The case study of Oyster Bilingual School demonstrates that schools can collectively organize and construct alternative discourses that position minority students more favorably than mainstream US discourse does" (p. 238).

Yet, despite the apparent success of the dual-immersion approach at Oyster School, Duff and Early report that some of the students have difficulty maintaining the language and values they have acquired there when they transition to junior high school. This underscores the need for maintaining not only two languages but also a pluralistic environment throughout schooling.

Majority students are certainly not hampered in their progress in English or in their academic subjects by their study of a second language. However, it seems that while these students do gain skills in their second language in DL programs, they do not necessarily gain nativelike fluency by the time they graduate, and they do not necessarily gain as much of their second language as their Spanish-speaking peers gain of English. Why this difference is present, and how/whether it can be overcome, is not yet clear and is a subject for further research.

ENGLISH-LANGUAGE DEVELOPMENT IN A BILINGUAL PROGRAM

The widely accepted view in the ESL research and pedagogical community is that the ideal for all English-language learners is to maintain or enrich their native languages while acquiring English as a second language (Eisenstein, Bodman, & Carpenter, 1995; Gass & Neu, 1995; Kasper & Blum-Kulka, 1993). Thus, by definition, a bilingual program in which English is to be learned will include a second-language-acquisition component—often referred to as English as a second language. Like bilingual education, second-language acquisition/English as a second language (SLA/ESL) are umbrella terms that can refer to a large number of possible educational models, including not only the more traditional pull-out efforts in which SLA/ESL teachers work outside of the regular classroom but also push-in programs in which SLA/ESL teachers collaborate with regular classroom teachers in their regular classes to promote language development, understanding of content, and sociocultural insights among all students. SLA/ESL alternatives also include self-contained classrooms that offer content through an ESL approach called sheltered English (Stern, 1992).

When it is not possible to provide bilingual education (including some form of English-language development, ELD), then SLA/ESL alone is the next-best alternative to submersion—the option of offering no special assistance to bilingual students. Multilingual populations, small numbers of learners, and/or limited availability of bilingual staff can all contribute to the logistics of such educational decisions. SLA/ESL specialists are trained to promote additive bilingualism and to provide comprehensible input to learners in a supportive environment. It is a mainstay of the SLA/ESL professional to respect linguistic and cultural diversity and to communicate to all learners that their heritage languages and cultures are treasures to be preserved.

It is also clear that a second language is best acquired through content that is meaningful to learners (Chamot & O'Malley, 1994). This approach has several names, including "language through content" and "sheltered English." In addition, the "task-based syllabus" also promotes meaningful and cognitively challenging second-language experiences (Long & Crookes, 1992). A good example of such second-language teaching is the CALLA approach (Chamot & O'Malley, 1994).

The compatibility of bilingual education and SLA/ESL is illustrated by Rivera (1999), who describes the "El Barrio Popular Education Program as one . . . including literacy and basic education and Spanish and SLA/ESL" (p. 488). In this community-based program, English and Spanish are each viewed as powerful and relevant for individual development and self-determination. The curriculum involves thematic units that stress issues important in the students' lives. Ovando, Collier and Combs (2002), in their discussion of literacy and SLA/ESL, also note that concerns with ideology and the social distribution of power have had a substantial impact on the fields of language and literacy education. They note that "the impact has manifested itself in new ways of theorizing language and literacy development and, in particular, with an increased interest in critical literacy in both mother tongue and ESOL education." Indeed, the usefulness of first language support in SLA/ESL efforts has also been widely recognized.

Ebsworth and Sanchez (1997) report that in a middle school program at-risk bilingual students made dramatic gains in language and developed higher educational aspirations in a primarily SLA/ESL program that allowed for L1 use when needed. The knowledge that L1 support was available often encouraged learners to experiment with English. Similar results are reported by Shamash (1990). Many SLA/ESL programs today do allow for a degree of L1 use. Rather than present SLA/ESL and bilingual education as a dichotomy, it might be more reflective of classroom practice to conceive of both SLA/ESL and bilingual education as promoting additive bilingualism. The degree to which L1 and L2 may be used in this process would involve a range of L1 use for a variety of purposes. The actual demarcation of when an educational approach is purely SLA/ESL as opposed to bilingual (which includes SLA/ESL) may be somewhat similar to the dialect/language issue mentioned by Garcia (2001a)—that programs on the borderline receive their labels as much for political reasons as to reflect actual practice.

The instruction of English in academic settings has begun to acknowledge the importance of attending to the form and structure of English. Ellis (1993) comments on the *intake facilitation* role of conscious grammar, which causes "learners to pay attention to specific formal features in the input and to notice the gap between these features and the ones they typically use in their output" (p. 91). Van Patten and Sanz (1996) discuss the relative merits of explanation as opposed to structured input in second-language acquisition. White (1998) identifies a number of variables thought to be involved in the efficacy of attention to form in SLA. These include salience (how easy a form is to notice), explicitness (obvious reference to a form through devices such as statement of rules or corrective feedback), stage of acquisition of a particular form (from pre-emergence through targetlike use), and the relationship of L1 to L2 (similarities and differences in structure). Lightbown and Spada's (1990) "teachability" hypothesis (first suggested in 1985) matches conscious instruction to the developmental stage of the learner. Lightbown (1998) more directly favors some kind of conscious focus on language features to support acquisition. Furthermore, like the positive results of bilingual education, "effects of instruction attributable to noticing may not be immediate and may result from the delayed interaction of materials noticed and available for recall (rather than simply detected)" (Long & Robinson, 1998, p. 40).

The separateness of acquisition and learning also has a parallel in the discussion of declarative and procedural knowledge, that is, information about how language works and the ability to use language in communicative settings (Anderson, 1983). In the view of McLaughlin (1990), proceduralization (of declarative knowledge) comes about through practice and restructuring. Anderson and Fincham (cited in DeKeyser, 1997) state, "It is too strong to argue that procedural knowledge can never be acquired without a declarative representation" (p. 213).

DEVELOPING "ACADEMIC" ENGLISH
IN U.S. BILINGUALS

English "academic" proficiency requires a mastery of a more extensive range of features than "everyday" English. As was made evident in Chapter 1, an increasing number of children in the United States come from a non-English background. One of the most important yet difficult aspects of English-language development for students from non-English backgrounds, here referred to as bilinguals, is the development of English in academic contexts (Garcia, 2002).

Despite its importance, English academic proficiency among all U.S. students is generally low. Nationally, only 31% of all eighth-grade students were rated as proficient or higher in the 1998 National Assessment of Educational Progress (NAEP) reading assessment and 24% were rated as proficient or higher in the 1998 NAEP writing assessment. Proficiency levels for Blacks and Hispanics were even lower—only 11% and 14%, respectively, were proficient in reading in 1998 and only 8% and 11%, respectively, were proficient in writing in 1998.

While the research on reading and writing is fairly extensive, research on second-language teaching and learning is not. Two National Research Council (NRC) reports (August & Hakuta, 1997; Snow, Burns, & Griffin, 1998) point out the paucity of research on how best to teach English to bilinguals: "Researchers and educators possess scant empirical guidance [on] how best to design literacy instruction for such [limited-English-speaking] children in either their primary language or English, much less both" (Snow et al., 1998, p.339). A third NRC report (Meyer & Fienberg, 1992) reviewed methodological shortcomings of prior research studies designed to assess the effectiveness of instructional strategies for teaching bilinguals. Together, these studies have identified a number of problems with the current research on English-language development in schools:

- Failure of theories and research to take into account "the complexity of issues" (Garcia, 2001a)
- Lack of explicit theories and objectives in existing programs that make it difficult to sensibly design evaluation studies (Meyer & Fienberg, 1992, p. 90)
- Inability of "school and classroom effectiveness studies to identify particular attributes of programs and their relationship to student outcomes " (August & Hakuta, 1997, p. 162)
- Selection and attrition effects that make it difficult to make meaningful comparisons between studies in different educational programs (Meyer & Fienberg, 1992, pp. 17, 71–73)

The advanced language/literacy skills in reading, writing, speaking, and listening needed to succeed in school are often referred to as "academic" English (Garcia, 2001a; Scarcella, 2001; Wong Fillmore & Snow, 1999). A variety of models have been proposed to explain the role of academic language proficiency in educational attainment. Some, like Cummins (1981, 1997), have focused on the cognitive load and degree of context students manipulate as they respond to academic tasks. Some (e.g., Crandall, Dale, Rhodes, & Spanos, 1989) have focused on a close analysis of the language used in specific disciplines, considering academic English as a compilation of many subregisters, such as the language of mathematics. Canale and Swain (1980), in a widely discussed model, propose four key areas to consider: grammatical competence (encompassing lexical, syntactic, and phonological knowledge in an integrated whole), sociolinguistic knowledge (knowing which lexicogrammatical form to choose given the topic, the social setting, and the interlocutor), discourse competence (knowing how to put sentence-level propositions in sequence to form coherent text), and strategic competence (knowing how to negotiate clarification when lack of competence impedes communication). This model implies that unique aspects of language proficiency are tapped by each knowledge type and gives a broader perspective from which to view academic English.

Wong Fillmore and Snow (1999) report a recent examination of prototype test items for a high school qualifying examination for one of the 23 states that has adopted this requirement. Their analysis reveals that students must have competence in academic English to do well on the test. The language used in the test is not different from that ordinarily used in school textbooks and academic discussions about science, mathematics, literature, or social studies. To deal with this test successfully, students must be able to do the following:

- Summarize texts, using linguistic cues to interpret and infer the writer's intentions and messages
- Analyze texts, assessing the writer's use of language for rhetorical and aesthetic purposes and to express perspective, mood, and so on
- Extract meaning and information from texts, and relate it to other ideas and information
- Evaluate evidence and arguments presented in texts and critique the logic of arguments made in them
- Recognize and analyze textual conventions used in various genres for special effect, to trigger background knowledge, or for perlocutionary effect
- Recognize ungrammatical and infelicitous usage in written language and make necessary corrections to texts in grammar, punctuation, and capitalization
- Use grammatical devices for combining sentences into concise and more effective new ones and use various devices to combine sentences into coherent and cohesive texts
- Compose and write an extended, reasoned text that is well developed and supported with evidence and details

- Recognize specialized meaning; for example, that "share equally among them" means to divide a whole into equal parts
- Extract precise information from a written text and devise an appropriate strategy to solve the problem based on information provided in the text (Wong Fillmore & Snow, 1999).

Scarcella (2001, 2003) has undertaken both conceptual and empirical studies in English academic language. Her framework provides an analysis of the various social, cognitive, and linguistic components that students must master to communicate competently in a range of informal and academic situations. She argues that the features that enable students to use English in both everyday situations and academic situations are acquired at different rates over time; that some are easily acquired and some are not; and that most features of academic English depend largely on the development of basic English proficiency but there are many others (including formulaic expressions and simple word forms and transitional devices) that may depend less on the development of general language proficiency. In general, academic English and general English proficiency have a symbiotic relationship; the acquisition of academic English indicates that general English proficiency is in the advanced stages because academic English constitutes an important part of a student's general language proficiency that rests on the development of general English language proficiency. General English proficiency, on the other hand, is viewed as an integral component of academic English, for it is through the acquisition of academic English that general English proficiency is advanced (Scarcella, 2000).

In addition, some features may be more important than others. For instance, specific linguistic *functions* (such as persuading, arguing, and hypothesizing) are more characteristic of academic English than of ordinary English. Also, academic English makes more extensive use of reading and writing, while ordinary English makes more extensive use of listening and reading. In addition, Cummins (1981, 1984) points out that academic English, in comparison to ordinary English, is cognitively demanding and relatively decontextualized. All students, including those acquiring English as their second language in a bilingual schooling context, rely on their prior knowledge of words, phraseology, grammar, and pragmatic conventions to understand and interpret it. However—perhaps most importantly—academic English requires a much greater mastery of a wider range of linguistic features than ordinary English. It is important to note that despite these differences, both academic English and ordinary English require proficiency in the same linguistic components: phonological, grammatical, lexical, sociolinguistic, and discourse.

Although both theory and empirical research suggest that it takes many years for English learners to attain proficiency (Thomas & Collier, 1995), few studies have charted this development over an extended period. Most studies tend to target cross-sectional snapshots of student writing or examine development over a short period of time (e.g., Colombi, 2000; Gomez, Parker & Lara-Alecio, 1996). The few longitudinal studies are usually very small case studies. Sahakian (1997), for example, studied the writing development of four Hong boys from their entry into high school to graduation, exploring its development over time through the analysis of their school writing portfolios. In her case study research of four bilingual Hispanic students, Valdes (1996) found that the benefits of intensive ESL instruction and sheltered academic content class are mixed, since they often isolate students from native English-speaking peers and the more rigorous classes necessary to succeed in schools.

At the theoretical level, psychologists, linguists, and anthropologists have sought to define language and literacy through a variety of disciplinary lenses and develop models that address their particular disciplinary perspective, although some researches have sought to integrate these multiple perspectives (Bernhardt, 1991; Garcia, 1983). Linguists tend to focus on the *linguistic* dimensions, such as the features, forms, and uses of language (e.g., Halliday, 1989). Psychologists tend to focus on the *cognitive* dimensions, often from an information-processing perspective (e.g., Just & Carpenter, 1992). Anthropologists and sociolinguists tend to focus on the *sociocultural* dimensions, in which discourse and texts are viewed as social and cultural artifacts reflecting group values and norms, co-constructed in particular social situations (e.g., Freire & Macedo, 1987; Heath, 1983; Hornberger, 1989). Although each of these perspectives is important in understanding the development of English in formal schooling situations, each fails to provide a comprehensive view. The separate approaches do help us understand the multiple characteristics of this academic task and the need for a broader, multidimensional perspective with respect to research on second-language acquisition (Firth & Wagner, 1997).

At the empirical level, prior research has examined several issues relevant to this issue. One body of research has examined the issue of language transfer between the native language (L1) and English (L2). In an exploration of language transfer, Zentella (1997) defines transfer as "the influence resulting from similarities and differences between the target language and any other language that has been previously and (perhaps imperfectly) acquired" (p. 27). The exploration of transfer in a study of bilingual learners acquiring literacy is important because, depending on the relationship of the primary language to the target language, skills acquired in L1 may act as facilitators of the acquisition of literacy in L2. The similarities between English and Spanish have been shown to be so extensive that bilingual learners can considerably reduce the time needed to become literate (Zentella, 1997). Genesee

(1979) has shown that among trilinguals, there will be more transfer among languages that are closely related, such as French and English, than between those whose writing systems are more different, such as Hebrew and English. The age at onset of L2 acquisition, the amount of formal education, and pedagogical variables (such as the degree to which teachers help students see the relationship between their L1 and L2) are among the many factors that have been shown to influence transfer.

Studies contrasting writing development in English and Spanish also show some unique features that may be due to unique rhetorical traditions. For example, Montano-Harmon (1991), in a comparison of secondary school Spanish writers in Mexico and English L1 writers in the United States, reported that Spanish writers wrote longer sentences, used fewer simple sentences, and used more coordinating clauses. Reppen and Grabe (1993), comparing the writing of Spanish-speaking elementary ESL students with English L1 students of low socioeconomic status, also found that Spanish writers wrote longer sentences in English, with more coordinate and subordinate clauses. We will explore how age of onset of L2 acquisition of writing, level of writing development in L1, and instructional variables affect the writing performance of bilingual learners.

Another body of research has examined the development of writing in bilingual learners. Much of this research has focused on elementary school children (e.g., Carlisle, 1989; Edelsky, 1986; Gomez et al., 1996). One exception is a study by Valdes (1998) that provides a very rich longitudinal analysis of four English-language learners developing and not developing writing in middle school. Most research on writing, especially among elementary-age children, has explored the development of narrative writing from a personal perspective (Edelsky, 1986; Swain, 1975). This emphasis is understandable, given the stress schools place on narratives in both reading and writing throughout the elementary years.

School districts and teachers also vary in the teaching of writing in significant ways, with some teachers focusing on mechanics alone and others focusing on the content of the message, especially on academic content writing in science (Merino & Hammond, 2001). Other research has examined the nature and impact of feedback on writing development (e.g., Clare-Matsumura, Patthey-Chavez, Valdés, & Garnier, 2000; Ferris, 1999; Olson, 1990; Olson & Raffeld, 1987). Genre is another aspect of writing instruction that has been explored to a limited degree. Genre has been broadly defined by Grabe and Kaplan (1996) as "discourse types that have identifiable formal properties, identifiable purposes, and a complete structure (i.e., a beginning, a middle and an end)" (p. 206). Genre is important because students must become proficient in several different genres to be successful in academic settings (Scarcella, 2000).

Research also exists on the influence of contextual factors in literacy development. As August and Hakuta (1997) point out, the education of bilinguals is complicated by a number of contextual issues at various levels of the educational process, from the classroom to the larger community. At the classroom level, the composition (relative numbers of English-language learners and fluent English speakers) and structure (opportunities for inter-action) of the classroom can affect the social and linguistic processes that lead to meaningful second-language acquisition (Hornberger, 1989; Wong Fillmore, 1991). The attitudes and beliefs of the fluent English speakers are important contextual variables (Wong Fillmore, 1991). At the school level, the social composition of the student body can also be important in providing not only opportunities for interaction between English learners and English speakers but also a more supportive environment for learning generally (Rumberger & Palardy, 2001). At the family level, English learners generally come from poor immigrant families with low levels of parent education (García, 2001a), different cultural models of child development (Gallimore & Goldenberg, 2001), and a lack of knowledge and understanding of U.S. schooling and their role in it (Delgado-Gaitan, 1990). These factors have been shown to affect the development and academic achievement of English learners (Delgado-Gaitan, 1990; Goldenberg, Reese, & Gallimore, 1992; Rumberger & Larson, 1998). Many English learners live in communities that lack resources and opportunities for developing literacy competency (Rumbaut, 1994).

Merino (1992) has undertaken a number of studies on the teaching of writing to bilinguals. The focus of inquiry has been the intersection of teaching and learning as bilinguals develop their writing abilities in English and Spanish. This research has focused on exploring how teachers at the upper elementary level scaffold the development of writing in a variety of genres but with a focus on scientific discourse, exploring different kinds of science activities, and analyzing the products students produce in these activities and their relationship to standards (Merino & Hammond, 2001). Merino and Hammond (2001) studied two teachers who taught writing to bilingual learners. One teacher targeted the longitudinal development of her students through cross-sequential sampling, looking at students over time and across language proficiency levels. The other conducted a systematic cross-sectional sampling of her students' work, targeting students from different levels of language proficiency but capturing her students' writing as they first constructed it while going step-by-step through an experiment. Building on the preliminary analysis of the teachers, they applied several different types of methodologies, showing that pupil learning was incredibly rich in a wide range of discourse acts. In some cases, teachers missed the complexity of the growth in their students because of their use of traditional approaches to assessment.

Other studies on writing development in bilinguals have focused on elementary and middle school students from linguistically diverse backgrounds (Gutierrez, Baquedaño-Lopez, Alvarez, & Chiu, 1999; Gutierrez & Stone, 2000). These long-term ethnographic studies have focused both on writing/literacy development and on the consequences of particular writing/literacy reforms on linguistically and culturally diverse students in both formal and nonformal learning environments. Of particular relevance, these studies have documented the opportunity for participation structures or ways of organizing learning (or scripts) across both reform-minded and traditional classrooms (Gutierrez, 1992; Gutierrez, Rymes, & Larson, 1995). Gutierrez and her colleagues have illustrated how strikingly different microcultures for the teaching and learning of literacy emerge. They report that both reform-minded and more traditional classrooms continue to exclude bilingual students from rich writing opportunities in extremely low-level scripted lessons (Gutierrez et al., 1995).

Recent research has focused on the implementation of the process approach to writing instruction in urban schools (Clare-Matsumura, Patthey-Chavez, Valdés, & Garnier, 2000). Despite the codification of the process approach to writing instruction in many district and state standards, few studies have investigated how these standards are being implemented in practice. To address this issue, Clare-Matsumura and colleagues (2000) focused specifically on the nature of teachers' written feedback on students' work and the relation of this feedback to improvement in students' work from first to final drafts of their compositions. Results indicated that elementary and middle school teachers serving primarily poor and bilingual students tended to focus mostly on standardizing their students' written work with measurable success. Students received little feedback on the content and organization of their work, and these qualities generally did not change over successive drafts. Further research investigated the relation of teacher feedback and writing assignment quality to student improvement across drafts of their written work in elementary schools serving more and less privileged students. Results indicated that the amount and type of feedback students received and writing assignment quality each predicted a significant, although small, proportion of the variance in the quality of students' final drafts (Clare-Matsumura, Patthey-Chavez, Valdés, & Garnier, 2000). Results also indicated that regardless of students' level of academic achievement, when they had access to higher-quality feedback, they tended to incorporate this feedback into their written work with measurable success.

Although there is no consensus regarding the development of academic English in bilingual schooling, considerable agreement is beginning to emerge concerning the factors that affect its development (see, e.g., Fitzgerald, 1995; Garcia, 1999; Snow et al., 1998). The development of academic English is affected by political, social, psychological, and linguistic variables. Instruction also has an enormous effect on the acquisition of academic English. Academic English seems to develop successfully in classroom in the following circumstances:

1. *Teachers provide students with ample exposure to academic English.* Teachers make regular use of classroom activities and assignments that call on students to use academic English; they provide students with extensive practice in the use of academic English in speech and in writing, including in meaningful academic discussions about the texts that the students use and in writing expository essays.
2. *Teachers get students to attend closely to the features of academic English.* Teachers regularly use classroom activities and assignments that call on students to attend closely to the features of academic English.
3. *Teachers provide direct, explicit language instruction.* Such instruction includes particular features of academic English, including, for instance, word formation skills and specific uses of grammar.
4. *Teachers provide multiple assessments of bilinguals' academic English.* Teachers provide learners with honest feedback concerning their English development. They provide valid, reliable, and frequent assessments (including entry-level assessment; diagnostic, formative assessments; and summative assessments) using multiple measures. These measures (1) allow teachers to measure their students' developing academic English and to tailor their instruction appropriately, (2) provide parents with information that help them support their children's learning, and (3) give instructional information to all students that helps them learn English.

SPECIALLY DESIGNED ACADEMIC INSTRUCTION

Of particular significance for teachers of non-English-speaking students is the use of Specially Designed Academic Instruction in English (SDAIE) techniques (Becijos, 1997; Garcia, 1999; Krashen, 1999). These strategies attempt to minimize the use of English as the primary mode of delivering instruction while tapping the existing knowledge base of the students during content-based instruction. Students are not asked to learn English before being challenged in subject-matter learning. In particular, SDAIE attempts to match content instruction to students' language/communicative abilities where the instruction is not delivered in the student's primary language. These techniques allow the students to do the following:

- Show their abilities in ways that do not depend only on English proficiency, such as using pictures to depict a science concept
- Connect their real-world experiences to the content material under study (begin with fiction the students have read in their primary language then allow analysis of biological phenomenon present in their lives)
- Utilize talents not normally interjected into academic content learning, such as using music or dramatic presentations
- Seek and receive support from their peers, such as using group projects and community-based data gathering
- Utilize diverse ways to focus on and attack the assigned material, such as journal writing, quick-writes, and graphic organizers
- Connect content-area material through thematic units, such as interdisciplinary organization of content material around a theme

Although there is little research that specifically addresses the effectiveness of these instructional practices, they are making their way into teacher training programs and classroom instruction in U.S. schools.

CONCLUSION

This chapter has highlighted theories and related educational practices that provide a broad understanding of important issues in the schooling of bilingual students. The knowledge base continues to expand but is in no way complete. In addition, it would be incorrect to conclude that the data and theory that have emerged have been primary factors in determining the educational treatment of bilingual students. However, it does seem appropriate to identify possible program, policy, and research implications derived from research and practice as highlighted by this and previous reviews (August & Hakuta, 1997; Ovando & Collier, 1998):

1. One major goal in the education of bilingual students should be the development of the full repertoire of linguistic skills in English, in preparation for participation in mainstream classes. Future research should delineate alternative routes that will allow for effective achievement of this "academic English" goal.
2. Time spent learning the native language is not time lost in developing English. Children can become fluent in a second language without losing the first language, and can maintain the first language without retarding the development of the second language. Presently, it is not clear what processes or mechanisms best facilitate positive transfer. Identifying such processes is a challenge for future researchers.

3. There is no cognitive cost in the development of more than one language in children during the schooling process. Further research that explores specific cognitive/academic functioning of bilingualism is needed.
4. Programs for bilingual students should be flexible enough to adjust to individual and cultural differences among children. Furthermore, educators should recognize that it is not abnormal for some students to need instruction in two languages for relatively long periods of time. We do not yet know how much time in the first language positively or negatively influences academic outcomes in the second language. This type of research will greatly enhance educational outcomes for language-minority students.
5. Educators should expect that young children will take several years to learn a second language at a level comparable to that of a native speaker. At the same time, they should not have lower expectations of older learners, who can typically learn languages quite quickly and often end up speaking them just as well as younger learners. The clear distinction between "young" and "older" learners requires further research.
6. Particularly for children who are at risk of reading failure, reading should be taught in the native language. Reading skills acquired in the native language will transfer readily and quickly to English and result in higher reading achievement in English. Future research should connect overall literacy in the native and second languages.
7. A major problem for minority students in the United States is that many English-speaking children share the negative stereotypes of their parents and the society at large. Any action that upgrades the status of the minority child's language contributes to the child's opportunities for friendship with native English-speaking children. Future research with these children should link issues of ethnic identity, general self-concept, and specific academic status.

CHAPTER 4

Bilinguals in the United States Speak More Than a Foreign Language

Because the United States has been dominated by immigrants coming to its shore speaking languages other than English, we often forget that a significant number of students come to our schools speaking languages that are native to this country. Most obvious are the indigenous peoples of this country, including Alaska and Hawaii. Early in U.S. history, more than 200 indigenous languages were spoken here (McCarty, 2001, 2002). Very few of these languages remain today, although efforts are being made not only to record them but to sustain and in some cases revitalize their everyday use. Although not exactly in the same category, hard-of-hearing and deaf students also come to school speaking a language other than English that is not derived from an immigrant experience. In the United States, this is typically American Sign Language (ASL). These students also are immersed in non-English-language experiences during their early years and become proficient in their primary language, ASL. Issues related to the education of these newly "discovered" bilingual student populations is the focus of this chapter. They are new to this discussion only because they are not normally included in educational overviews of bilingual student education (August & Hakuta, 1997; Garcia, 1999; Ovando & Collier, 1998). A research and practice base of knowledge has developed in the last few decades on the education of these students.

DIALECTS AND BILINGUALISM

The terms *dialect* and *language* are sufficiently unclear to cause much confusion among educators; they are not even well defined by linguists (Fasold, 1984). However, linguists have learned to live with these ambiguities. It helps in understanding these terms to recall that everyone grows up speaking a language. If there are noticeable differences in several aspects of the language two individual speak, we might conclude that these individuals speak different dialects. The term *language* is also used to refer to a group of related dialects, but there is not a clear-cut way of deciding when to distinguish these groups as different dialects or different languages. There are criteria, usually based on the historical relationship of the languages, that are used to make such distinctions, but these are quite arbitrary and depend on good historical records and sometimes formal analysis of written documents that have been preserved. Much arbitrariness exists in deciding whether the forms of English spoken by Appalachian miners, New York City children, New Orleans hairdressers, and El Paso gardeners are different dialects. This is not a precise or scientific undertaking.

This decision is further complicated by the social and political reasons one dialect comes to be the preferred means of communication in formal social institutions such as schools, churches, and business establishments. According to Wolfram (1994), this preferred means of communication can come to be known as the "language" of society, with all other dialects perceived as failing the test of being a real language. This is just not the case. Each of the dialects can have well-defined linguistic structures, operate effectively and efficiently, and still be perceived as "less than" the standard. Although the standard does not have higher linguistic standing, it usually has higher social and political standing. A common myth, then, is that the standard is pure while dialects are full of errors (Perry & Delpit, 1998).

Negative attitudes about speech start with the belief that some dialects are linguistically inferior to the standard version of the language. Until the 1960s, the language of low-income children was viewed as limited and debilitating and as affecting every aspect of schoolwork. The language of Black children was described as inarticulate and underdeveloped (Labov, 1972). However, linguistic research (Labov, 1972) indicates that language variation is a natural reflection of culture and community differences. People's attitudes toward languages in general and dialects in particular stem from the social-class structure. If some dialects of English are more highly regarded than others, this reflects a socially constructed hierarchy, "so deviations from them are seen as unnatural, incorrect and inferior" (Thorton, 1981, p. 49).

Black English, also referred to as Black English Vernacular or Ebonics, is the most studied nonstandard American English dialect. It is based on African Creole and English but has certain distinct syntactic, phonological, semantic, and vocabulary rules. Labov (1972) estimated that 80% of the African American population in the United States speaks some distinct version of English. He notes that some Puerto Ricans in New York City speak a version of English as well as version of "Puerto Rican Spanish." A suggested estimate is that 60% to 70% of African Americans speak different varieties of English that can be identified as Black English, Ebonics, or Black English Vernacular (Lucas, 1997).

Despite linguistic equality among dialects, a student's language may influence his or her chances for success in the classroom. For some, the variation may involve pronunciation and vocabulary (e.g., Boston dialect); for others, it may also include syntactic changes (e.g., Ebonics). In the classroom and out, the dialect speaker will confront negative social attitudes toward dialects other than "standard English."

At a high school in northern California, an African American student almost missed her opportunity to be class valedictorian because of her Mississippi dialect. She was initially judged as not capable of competing in college-level high school courses based on this language judgment by local educators, despite her straight "A" grades (California Tomorrow, 1997). She was able to overcome this initial judgment only after her parents became adamant about her academic abilities and record and convinced teachers to give her the opportunity to excel or fail in the courses independent of her dialect.

For students like this one and others, such as Chicano students in the same high school who spoke a dialect identified as "Calo" or "Spanglish" (a mix of Spanish and English) (Garcia, 1983), dialects can represent important connections to their communities while being perceived as a liability by educators. A student can come to school with five present tenses (as in Ebonics) or the ability to create meaning by switching from one language to another (as with Calo) only to meet a language that is less linguistically adept or expressive. The students who never manage to impress the teacher with "I be good" or "estoy leyendo" are more than likely to withdraw from the conversation and subsequently fail to thrive in the classroom. For too many educators, the effect can be too easily mistaken for the cause (Wolfram, 1994).

Harrison (1985) concludes that a dialect can affect the initial judgment about how smart children are likely to be, how well they will fare as learners, how they are grouped for instruction, and how their contributions in class will be treated. And that, in turn, may affect the children's attitude about themselves as school learners, their willingness to participate, and their expectations about the results of participation. Children's competence in other skills is not easily predicted from the dialect they speak. Edwards (1981) found that it is probable that teachers, who expect problems with some children based on judgments of their dialects, may deal with those children differently in a type of self-fulfilling prophecy.

Studies have shown that children quickly learn to use more standard dialects in the classroom as they grow older (Dwyer, 1991; Lucas, 1997). In particular, studies of code-switching in children whose original dialect was Black English support this conclusion. Destefano (1972) recorded the classroom and nonschool speech of 8- to 11-year-old Black children. Their classroom speech appeared to be more formal or careful and to contain a greater frequency of standard features than their nonschool speech. Furthermore, it was reported that in a repetition task, Black English–speaking first graders responded in standard English 56% of the time. It is possible that even young children already knew most of the standard forms and were learning to use them in the appropriate contexts. A study conducted by Melmed (1971) revealed that third-grade African American children used standard English 70% of the time in school-related tasks.

Lucas (1997) refers to an instructional discourse study describing dialect features in predominantly African American classrooms in Washington, D.C. The study reports a developmental progression in the use of dialect from kindergarten through sixth grade. Children in kindergarten are still in the process of learning in which situation dialect is appropriate or inappropriate. By fourth or sixth grade, the learning process is practically complete. Group interviews showed dialect awareness mostly in the fourth and sixth grades. Few data are presently available regarding the instructional use and effects of dialect on academic outcomes. Wolfram (cited in Dwyer, 1991) proposed that it is possible to introduce students to dialect as a type of language study in its own right. He suggested that the dialect study would give students an understanding of language variation along with a deeper appreciation of the richness of U.S. dialects. Moreover, he concluded that there is no evidence to suggest that Black English, as a dialect for school-age children, negatively affect academic achievement.

In December 1996, the Oakland School District in California formally adopted a resolution calling for the recognition of Ebonics as a language and requiring that instructional strategies using Ebonics be used to teach Standard English to its African American students, who made up over 50% of the student body. This resolution generated a national and highly polarized debate about Ebonics, its linguistic characteristics, its varieties, and its advantages and disadvantages socially, educationally, and economically for its speakers. The debate led to the following resolution by the Linguistic Society of America (Linguistic Society of America, 1997):

> Whereas there has been a great deal of discussion in the media and among the American public about the 18 December 1996 decision of the Oakland School Board to recognize the language variety spoken by many African American students and to take it into account in teaching Standard English, the Linguistic Society of America (LSA), as a society of scholars engaged in the scientific study of language, hereby resolves to make it known that;
>
> • The variety known as "Ebonics," "African American Vernacular English" (AAVE), and "Vernacular Black English" and by other names is systematic and rule-governed like all natural speech varieties. In fact, all human linguistic

systems—spoken, signed, and written—are fundamentally regular. The systematic and expressive nature of the grammar and pronunciation patterns of the African American vernacular has been established by numerous scientific studies over the past thirty years. Characterizations of Ebonics as "slang," "mutant," "lazy," "defective," "ungrammatical," or "broken English" are incorrect and demeaning.

- The distinction between "languages" and "dialects" is usually made more on social and political grounds than on purely linguistic ones. For example, different varieties of Chinese are popularly regarded as "dialects," though their speakers cannot understand each other, but speakers of Swedish and Norwegian, which are regarded as separate "languages," generally understand each other. What is important from a linguistic and educational point of view is not whether (AAVE) is called a "language," or a "dialect," but rather that its systematicity be recognized.

- As affirmed in the LSA Statement of Language Rights (June 1996), there are individual and group benefits to maintaining vernacular speech varieties and there are scientific and human advantages to linguistic diversity. For those living in the United States there are also benefits in acquiring Standard English. The Oakland School Board's commitment to helping students' master Standard English is commendable.

- There is evidence from Sweden, the United States, and other countries that speakers of other varieties can be aided in their learning of the standard variety by pedagogical approaches that recognize the legitimacy of the other varieties of a language. From this perspective, the Oakland School Board's decision to recognize the vernacular of African American students in teaching them Standard English is linguistically and pedagogically sound. (Linguistic Society of America, 1997)

Controversies over Ebonics, how it relates to Standard English, how families should address their children's use of nonstandard varieties of English, and how such varieties should be used in formal educational circumstances are not new to the United States. Perry and Delpit (1998) comment on these controversies:

> These debates go beyond linguistics. It is a debate about culture, power, identity, and control. It is a debate about how best to acknowledge and change the reality that our nation's schools are failing African American students. It is a debate that will never end until our society and our schools provide true access and opportunity to African Americans. (p. 47)

This conclusion regarding Ebonics, although controversial, recognizes the complex interaction among issues of language development, culture, and schooling that continue to shape the educational circumstances of U.S. schools. It is both a challenge and an opportunity to address the linguistic diversity that resides in our families, homes, and communities, while at the same time realizing the significance of achieving communication in Standard English in schooling endeavors.

This research base and the understandings it has generated make clear that language variation is a common trait of U.S. students—they come in many linguistic shapes and forms. When we address such variation in classrooms, the question always arises: How should we treat such variation? This same research base suggests that educators cannot legislate or regulate the use of language, particularly in the home and in the community. We should never try to do so. We should know that such variation is the result of the social roots of language. This variability will persist because it feeds into a whole alternative set of identities, purposes, and cultures that speakers find rewarding and valuable.

We should recognize that the variations of languages that students bring to the classroom should be perceived as linguistic capital that can be used to achieve the goals of the schooling process—one of which is to teach a common standard of English. In these additive responses to language variation, we are building on the languages that children already have to help them acquire the language and the subject matter they need to succeed in school.

U.S. INDIGENOUS BILINGUAL STUDENTS

Language loss and language revitalization in North America are becoming issues of interest to U.S. bilingual researchers and educators. Kraus (1992) concludes that about 150 of some 300 original indigenous languages are still spoken in the United States. However, he notes that 87% of these are close to being lost. McCarty and Watahomigie (1999) report that 34 languages are still spoken by all generations, 35 languages are spoken only by the parental and older generations, 84 languages are spoken by grandparental generation, and 57 are spoken only by the very elderly. These languages consist of 136 different groupings; 47 were spoken in the home by fewer than 100 persons, and an additional 22 were spoken by fewer than 200 persons.

As Sells Dick and McCarty (1998) point out, a rapid shift to English is evident even among speakers of the healthiest indigenous languages such as the Navajo, who were historically among the slowest to become bilingual. As late as 1930, 71% of Navajos spoke no English, as compared with only 17% of all American Indians at the time (U.S. Bureau of the Census, 1937). The number who speak Navajo in the home remains substantial—164,286 in 2000, or 45% of all Native American language speakers (U.S. Census Bureau, 2001).

But the percentage of Navajos who speak only English is growing, predictably among those who have migrated from their tribal homeland, but also among those who have remained. For Navajos living on the reservation, age 5 and older, the proportion of English-only speakers rose from 7.2% in 1980 to 15.0% in 2000. For those aged 5–17, the increase was even more dramatic: from 11.8% to 28.4%. Among school-age children living on the reservation, the number of monolingual English speakers more than doubled, from 5,103 to 12,207.

As Crawford (1995) concludes, the crisis of Native American languages can be summarized as follows: "Unless current trends are reversed, and soon, the number of extinctions seems certain to increase. Numerous tongues— perhaps one-third of the total—are on the verge of disappearing along with their last elderly speakers" (p. 28). Native American languages are becoming endangered, as are the cultural attributes that reside in their essence.

Language loss among Native Americans did not arise as a result of recent policies and practices. The United States has singled out indigenous-language issues for quite some time. In 1868, federal policy regarding American Indians made clear that the schools should be established to eliminate "barbaric dialects" and substitute English (Crawford, 1995). These same sentiments and policies continued as the Bureau of Indian Affairs (BIA) established boarding schools and instituted an English-only curriculum. In addition to these policies, the migration of native people to urban areas, the penetration of English via economic efforts, English-language media (particularly video/TV), and the general positive social status of English have further exacerbated language loss (Fishman, 1991).

Sells Dick and McCarty (1998) report a useful analysis of the Navajo language. First, they conclude that the Navajo language is an endangered language. The causes for this situation are multifaceted (Fishman, 1991). At the center of these causes is the continued presence of a federal policy aimed at substituting English for Navajo. Until recently, schools independently supported and administered by the BIA represented the single most important institution charged with carrying out this language policy. Historically, they have been the only social institution to demand exclusive use of English and prohibit the use of students' native tongues (Crawford, 1995).

As McCarty and Watahomigie (1999) describe, the legacy of the past has begun to generate active resistance to language assimilation and blatant educational inequities among the Navajo. This is also the case for southwestern Pueblo people, who are beginning small-scale efforts to revitalize some eight related Tesra languages (Benjamin, Pecos, & Romero, 1997). In these efforts, Fishman (1991) describes the difficulties associated with these efforts, particularly since schools are influenced by the social and economic circumstances in which they reside. The tribe itself may wish to restrict the language taught in schools due to the particular language roles prescribed by its culture and religion (McCarty & Watahomigie, 1999).

More important than curriculum and pedagogy, school-based decisions about language influence what happens outside of school. At the Navajo Rough Rock School, bilingual education is organized consciously to revitalize the Navajo language in the broader community. The schooling activities are meant to reinforce the positive notions of bilingualism and to forestall the strong propensity for the students and community to speak only English. The specific intent here is not just education, but social "engineering" aimed at recapturing the use and well-being of the Navajo language. Initial signs from efforts by the Navajo (McCarty & Watahomigie, 1999) and Pueblo (Benjamin et al., 1997) cultures in reclaiming indigenous languages are hopeful. Others, including Hinton (1994), conclude that limited progress is being made in retarding the overall phenomenon of language loss among U.S. indigenous people.

As we address issues of bilingualism and schooling in the United States, language loss will continue to require attention. With the roots of bilingual education in the domain of social justice, the human, particularly educational, cost of native-language extinction has not received extensive attention. At the core of this phenomenon of language extinction, Fishman (1991) points out, is the issue of "rooted identity." In essence, Fishman reminds bilingual educators that self-worth is a critical element in educating language-minority students. Crawford (1995) points out that language and cultural loss is a characteristic of dispersed and disempowered communities—those that may need their language and culture most. It is not a phenomenon of privileged communities.

BILINGUAL/BICULTURAL U.S. DEAF STUDENTS

The options for language of instruction available to educators of the deaf in the United States have included spoken English, invented representations of English on the hands, written forms of English, American Sign Language (ASL), or some combination thereof. The current choice for language of instruction advocated by some deaf education researchers and members of the Deaf[1] community is the use of both ASL and written English (e.g., Ahlgren & Hyltenstam, 1994; Hoffmeister, 1990; Mahshie, 1995). Instruction that includes ASL and written English is commonly referred to as bilingual/bicultural education. The bicultural component refers to the inclusion of explicit instruction on the "beliefs, lives, and activities" that are embedded in and unique to the distinct communities of hearing and deaf people (Padden, 1996, p. 87).

I will briefly examine what a bilingual/bicultural model for deaf education entails and relate it to other models that seem optimal for supporting the social and academic development of "bilingual" children.

In the United States, ASL has been in existence for almost 200 years. During the early half of the 19th century, ASL was the primary medium of instruction in educational settings for deaf students. In the mid- to late 1800s, a growing sentiment that the use of sign language in education interferes with deaf children's learning of English led to the replacement of signed instruction with oral instruction (Hoffmeister, 1990). The official turning point to oralism[2] was the Second International Congress on Education of the Deaf in Milan in 1880, at which it was declared that "the method of articulation [i.e., speech] should have preference over that of signs in the instruction and education of the deaf and dumb. The convention declared that the pure oral method ought to be preferred" (Gallaudet, 1881, cited in Jankowski, 1993, p. 6). The result of this declaration was a sweeping eradication of sign language from the classroom and a direct shift to oralism.

The period following the Milan Congress was one of considerable challenge for deaf people. During this time, Alexander Graham Bell led a movement in the United States to prevent the development of a deaf "race" by attempting to impose rules preventing the deaf from marrying one another, preventing deaf people from having children, and prohibiting the use of sign language in public (Hoffmeister, 1990; Jankowski, 1993). Mas (1994) refers to this era following the Milan Congress as a time of "hearing 'colonialism'" (p. 72). The impact of the Milan Congress was felt worldwide, with many deaf teachers losing their jobs (Bergmann, 1994) and with sign language becoming "pathologized" (Jankowski, 1993, p. 7). During this period of public intolerance of sign language, the Deaf community managed to keep their language alive, albeit only in informal settings.

In the ensuing period of oralism, few deaf people successfully acquired spoken English or attained high academic achievements. After nearly 100 years of oralism, members of the Deaf community began to argue for inclusion of manual communication in the education of their children (Jankowski, 1993). Starting in the 1960s, some professionals in the United States and elsewhere began to acknowledge the failure of oral methods and began incorporating signs into their instruction of deaf students. What followed was the development of a variety of sign systems used to represent spoken language manually. These artificial systems included vocabulary items from the surrounding community's natural sign language as well as invented signs to represent grammatical morphemes and lexical items unique to the spoken language.

The invention of sign systems contributed to the rise of an instructional approach known as Total Communication. Though it has been defined and applied in various ways, Total Communication was intended to be the use of multiple communication forms including signing, finger-spelling, speaking, lip reading, and amplification to provide linguistic input to deaf students based on their communicative needs (Stewart, 1993). In application, though, Total Communication has come to mean using an artificial sign system while simultaneously speaking—regardless of students' needs. The use of Total Communication became increasingly popular in the 1970s and continues to be the most commonly used method in deaf education in the United States today (Jankowski, 1993).

Although the incorporation of signs into the instruction of deaf children has improved communication between students and teachers, the purported language skills in the majority language have not followed (Mahshie, 1995). While the United States continues to use artificial sign systems in conjunction with speech, many European countries, such as Sweden, Denmark, and the Netherlands, have abandoned sign systems in favor of the natural sign language of each country's Deaf community. This shift is the result of linguistic research that demonstrates the inherent limitations of artificial sign systems that attempt to mimic a spoken language along with the linguistic research highlighting the completeness and naturalness of the sign languages used by the deaf (Bergmann, 1994). The dissemination of these findings together with collaboration among deaf adults, parents of deaf children, and educators of the deaf have led to the renewed appreciation of signed language (Bergmann, 1994).

Linguists in the United States have shown that American Sign Language is a natural and autonomous language with a complete lexicon and grammar (Wilbur, 1987). Research examining signed English systems in the United States paralleled the European studies generating findings that these systems are incomplete, unnatural, and fail to adequately represent English (e.g., Drasgow, 1993).

Despite parallel efforts, the research findings in the United States have not had the same impact as those in Europe and have been largely ignored or rejected by many educators and parents of the deaf (Mahshie, 1995). Davies (1991) attributes the different outcomes to two important factors—namely, governmental support for multilingualism and multiculturalism and a high level of societal multilingualism in Europe. These factors are coupled with a highly centralized school system that applies national standards of education. The story in the United States is quite the opposite, with the nation as a whole continuing to promote monolingualism (Crawford, 1998). In addition, the United States lacks any cohesive educational strategy, so even if the federal government were to recognize the merits of sign language, local communities would still have final say over how deaf students are taught.

In spite of the political and social situation surrounding linguistic minorities in the United States, a bilingual model for the education of deaf students that includes the use of both ASL and English is *slowly* gaining popularity. The pendulum in deaf education is starting to swing back to using

ASL as the medium of instruction, as was done 150 years ago. However, as Mahshie (1995) notes, "Widespread implementation of a model that promotes fluency in both the language of the majority and of the Deaf community would represent a significant departure from current practices in the United States" (p. xviii). Jankowski (1993) indicates that most deaf students in the United States are currently educated monolingually—41.1% are taught in auditory/aural methods (spoken English only); 56.1% are taught in both speech and sign (spoken English accompanied by signs in English word order); and 1.9% in sign only (Mahshie, 1995, pp. xii-xiv). Furthermore, over half of the schools serving deaf students have only one or two deaf students (Ramsey, 1998). Consequently, very few deaf students have regular contact with other deaf children (Ramsey, 1998).

The academic achievement of most deaf students in the current system is alarmingly low. As Mahshie (1995) aptly observes, "Patterns of depressed English skills and school achievement of deaf children in the United States persist" (p. xiv). This contrasts sharply with the academic achievement of deaf students in European countries, where an improvement in academic outcomes has resulted from the use of natural sign languages for instruction.

The poor reading and writing abilities of most deaf people, together with their low achievement in other academic areas, has led some commentators to conclude that deaf education in the United States is a failure (Mahshie, 1995). The academic nonsuccess of generations of deaf children with normal intellectual capabilities indicates the need for an immediate change in the way deaf education is structured and delivered. For this reason, researchers, educators, and, most importantly, Deaf people themselves are taking steps to encourage a change in deaf education. They want a shift to use of ASL as the medium of instruction within a bilingual/bicultural model of education.

The debate over the best methods to educate deaf students in the United States is now becoming more intense. As this debate continues, Grosjean (1996) reminds us that the deaf child has to attain a number of goals with language:

- *Learn to communicate with parents and family members as soon as possible.* Hearing children normally acquire language in the very first years of life on the condition that they are exposed to a language and can perceive it. Language, in turn, is an important means of establishing and solidifying social and personal ties between children and their parents. What is true of hearing children should also become true of deaf children. They should be able to communicate with their parents by means of a natural language as soon, and as fully, as possible. It is through language that much of parent–child affective bonding takes place.

- *Develop cognitive abilities in infancy.* Through language, children develop cognitive abilities that are critical to their personal development. Among these we find various types of reasoning: abstracting, memorizing, and so on. The total absence of language, the adoption of a non-natural language, or the use of a language that is poorly perceived or known can have significant negative consequences for children's cognitive development.
- *Acquire world knowledge.* Children will acquire knowledge about the world mainly through language. As they communicate with parents, other family members, children, and adults, information about the world will be processed—and that will take place in school. It is also world knowledge that facilitates language comprehension; there is no real language understanding without the support of this knowledge.
- *Communicate fully with the surrounding world.* Deaf children, like hearing children, must be able to communicate fully with those who are part of their lives (parents, brothers and sisters, peers, teachers, various adults, etc.). Communication should take place at an optimal rate of information in a language that is appropriate to the end situation. In some cases it will be sign language, in other cases it will be oral language (in one of its modalities), and sometimes it will be the two languages in alternation.
- *Acculturate into two worlds.* Through language, deaf children must progressively become a member of both the hearing and of the Deaf worlds. They must identify, at least in part, with the hearing world, which is almost always the world of their parents and family members (90% of deaf children have hearing parents). But deaf children must also come into contact as early as possible with the world of the Deaf, their other world. Deaf children should feel comfortable in these two worlds and be able to identify with each as much as possible.

Consideration of these issues related to bilingualism and schooling suggests a much broader inclusion of research and practice in the United States. That includes research with deaf students. They are too often overlooked as a significant bilingual population.

CONCLUSION

Not all programs that serve bilingual students in U.S. schools serve immigrants or the offspring of immigrants. Indigenous students speak a large variety of languages, and children in the large deaf community in the United States come to school with ASL expertise. And a significant number of Ebonics speakers enter U.S. schools. Too often, these students are educationally invisible during discussions about the schooling of bilingual students. They do not deserve to be on the fringe of these discussions, debates, policies, or practices. These populations, much like the majority of Spanish/English bilinguals in the United States, offer a special set of challenges and opportunities to U.S. schools. The challenges have frequently gone unmet and the opportunities unrealized. It seems time to bring these populations into the broader discussion of bilingualism in the U.S. schooling process.

NOTES

1. *Deaf* with an uppercase *D* refers to a particular group of deaf people who share a language and a culture. Lowercase *deaf* refers to the audiological condition of not hearing.

2. Oralism refers to instruction that focuses on speech training and lip reading. Under this method, deaf children receive many hours of speech therapy during which they are trained to produce English phonemes and recognize spoken words on the lips. Oral teachers use only spoken English and do not incorporate any form of gestural communication. Children are not allowed to use any form of sign language; rather they are encouraged to use their speech skills to express themselves and their lip-reading skills to comprehend others.

CHAPTER 5

The Policy Debate and Related Policies Regarding U.S. Bilinguals

Educating children from bilingual immigrant and nonimmigrant families is a major concern of school systems throughout the United States. Policy makers understand that American education is not a successful experience for these students. One-third of Hispanics and two-thirds of immigrant students drop out of school (National Research Council, 1997). Confronted with this reality, policy makers (state and federal executive branches, legislative branches, and the courts) and the public have urged changing teaching methods, adopting new curricula, allocating more funding, and holding educational institutions accountable. Such actions at the federal, state, and local school district levels have and will continue to affect bilingual students directly.

The present discussion is an attempt to describe federal, state, and local policy and to help further our understanding of how such declarations attempt to either disadvantage or enhance the education of bilingual students. The education of these populations in the United States is a continuous story of underachievement. It need not be that way in the future. Educational institutions today should address issues of both equity and excellence. Our national educational goal for underachieving students has been to provide equal educational opportunity. The challenge today is for those opportunities to produce excellence in academic outcomes. Our five-decade effort in serving these students since the historic *Brown v. Board of Education* ruling in the 1950s must change from compensatory educational "inputs" to academically successful "outputs."

THE FEDERAL COURTS

The 1974 Supreme Court decision in *Lau v. Nichols* is the landmark statement of the rights of language-minority students, indicating that limited-English-proficient (LEP) students must be provided with language support:

[T]here is no equality of treatment merely by providing students with English instruction. Students without the ability to understand English are effectively foreclosed from any meaningful discourse. Basic English skills are at the very core of what these public schools teach. Imposition of a requirement that, before a child can effectively participate in the education program he must already have acquired those basic skills is to make a mockery of public education. We know that those who do not understand English are certain to find their classroom experiences wholly incomprehensible and in no way meaningful. (p. 18)

This articulation of the rights of language-minority students prevails today. The court suit was filed on March 25, 1970, and involved 12 American-born and foreign-born Chinese students. Prior to the suit, in 1966, at the request of parents, an English as a second language (ESL) pull-out program was initiated by the district, and in a 1967 school census, the district identified 2,456 limited-English-speaking Chinese students. By 1970, the district had identified 2,856 such students. Of this number, more than half (1,790) received no special instruction. In addition, more than 2,600 of these students were taught by teachers who could not speak Chinese. The district had made initial attempts to serve this population. The Supreme Court's majority opinion overruled an appeals court that had ruled in favor of the district and instead supported the pupils and parents.

The opinion relied on statutory (legislative) grounds and avoided any reference to constitutional determination, although plaintiffs had argued that the equal protection clause (of the Fourteenth Amendment) of the U.S. Constitution was relevant to the case. Pupils' right to special education services flowed from the district's obligations under the Title VII of the 1964 Civil Rights Act and the HEW qualifying regulation articulated in its memorandum of May 25, 1970. The plaintiffs did not request an explicit remedy, such as a bilingual or ESL program, nor did the Court address this issue. Thus *Lau* does not endorse the proposition that children must receive a particular educational service, but instead that some form of effective educational programming must be available to "open the instruction" to language-minority students. This explicit avoidance of specifying a particular remedy has plagued efforts to identify primary-language instruction as an essential ingredient for instruction of bilingual students, as in *Otero v. Mesa County School District No. 51* (1977) and *Guadalupe v. Tempe School District No. 3* (1978).

After *Lau*, the domain of the language-minority education lawsuits belonged almost exclusively to Hispanic bilingual litigants. Although some cases were litigated to ensure compliance with the *Lau* requirements of some special assistance, most subsequent cases were about the issues left unanswered in *Lau*: Who are these students, and what form of additional educational services must be provided?

In *Aspira of New York, Inc. v. Board of Education* (1975), a suit was brought by a community action group on behalf of all Hispanic children in the New York School District whose English-language deficiency prevented effective participation in an English schooling context but who could effectively participate in a Spanish-language curriculum (Roos, 1984). The district court hearing this case adopted a language-dominance procedure to identify those students eligible for non-English, Spanish-language instructional programs.

The procedure called for parallel examinations to obtain language-proficiency estimates on Spanish and English standardized achievement tests. All students scoring below the 20th percentile on an English-language test were given the same (or a parallel) achievement test in Spanish. Students who scored higher on the Spanish achievement test and Spanish-language proficiency test were to be placed in a Spanish-language program. These procedures assumed adequate reliability and validity for the language and achievement tests administered. Such an assumption was and still is highly questionable. However, the court argued that it acted in a "reasonable manner," admitting that in the absence of better assessment procedures it was forced to follow previous (*Lau*) precedents.

In the key Fifth Circuit decision of *Castañeda v. Pickard* (1981), the court interpreted Section 1703(f) of the Equal Education Opportunities Act of 1974 as substantiating the holding of *Lau* that schools cannot ignore the special language needs of students. Moreover, this court then pondered whether the statutory requirement that districts take "appropriate action" suggested a more precise obligation than the Civil Rights Act requirement that districts do something. The plaintiffs predictably urged on the court a construction of "appropriate action" that would necessitate bilingual programs that required the utilization of the bilingual student's primary language. The court concluded, however, that Section 1703(f) did not embody a congressional mandate that any particular form of remedy be uniformly adopted. If Congress wished to intrude so extraordinarily on the local districts' traditional curricular discretion, it must speak more explicitly. This conclusion, the court argued, was buttressed by the congressional use of "appropriate action" in the statute, instead of "bilingual education" or any other educational terminology.

However, the court concluded that Congress did require districts to adopt an appropriate program and that by creating a cause of action in federal court to enforce Section 1703(f), it left federal judges the task of determining whether a given program is appropriate. The court noted that Congress had not provided guidance in that statute or in its brief legislative history on what it intended by selecting "appropriateness" as the operative standard.

Continuing with clear reluctance and hesitancy, the court described a mode of analysis for a Section 1703(f) case:

1. The court will determine whether a district's program is "informed by an educational theory recognized as sound by some experts in the field or, at least, deemed a legitimate experimental strategy." The court explicitly declined to be an arbiter among competing theorists. The appropriate question is whether some justification exists, not the relative merits of competing alternatives.
2. The court will determine whether the district is implementing its program in a reasonably effective manner (e.g., adequate funding, qualified staffing).
3. The court will determine whether the program, after operating long enough to be a legitimate trial, produces results that indicate the language barriers are being overcome. A plan that is initially appropriate may have to be revised if expectations are not met or if the district's circumstances significantly change in such a way that the original plan is no longer sufficient. (p. 73)

After *Castañeda* it became legally possible to substantiate a violation of Section 1703(f), following from *Lau*, on three grounds: (1) The program providing special language services to eligible language-minority students is not based on sound educational theory; (2) the program is not being implemented in an effective manner; and (3) the program, after a period of "reasonable implementation," does not produce results that substantiate language barriers are being overcome so as to eliminate achievement gaps between bilingual and English-speaking students.

It is obvious that these criteria allow a local school district to continue to implement a program with some educational theoretical support for a "reasonable" time before it will make judgments upon its "positive" or "negative" effects. However, the *Castañeda* court, again reluctantly but firmly, spoke to the issue of program implementation. Particularly, the court indicated that the district must provide adequate resources, including trained instructional personnel, materials, and other relevant support that would ensure effective program implementation. Therefore, a district that chooses a particular program model for addressing the needs of its bilingual students must demonstrate that its staffing and materials are adequate for such a program. Implicit in these standards is the requirement that districts staff their programs with language-minority education specialists, typically defined by state-approved credentials or professional coursework (similar to devices used to judge professional expertise in other areas of professional education).

The decision in *Keyes v. School District No. 1* (1969) speaks directly to the issue of professionally competent personnel serving bilingual students. The case was originally initiated in 1969 by a class of minority parents on behalf of their minor children attending the Denver public schools in order to desegregate the public schools and to provide equal educational opportunities for all children. In granting the preliminary injunction, the trial court found that during the previous decade the school board had willfully undertaken to maintain and intensify racial segregation.

In 1974, during the development of a desegregation plan, intervention was sought by the Congress of Hispanic Educators (CHE) on behalf of themselves as educators and on behalf of their own minor children who attended the Denver schools. CHE was interested in ensuring that the desegregation plan ordered by the court include educational treatment of bilingual students to help them overcome the deficits created by many years of attendance in segregated and inferior schools. A sequence of additional proceedings and negotiations followed, with final comprehensive court hearings commencing in May 1982.

In December 1983, Judge Richard Matsch issued a 31-page opinion, which is the most complete language-programming discussion to date in a judicial decision. Judge Matsch, applying the *Castañeda* standards, found that Denver had failed to direct adequate resources to its language program, the question of teacher skills being a major concern. Moreover, this decision made it clear that any local school district in the United States must attend to the *Castañeda* standards. A few years later, the Seventh Circuit Court of Appeals, which includes Wisconsin, Illinois, and Indiana, ruled on the obligations of the states under the Equal Educational Opportunities Act of 1974 (EEOA). The court applied the tripartite test established in *Castañeda* and extended to state education agencies, as well as to local education agencies, the obligation to ensure that the needs of students with limited English proficiency be met. In doing so, the "Castañeda Standard," with deference to *Lau*, has become the most visible legal articulation of educational rights for Chicano language-minority students in public schools.

RIGHTS OF LANGUAGE-MINORITY STUDENTS

The previous discussion highlighted the increasing number of court initiatives influencing the educational services for language-minority students. The court opinions in particular have generated some understanding of a language-minority pupil's legal standing as it relates to the educational treatment received. At the national level, this legal standing stems from court opinions specifically interpreting Section 1703(f) of the 1974 EEOA. The courts have consistently refused to invoke a corollary to the Fourteenth Amendment within respect to educational treatment. Even so, it is evident that litigation has increased (and is likely to continue) and has been an avenue of educational reform that has produced significant changes in educational programs for language-minority students. However, like almost all litigation, it has been a long (a range of 4 to 13 years in court prior to an operational decision) and often highly complicated and resource-consuming enterprise.

Nevertheless, several important conclusions regarding the responsibilities of educational agencies have been established. The following, in a question-and-answer format, sets out some of these responsibilities. These are adapted from Roos (1984) and Garcia (2001b) and are still legally valid today. They represent a practical guide for understanding the legal status of bilingual students and the legal liability of the educational agencies that serve them.

Question: Is there a legally acceptable procedure for identifying language-minority students in need of special instructional treatment?

Answer: Yes. The legal obligation is to identify all students who have problems speaking, understanding, reading, or writing English because of a home-language background other than English. In order to do this, a two-phase approach is common and acceptable. First, the parents are asked, through a home-language survey or on a registration form, whether a language other than English is spoken in the child's home. If the answer is affirmative, the second phase is triggered. In the second phase, students identified through the home-language survey are given an oral language proficiency test and an assessment of their reading and writing skills.

Question: Once the students are identified, are there any minimal standards for the educational program provided to them?

Answer: Yes. First, a number of courts have recognized that special training is necessary to equip a teacher to provide meaningful assistance to LEP students. The teacher (and it is clear that it must be a teacher, not an aide) must have training in second-language acquisition techniques in order to teach English as a second language.

Second, the time spent on assisting these students must be sufficient to assure that they acquire English skills quickly enough to assure that their disadvantages in the English-language classroom does not harden into a permanent educational disadvantage.

Question: Must students be provided with instruction in their native language as well as English?

Answer: At the present time, the federal obligation has not been construed to compel such a program. However, the federal mandate is not fully satisfied by an ESL program. The mandate requires English-language help plus programs to assure that students not be substantively handicapped by any delay in learning English. To do this requires either (1) a bilingual program that keeps the students up in their coursework while learning English or (2) a specially designed compensatory program to address the educational loss suffered by any delay in providing understandable substantive instruction. Given these alternatives, the legally "safe" posture is to offer native-language instruction whenever possible. Finally, it is legally necessary to provide the material resources necessary for the instructional components. The program must be reasonably designed to succeed. Without adequate resources, this requirement cannot be met.

Question: What minimal standards must be met if a bilingual program is to be offered?

Answer: The heart of a basic bilingual program is a teacher who can speak the language of the students as well as address the students' limited English proficiency. Thus, a district offering a bilingual program must take affirmative steps to match teachers with these characteristics. These might include allocating teachers with language skills to bilingual classrooms and active recruitment of bilingual teachers. Additionally, it requires the district to establish a formal system to assess teachers to ensure that they have the prerequisite skills. Finally, where there are insufficient teachers, there must be a system to ensure that teachers with most (but not all) of the skills are in bilingual classrooms, that those teachers are on a track to obtain the necessary skills, and that bilingual aides are hired whenever the teacher lacks the necessary language skills.

Question: Must there be standards for removal of a student from a program? What might these be?

Answer: There must be definite standards. These generally mirror the standards for determining whether a student is in need of special language services in the first place. Thus, objective evidence that the student can compete with English-speaking peers without a lingering language disability is necessary.

Several common practices are unlawful. First, the establishment of an arbitrary cap on the amount of time a student can remain in a program fails to meet the requirement that all language-minority students be assisted. Second, it is common to have programs terminate at a certain grade level, for example, sixth grade. While programs may change to accommodate different realities, it is unlawful to deny a student access to a program merely because of grade level.

Question: Must a district develop a design to monitor the success of its program?

Answer: Yes. The district is obligated to monitor the program and to make reasonable adjustments when the evidence suggests that the program is not successful.

Monitoring is necessarily a two-part process. First, it is necessary to monitor the progress of students in the program to assure (1) that they are making reasonable progress toward learning and (2) that the program is providing the students with substantive instruction comparable to that given to English-proficient pupils. Second, any assessment of the program must include a system to monitor the progress of students after they leave the program. The primary purpose of the program is to assure that the LEP students ultimately are able to compete on an equal footing with their English-speaking peers. This cannot be determined in the absence of such a post-reclassification monitoring system.

Question: May a district deny services to a student because there are few students in the district who speak her or his language?

Answer: No. The 1974 Equal Educational Opportunity Act and subsequent court decisions make it clear that every student is entitled to a program that is reasonably designed to overcome any handicaps occasioned by a language deficit. Numbers may, obviously, be considered in determining how to address the student's needs. They are not a proper consideration in determining whether a program should be provided.

Although reluctant, courts have played a significant role in shaping educational policy for U.S. bilingual students. They have spoken to issues of student identification, program implementation, resource allocation, professional staffing, and program effectiveness. Moreover, they have obligated both local and state educational agencies to language-minority education responsibilities. Most significantly, they have offered to language-minority students and their families a forum in which minority status is not disadvantageous. It has been a highly ritualized forum, extremely time- and resource-consuming, and always reluctant. But it has been a responsive institution and will likely continue to be used as a mechanism to air and resolve the challenges of educating language minority students.

Skutnabb-Kangas (2000, 2002) and Crawford (2002) remind us that the United States is only one of many nations that must deal with issues of students coming to public schools not speaking the schooling language. In particular, the United Nations has spoken directly to the rights of a minority group to its language:

> Prohibiting the use of the language of a group in daily discourse or in schools or the printing and circulation of publications in the language of the group falls within the agreed upon constraints regarding linguistic genocide. (United Nations, Convention on the Prevention and Punishment of the Crime of Genocide, e794, 1948)

In 1994, the United Nations Human Rights Committee spoke again to this international issue (UN Doc.CCPR/C/21/Rev.1/Add.5, 1994). It is the most far-reaching human rights articulation of an international body addressing linguistic rights:

In those states in which ethnic, religious or linguistic minorities exist, persons belonging to such minorities shall not be denied the right, in community with other members of their group, to enjoy their own culture, to profess and practice their own religion, or to use their own language.

Skutnabb-Kangas (2002) has summarized Article 27 as doing the following:

- Protecting all individuals on the state's territory or under its jurisdiction, such as immigrants and refugees, irrespective of their legal status
- Recognizing the existence of a linguistic "right"
- Imposing positive obligations on the state to protect that "right"

Under this interpretation, the United States is in violation of this international standard.

STATE AND LOCAL POLICIES

Through state legislation, 12 states mandate special educational services for language-minority students, 12 states permit these services, and 1 state prohibits them. Twenty-six states and Puerto Rico have no legislation that directly addresses language-minority students.

State program policy for language-minority students can be characterized as follows:

1. Implementing instructional programs that allow or require instruction in a language other than English (17 states)
2. Establishing special qualifications for the certification of professional instructional staff (15 states)
3. Providing school districts supplementary funds to support educational programs (15 states)
4. Mandating a cultural component (15 states)
5. Requiring parental consent for enrollment of students (11 states).

Eight states (Arizona, California, Colorado, Illinois, Indiana, Massachusetts, Rhode Island, and Texas) impose all of the above requirements concurrently.

Such a pattern suggests continued attention by states to issues related to language-minority students (for details, see Garcia, 2001a). Of particular interest is a set of states that are home to almost two-thirds of this nation's language-minority students: California, Florida, Illinois, New York, New

Jersey, and Texas. In these states, bilingual credentialing and ESL or some other related credential/endorsement is available. However, in only three of the six states is such credentialing mandated. Therefore, even in states that are highly "impacted" by language-minority students, there is no direct concern for the specific mandating of professional standards. Valencia (1991) has suggested that with the segregation of language-minority students, particularly Chicano students in the Southwest, state school systems are not equally affected by these students. These students tend to be concentrated in a few school districts within the state, and even though their academic presence is felt strongly in these individual districts, they do not exert this same pressure statewide.

ENGLISH-ONLY STATE POLICIES

Three state initiatives in California (1998), Arizona (2000), and Massachusetts (2002) are the most recent efforts by states to restrict the use of a language other than English in the delivery of educational services to Chicano children. In California, the 1998 ballot measure identified as "English for all Children" and the related state education code do the following:

1. Require that all children be placed in English-language classrooms and that English-language learners be educated through a prescribed methodology identified as "structured English immersion."
2. Prescribe methodology that would be provided during a temporary transition period not normally to exceed 1 year.
3. Allow instruction in the child's native language only when parents annually sign a waiver and visit the school.
4. Prohibit native-language instruction only if the student has already mastered English and is over 10 years of age and when such instruction is approved by the principal and the teacher.

Therefore, this English-only policy allows native-language instruction only through an exclusionary and complicated process for the 1.6 million students in the state who are identified as limited in their English proficiency. Moreover, teachers, administrators, and school board members can be held personally liable for fees and damages by the child's parents and guardians.

The Arizona and Massachusetts statutes, passed in 2000 and 2002 respectively, are much like California's and require that all public school instruction be conducted in English, with some limiting provisions. Children not fluent in English are to "normally" be placed in an intensive 1-year English immersion program to teach them the language as quickly as possible while also teaching academic subjects. Parents may request a waiver of these requirements for children who already know English, are 10 years of age or older, or have special needs best suited to a different educational approach. It is the waiver provision that becomes more restrictive than California's. Waivers for primary-language use fall into three categories:

1. *Children who already know English.* The child already possesses good English-language skills, as measured by oral evaluation or standardized tests of English vocabulary comprehension, reading, and writing, in which the child scores approximately at or above the state average for his or her grade level or at or above the fifth-grade average, whichever is lower.

2. *Older children.* The child is 10 years of age or older, and it is the informed belief of the school principal and educational staff that an alternate course of educational study would be better suited to the child's overall educational progress and rapid acquisition of basic English-language skills.

3. *Children with special individual needs.* The child has already been placed for a period of not less than 30 calendar days during that schoolyear in an English-language classroom and it is subsequently the informed belief of the school principal and educational staff that the child has such special and individual physical or psychological needs, above and beyond the lack of English proficiency, that an alternate course of educational study would be better suited to the child's overall educational development and rapid acquisition of English. A written description of no less than 250 words documenting these special individual needs for the specific child must be provided and permanently added to the child's official school records, and the waiver application must contain the original authorizing signatures of both the school principal and the local superintendent of schools. Any such decision to issue such an individual waiver is to be made subject to the examination and approval of the local school superintendent, under guidelines established by, and subject to, the review of the local governing board and ultimately the state board of education. Teachers and local school districts may reject waiver requests without explanation or legal consequence, the existence of such special individual needs will not compel issuance of a waiver, and the parents will be fully informed of their right to refuse to agree to a waiver.

It should be noted that a proposition similar to those of Arizona and Massachusetts was defeated in Colorado in 2002. This defeat was the first rejection of such a state referendum.

In recent efforts to document the implementation of Proposition 227 in California, yet another "English-only" policy was reported to be substantially influencing the organizational environments of bilingual students. That policy is embedded in California's use of an English academic test (Stanford 9) within a newly defined Academic Performance Index (API) designed by the state to either reward or sanction schools for measured progress or failure of such progress (García & Curry, 2000; Palmer & García, 2000). In these empirical reports, school district administrators, including principals, and classroom teachers indicate that Chicano students are receiving more instructional emphasis in English, even in school districts and schools that have used the Proposition 227 waiver process to maintain their bilingual education programs. This new accountability policy, by providing only "high-stakes" assessment in English, is doing more than Proposition 227 to move instruction into English for non-English-speaking students (Palmer & García, 2000). (It is important to note that Texas accountability policies allow for the use of a Spanish-language academic test.)

These California and Arizona policy provisions, taken together, are the most restrictive measures proposed yet for serving bilingual language-minority students either nationally or within any state, via legislation or the courts. It is anticipated that the results of these policies will have substantive effects on the future on bilingual education and its practice within and outside the states of California and Arizona.

CONVERGENCE OF OTHER STATE AND LOCAL POLICIES

Because of the contemporary educational zeitgeist that embraces excellence and equity for all students—best reflected in the National Commission on Excellence in Education's final report, *A Nation at Risk* (1983), the articulation of national goals, *Goals 2000*, and the "No Child Left Behind" Act—attention to bilingual and immigrant children, families, and students has been significant. The major thrust of efforts aimed at these populations has been to identify why such populations are not thriving and how institutions serving them can be "reformed" or "restructured" to meet this educational challenge.

Such efforts include the California State Department of Education's attempt to better train infant and toddler caregivers in state-supported programs and the U.S. Department of Education's attempts to reform federally funded education programs (García & Gonzalez, 1995; U.S. Department of Education, 1997). Other agencies have also addressed this issue, including the Roundtable on Head Start Research of the National Research Council in its efforts to provide an issue analysis of research needed to produce a successful future for Head Start for a highly diverse population of children and families (Phillips & Cabrera, 1996), the National Council of Teachers of English and the International Reading Association in their treatment of language arts standards (NCTE/IRA, 1996), and the National Association for the Education of Young Children's position statement regarding linguistic and cultural diversity (NAEYC, 1997).

More directly relevant are the contributions to this discourse by the Initiative on Educational Excellence for Hispanic Americans (2003). All these articulations have attended to the "vulnerabilities" of bilingual students and have addressed issues of language and culture given the country's past treatment of Latinos and the present conceptual and empirical understanding of how institutions must be more responsive.

Reform initiatives addressed in the above publications have been used to construct new educational initiatives for bilingual students throughout the United States. Historically, educational reform aimed at bilingual students in California has diverged from many of these recommendations. The following discussion will deal with three substantive challenges regarding the schools reform response to bilingual students in California and to some degree in Texas, suggesting that new English-only policy initiatives converge with other "reform" policies to affect the schooling of bilingual students at the state and school district levels. Recall that at the state level, a new California reform has targeted "language of instruction" through the passage of Proposition 227 in 1998 (García & Curry, 2000). In 1999, the adoption of an English-only state school accountability program followed (García, 2001b). These two recent state policies, further enhanced by district-level policies, dictate the move toward English-only reading programs (Stritikus, 2002). In California, and to some degree in other states like Texas, these policy initiatives work together to determine the form and outcome of bilingual student education today. These policies and related practices are having and will continue to have negative effects on bilingual students. They are subtractive in nature, ignoring the linguistic resources Latino students bring to the classroom, and are out of alignment with responsive learning attributes of programs that work well for these students.

Since the passage of Proposition 227 in California, additional policy shifts—including high-stakes testing, supplemental curriculum focused on English acquisition, and high accountability—have converged to influence the education of language-minority students. Unfortunately, the effect of these multiple policies has not been all positive and the implications are not promising.

What emerges from the varied perspectives of teachers and principals (Stritikus, 2002) is that these policies are significantly altering the educational landscape for California's student population, especially bilingual students. Teachers are experiencing these policies as top-down reforms. This has in effect reduced teacher autonomy regarding classroom instruction. As teachers suggested, current educational trends posit higher test scores and a school's API ranking as the educational goals of students and teachers. This misplaced focus, argue teachers, leads to the impoverishment of student learning in the classroom (Stritikus, 2002). For bilingual educators, this further means the erosion of their primary-language instruction and curriculum. (See Figure 5.1.)

Most disheartening is the recent analysis of the achievement gap between bilingual and nonbilingual students in California. According to Stanford 9 data published in 2002 (California State Department of Education, 2002), the gap between English-fluent and non-English-fluent students has increased. According to this same data, since California's Proposition 227 passed in 1998, 88% of California's non-English-fluent students have been placed in English immersion classes that are designed to not normally exceed 1 year.

Figure 5.1. Instructional Services for English Learners, 1997–1998 to 2001–2002

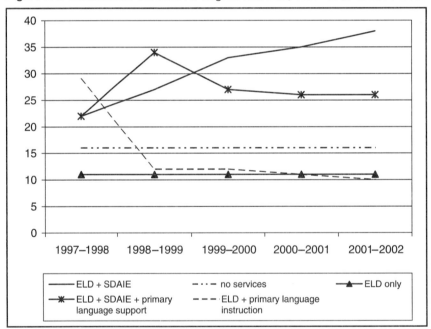

Source: California Department of Education, DataQuest. Retrieved November 21, 2002 from *http://data1.cde.ca.gov/dataquest/dataquest.asp*

Since 1998, SAT-9 test scores have shown a widening gap between non-English-fluent and English-fluent students, as Figures 5.2 and 5.3 indicate.

The impact of California's English-only reform policies on bilingual students finds strong parallels in the research findings of McNeil and Valenzuela (2001). Drawing on emerging research on high-stakes testing and their individual investigations (McNeil, 1988, 2000; Valenzuela, 1997, 1999), the authors identify a set of alarming educational trends regarding the impact of the Texas Assessment of Academic Skills (TAAS) in Texas. Some of the critical issues identified by McNeil and Valenzuela mirror the set of concerns raised by teachers in our study: TAAS-based teaching and test preparation are usurping a substantive curriculum; TAAS is divorced from children's experience and culture and is widening the educational gap between rich and poor, and between mainstream and language-minority students (McNeil & Valenzuela, 2001).

The educational trends in California and Texas are similar. Both states use one test to determine academic outcomes for students. Both have placed a tremendous emphasis on school ranking and are seeing a drastic increase in the implementation of mandated scripted reading programs at the expense of instructional practices for second-language learners known to be effective. California's educational system is growing more and more prescriptive,

Figure 5.2. California SAT-9 Testing Results Statewide 1998–2001; Class of 2008 Reading–National Percentile Ranking

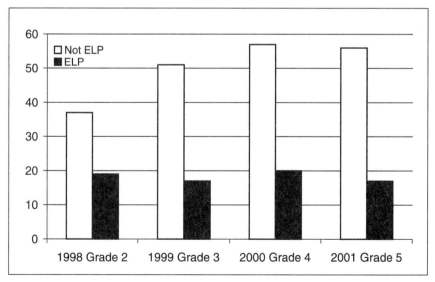

Figure 5.3. California SAT-9 Testing Results Statewide 1998–2001;
Class of 2008 Math–National Percentile Ranking

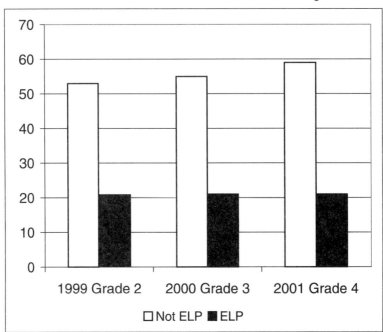

just as the Texas system has, discrediting the cultural and linguistic assets students bring to the classroom. McNeil and Valenzuela state that the TAAS system in Texas is "playing out its inherent logic at the expense of our poorest minority children" (p. 63).

FEDERAL POLICY

The Bilingual Education Act of 1968

Throughout our nation's history, Americans have maintained an intense faith in education. For more than 150 years, "Americans have transformed their cultural anxieties and hopes into dramatic demands for educational reform" (Tyack & Cuban, 1995, p.1). Although most groups made some advances in the quality of schooling during the first half of the 20th century, during the 1960s certain groups called attention to the deprivation and discrimination experienced by "disadvantaged" groups. As Tyack and Cuban

(1995) explain, African Americans, feminists, Hispanic Americans, Native Americans, and parents of disabled children entered the arena of educational politics and in the process created new goals and strategies of school reform. In particular, they moved issues of equity to the forefront of educational policy, as created in the legislatures and the courts.

The U. S. Congress set a minimum standard for the education of bilingual students with Title VI of the 1964 Civil Rights Act, which prohibits discrimination on the grounds of race, color, or national origin in programs or activities receiving federal financial assistance. In similar fashion, the subsequent passage of the Equal Educational Opportunities Act of 1974 (EEOA) made Title VI of the Civil Rights Act applicable to all educational institutions but did not prescribe a specific remedy. The EEOA was an effort by Congress to define what constitutes a denial of constitutionally guaranteed equal educational opportunity. The EEOA states that:

> No state shall deny equal educational opportunities to an individual on account of his or her race, color, sex, or national origin by the failure of an educational agency to take appropriate action to overcome language barriers that impede equal participation by its students in its instructional programs.

Still, while Title VI and the EEOA focused attention on educational equity and access, they did not define "equality" for policy makers. As the Office of Education Survey of Equality of Educational Opportunity stated, the definition of equality "will be an outcome of the interplay of a variety of interests and will certainly differ from time to time as these interests differ" (Coleman, 1966, p. 27).

On seven occasions, Congress has passed specific legislation related to the education of language-minority students (1968, 1974, 1978, 1984, 1988, 1994, 2002). The Bilingual Education Act (BEA) (1968) and Title VII of the Elementary and Secondary Education Act of 1965 serve as a guide for state and local policy regarding language-minority students. Since its inception, the primary aim of the BEA has been "providing meaningful and equitable access for English-language learners to the curriculum, rather than serving as an instrument of language policy for the nation through the development of their native languages" (August & Hakuta, 1997, p. 16). In other words, the BEA has aimed to address equal educational opportunity for language-minority students and has not evolved as a language policy.

The initial Title VII legislation built on the Civil Rights Act of 1964 and originated as part of the War on Poverty legislation. The legislation was primarily a "crisis intervention" (Garcia & Gonzalez, 1995), a political strategy to funnel poverty funds to the second-largest minority group in the Southwest,

Mexican Americans (Casanova, 1991). The BEA was intended as a demonstration program to meet the educational needs of low-income LEP children.

The War on Poverty legislation was largely based on the cultural deprivation theory (Erickson, 1987; Riessman, 1962), or culture of poverty theory, which dominated educational psychology. Instead of genetic inferiority, environmental factors were viewed as the main reasons for the underachievement of minority children. In theory, specific types of attitudes, language styles, work values, and other behaviors dampened the abilities necessary to overcome poverty (Levin, 1986). This implicitly encouraged a subtractive form of bilingual education, where the native language and culture were viewed not as resources to build on but as barriers to overcome (Cummins, 1991). Bilingual education was a remedial effort, aimed at overcoming students' "language deficiencies," and these "compensatory efforts were considered to be a sound educational response to the call for equality of educational opportunity" (Navarro, 1990, p. 291).

No particular program of instruction was recommended. In fact, financial assistance was to be provided to local educational agencies (LEA) "to develop and carry out new and imaginative . . . programs" (BEA, 1968, Sec. 702). Grants were awarded to LEAs or institutions of higher education working in collaboration with LEAs to (1) plan and develop programs "designed to meet the special educational needs" of language-minority students, (2) provide pre-service training to personnel such as teachers and teacher aides, and (3) establish, maintain, and operate programs (Sec. 704). Among the approved activities were the following programs: bilingual education, history and culture, early childhood education, and adult education for parents. Although bilingual education was mentioned as an approved activity, the legislation did not specify the role of native-language instruction.

BEA Reauthorization of 1974: A Definition of Bilingual Education

In line with the legislation and litigation that provided the initial foundation for the BEA, the 1974 reauthorization specifically incorporated language to address equal educational opportunity and linked it to bilingual education programs: "The Congress declares it the policy of the United States to establish equal educational opportunity for all children (A) to encourage the establishment and operation . . . of education programs using bilingual education practices, techniques, and methods" [BEA, 1974, Sec. 702(a)]. For the first time, bilingual education was defined as "instruction given in, and study of, English, and, to the extent necessary to allow a child to progress effectively through the educational system, the native language" [Sec. 703(a)(4)(A)(i)].

The inclusion of native-language instruction in the definition of bilingual education was influenced by bilingual programs in Dade County, Florida, which were founded to address the needs of the first wave of professional-class Cuban immigrants. The Cuban immigrants saw themselves as temporary residents of the United States who would soon return to their country and, therefore, wanted to preserve their culture and language. Thus, the bilingual programs encouraged Spanish-language maintenance and English-language acquisition (Casanova, 1991). At the same time, the success of the programs gave encouragement to the idea of bilingual education as a method of instruction for students from disadvantaged backgrounds (Hakuta, 1986). Native-language instruction could serve as a bridge to English-language acquisition by providing equal access to the curriculum until students were proficient in English. While the BEA acknowledged the role native language could play in supporting a transition to English, it did not promote bilingual education as an enrichment program in which the native language was maintained.

Other changes in the legislation included eliminating poverty as a requirement, the specific mention of Native American children as an eligible population, and a provision for English-speaking children to enroll in bilingual education programs to "acquire an understanding of the cultural heritage of the children of limited English-speaking ability" [Sec. 703 (a)(4)(B)]. In addition to the grant categories listed in 1968, new programs were funded, including a graduate fellowship program for training teachers for bilingual education programs, a program for planning and providing technical assistance to the development of programs, and a program to develop and disseminate instructional materials.

BEA Reauthorizations of 1978, 1984, 1988: Special Alternative Instructional Programs

During the years of the next three reauthorizations, public opinion reflected a strong aversion to the use of federal funds to preserve minority languages and cultures, claiming that federal funds should focus on English-language acquisition and assimilation into the mainstream (Crawford, 1999). As mentioned in the beginning of this volume (see Chapter 1), during times of peak immigration there is a decline in the acceptance of bilingualism. Increased immigration tends to create a feeling of instability, perhaps due to the unsettling aura of change, seemingly increased job competition, or fear of an inability to communicate with immigrants. This feeling of instability often leads to a fear of the unknown and an insistence on using English (Fitzgerald, 1995; Portes & Rumbaut, 1996). From 1981 to 1990, 7,388,062 people immigrated to the United States; this represented a 63% increase in the immigrant population as compared to the previous decade (Garcia & Gonzalez, 1995). Most new immigrants were not viewed as temporary residents like the

Cuban community of Dade County in the early 1970s. New immigrants were here to stay, which precipitated the danger of separatism in some people's minds. Preservation of minority languages could very possibly lead to the fragmentation of American society. Bilingual education programs that encouraged native-language maintenance would only foster children's allegiance to minority languages and cultures, and this was not an acceptable responsibility for schools. It should only be carried out by families, churches, and other institutions outside the school (Casanova, 1991; Crawford, 1999).

The 1978 reauthorization of the BEA added language to the 1974 definition of bilingual education which specified that instruction in English should "allow a child to achieve competence in the English language" [Sec. 703(a)(4)(A)(i)]; when enrolling English-speaking children, "the objective of the program shall be to assist children of limited English proficiency to improve their English language skills" [Sec. 703(a)(4)(B)]. Other changes in the legislation included the following: parents were given a greater role in program planning and operation; personnel were required to be proficient in the language of instruction and English; and grant recipients were to demonstrate how the program would continue once federal funds were withdrawn.

The 1984 reauthorization of the BEA marked a shift from mandating only bilingual programs to the acceptance of English-only programs. Transitional bilingual education programs were defined as providing "structured English-language instruction, and, to the extent necessary to allow a child to achieve competence in the English language, instruction in the child's native language" [Sec. 703(a)(4)(A)]. So the purpose of native-language instruction is to support transition to English instruction, and the allocation of funding reflected a preference for this program: 60% of Title VII funds were allocated to the various grant categories, and 75% of these funds were reserved for transitional bilingual education programs. In contrast, developmental bilingual education programs were defined as providing "structured English-language instruction and instruction in a second language. Such programs shall be designed to help children achieve competence in English and a second language, while mastering subject matter skills" [Sec. 703(a)(5)(A)]. So the goal of this program included native-language and English-language competence, yet no specific funding allocations were specified.

In addition to delineating these two bilingual education programs, the grant categories included special alternative instructional programs (SAIPs) that did not require the use of native language; 4% of Title VII funds were allocated to SAIPs. These programs were created in recognition "that in some school districts establishment of bilingual education programs may be administratively impractical" [Sec. 702(a)(7)]. While the 1984 grant categories remained the same for the 1988 reauthorization, funds allocated to SAIPs were increased to 25%. Furthermore, the legislation included a 3-year limit on an individual's participation in transitional bilingual education programs or SAIPs: "No student may be enrolled in a bilingual program . . . for a period of more than 3 years" [BEA, 1988, Sec. 7021(d)(3)(A)].

BEA Reauthorization of 1994: Bilingual Education, Language Enhancement, and Systemic Reform

Too often in the heat of legislation and the political process, policy development is highly centralized in the domains of various interest groups and professional policy makers. Therefore, the 1994 BEA national policy initiatives were crafted in consultation with diverse constituencies. For linguistically and culturally diverse communities, these included the National Association for Bilingual Education; the Mexican American Legal Defense Fund, which has made specific legislative recommendations of major proportion; and other educational groups, which have made recommendations related to their own interests and expertise.

Of particular significance in the reauthorization was the work of the Stanford Working Group. This group, funded by the Carnegie Corporation of New York, consulted widely with various individuals representing a broad spectrum of theoretical, practical, and policy expertise. In both published reports and forums, they put forward a comprehensive analysis and articulated precise recommendations for policy and legislation related to language-minority students. In the final report, the Stanford Working Group set forth a series of recommendations for Title I and Title VII of the Elementary and Secondary Education Act (ESA) as part of a comprehensive plan for systemwide reform. The following recommendations regarding the BEA were among several: (1) Reformulate the types of grants awarded to encourage innovation and limit fragmentation of services, (2) give priority to program applications that promote full bilingual development, (3) create a new part of the legislation to support language conservation and restoration efforts in schools and school districts serving Native American students, and (4) enhance the BEA's "lighthouse" role in language policy, particularly in promoting and maintaining language resources. As discussed below, the 1994 reauthorization reflected the recommendations set forth by the Stanford Working Group. The 1994 reauthorization of the BEA still aimed to "to ensure equal educational opportunity for all children and youth and to promote educational excellence . . . for children and youth of limited English proficiency" [BEA, 1994, Section 7102(c)]. In particular, the reauthorization introduced new grant categories, gave preference to programs that promote bilingualism, and emerged from a larger systemic reform effort.

Reauthorization of 2002: The Demise of Title VII

Title VII was eliminated as part of a larger 2002 reauthorization of ESEA measure known as "No Child Left Behind." Under provisions of this new reauthorization, specifically Title III, federal funds will continue to support the education of bilingual students, referred in the new law as English-language learners (ELLs). But the resources will be allocated in new ways, primarily through a formula-generated process supporting programs defined by the states. This differs markedly from the initial enactment of Title VII or any of its five reauthorizations. Moreover, "accountability" provisions mandate annual English assessments and attainment of "measurable achievement objectives," with the loss of funding a potential consequence.

This marks a complete reversal from the reauthorization of ESEA in 1994. Whereas the 1994 version of the Bilingual Education Act included among its goals "developing the English skills . . . and to the extent possible, the native-language skills" of LEP students, the new law stresses skills in English only. The word *bilingual* has been completely eliminated from the law. The new federal office created to oversee the provisions of this new law is identified as the Office of English Language Acquisition, Language Enhancement, and Academic Achievement for Limited-English-Proficient Students (OELALEAALEPS or, as it is becoming commonly referred to, OELA).

Federal resources to serve bilingual students will no longer be federally administered via competitive grants designed to ensure equity and promote. These resources will be distributed as formula grants to each state based on their enrollments of ELLs and immigrant students. State education agencies will have control over this funding. This set of resources will be spread more thinly than before—between more states, more programs, and more students. Title VII support for instructional programs previously served about 500,000 "eligible" bilingual students out of an estimated 3.5 million nationwide in districts that won competitive grants. Under the new law, districts will automatically receive funding based on their enrollments of ELLs and immigrant students. So the impact of federal dollars will be reduced. In 2001, for example, about $360 was spent per student in Title VII–supported instructional programs. In 2002, despite the overall increase in appropriations, Title III provided less than $135 per student.

Funding for all other purposes—including teacher training, research, and support services—will be restricted to 6.5% of the total budget. That amounts to about $43 million in 2002. By contrast, in 2001 $100 million was spent on professional development alone in order to address the critical shortage of teachers qualified to meet the needs of bilingual students.

In summary, federal policies have begun to mirror those in the states and local districts. They have begun to emphasize the teaching and learning of

English with little regard for the development of a truly academically bilingual program for those students coming to school speaking a language other than English. It is not clear if this reflects only a swing in policy direction or if it will "stay the course" in a political climate that is likely to change as the projected increase in U.S. bilingual populations become a reality.

CONCLUSION

As the United States anticipates policies for any of its students, it is even more important to understand the seismic changes in technology, globalization, and democratization that are reflected in similar changes in demography. They are almost characterized by a "blind spot" when it comes to the new demographic reality, particularly the growth in the number of bilingual students (Wiese & García, 2001).

These circumstances pose a particular challenge to educators and those among us who look to educational agencies for help in realizing the moral imperatives of equity and social justice. These agencies are being called on to develop and implement models of culturally competent practices for bilingual students that go beyond only addressing issues of language. As Wilson (1978) has noted, class has become increasingly more important in today's policy context than race, ethnicity, national origin, or English-speaking abilities in determining access to opportunities, power, and privilege in American society. West (1993) reminds us that race is still important, and Garcia (2001a, 2001b) indicates that language will continue to be at the forefront of federal and state policy activity. This chapter, with its emphasis on the educational policy related to bilingual students in the U.S., has attempted to deepen our understanding of their education. If we conclude that class and race count, we also conclude that language counts as well.

If we can attend to policy that "counts," then one could predict that as more bilingual students enter the "right" kind of schools, barriers to their academic, social, and economic success and mobility will fall. In that policy arena, language distinctions will blend with other features of our society to create a more "equalitarian" society (Garcia, 2001b): a society that is dominated by English in which negative effects of racial, ethnic, linguistic, and class differences are eliminated. This is, of course, a highly optimistic scenario of our future for bilingual students and American society in general. Yet it is most certainly preferable to a scenario in which America becomes a Bosnian nightmare, where racial and ethnic conflicts could escalate into major social unrest.

CHAPTER 6

Educational Reform and Schooling
U.S. Bilinguals

The contemporary educational zeitgeist embraces excellence and equity for all students, best reflected in the National Commission on Excellence in Education 1983 report, *A Nation at Risk*; the national goals legislation, *Goals 2000* (1994); reauthorization of the Elementary and Secondary Education Act, now known as the Improving America's School Act of 1994; and the most recent federal initiative of "No Child Left Behind" (2002).

Each of these policy articulations pays particular attention to the under-achievement of non-English-speaking students, referred in the 2002 legislation as English learners (ELs). This chapter addresses the conceptual framework for such reforms. This framework recognizes the significance of generating a schooling response that is comprehensive but pays particular attention to the linguistic, cultural, and broader circumstances of bilingual students in the United States.

AN INTEGRATED CONCEPTUAL FRAMEWORK
FOR THE INSTRUCTION OF U.S. BILINGUALS

Tharp and Gallimore (1988), in their research related to the schooling of Hawaiian native children, articulated the proposition that the interconnections between the culture of the home and the culture of schooling are significant. Put simply, they investigated whether there are forms of education that are specifically suited for the education of students from cultures that speak languages different from the language of schooling. Garcia (1994, 1999, 2001a) has proposed an answer to this question: The more the organization of instruction mirrors the organization of instruction in the home, the more likely school can enhance learning for students—students' previous learning is a resource for school-based learning. Schools have been operating in the opposite mode by assigning the types of homework that reflect the instructional activities of the classroom; these might be perceived as conscious efforts to make the home like the school.

Such compatibility frameworks argue against the notion that there are learning universals that can be prescriptively applied to members of any cultural group with the same learning outcomes. The extreme of the compatibility theory would suggest that each individual is a "culture" unto him- or herself and that instruction must be tailored to that unique culture. Placed somewhere in between these two extremes, conceptual alternatives provide a middle ground. This perspective recognizes the existence of universal principles—like those discussed earlier (Chapter 3) as "optimal learning features"—that make clear the interrelationship of the individual learner as a product of culture(s) and language(s) and the significant relevance of that culture(s) and language(s) to the instructional enterprise.

Moving from the conceptual to educational practice, the Oyster School in Washington, D.C., a bilingual effort, is one of the most studied models fitting this conceptual framework in the continental United States. It is known as a dual-immersion model, also known as two-way bilingual, bilingual immersion, two-way immersion, or developmental bilingual (Christian, 1994, 1997, see also Chapter 3 for more details on this model). In this scenario native English speakers are given the opportunity to become bilingual along with their native Spanish-speaking peers.

Freeman (1998) describes in detail the dual-immersion approach at the Oyster School, whose goals include bilingualism for all students combined with high academic achievement expectations for all and "a culturally pluralistic atmosphere" in which mutual acceptance is emphasized (p. 13). Freeman's research indicates that at Oyster, while academic achievement is more emphasized in English than in Spanish, the school is largely successful. The researcher also emphasizes that all knowledge—linguistic, social, and cultural—that students bring to school is valued. All students experience the esteem and concern of all the teachers. Hornberger and Skilton-Sylvester (2000) have stressed the importance of valuing what students from different sociolinguistic, educational, and social-class backgrounds bring with them to school.

In further research at Oyster, Duff and Early (1999) suggest that schools that do not follow the Oyster approach may produce students who transition into mainstream classes and have difficulty both academically and socially because they do not share the cultural knowledge of the mainstream students. Their follow-up of Oyster students after leaving the program indicated that they outperform students from other local schools that receive a different educational experience. They conclude: "The case study of Oyster Bilingual School demonstrates that schools can collectively organize and construct alternative discourses that position minority students more favorably than mainstream US discourse does" (p. 238).

How do we as educators begin to understand such a complex set of cultural, linguistic, and schooling variables? One framework for understanding is founded in the concept of "act psychology." First formulated at the end of the nineteenth century, the notion of act psychology proposes a model for human cognitive processes, or how we come to know. It focuses on the assertion that the mental functions of perceiving, remembering, and organizing—ultimately, knowing—are all acts of construction. It also asserts that what we know is closely related to the circumstances in which we come to know it.

The term *constructivist* really is an apt one. The constructivist perspective is rooted in the notion that for humans, knowing is a result of continual building and rebuilding. Our "construction materials" consist of give-and-take between the organization and content of old information and new information, processes of organizing that information, and the specific physical and social circumstances in which this all occurs. We come to understand a new concept by applying knowledge of previous concepts to the new information we are given.

For example, in order to teach negative numbers, a math teacher can use the analogy of digging a hole—the more dirt you take out of the hole, the greater the hole becomes; the more you subtract from a negative number, the greater the negative number becomes. But a math teacher cannot use this example with children who have no experience with digging holes. It won't work. This theory of how the mind works implies that continual revisions are to be expected. Therefore, when we organize teaching and learning environments, we must recognize the nature of those environments. As educators, we "build" teaching and learning environments out of what we know and how we come to know them. And we must continue to build. To ignore that is to discount the relevance of previous educational environments to the ones we are considering now.

Embedded in the constructivist approach is the understanding that language and culture, and the values that accompany them, are constructed in both home and community environments (Cummins, 1986; Goldman & Trueba, 1987; Heath, 1983). This approach acknowledges that children come to school with some constructed knowledge about many things (Goodman, 1980; Hall, 1987; Smith, 1971) and points out that children's development and learning are best understood as the interaction of past and present linguistic, sociocultural, and cognitive constructions (Cole & Cole, 2001). A more appropriate perspective of development and learning, then, is one that recognizes that development and learning are enhanced when they occur in contexts that are socioculturally, linguistically, and cognitively meaningful for the learner. These meaningful contexts bridge previous "constructions" to present "constructions" (Cole & Cole, 2001; Diaz, Moll, & Mehan, 1986; Heath, 1986; Scribner & Cole, 1981; Wertsch, 1985).

Such meaningful contexts have been notoriously inaccessible to linguistically and culturally diverse children. On the contrary, schooling practices often contribute to their educational vulnerability. The monolithic culture transmitted by U.S. schools in the form of pedagogy, curricula, instruction, classroom configuration, and language (Walker, 1987) dramatizes the lack of fit between the culturally diverse student and the school experience. The culture of the U.S. schools is reflected in such practices as the following:

1. The systematic exclusion of the histories, languages, experiences, and values of these students from classroom curricula and activities (Banks & Banks, 1995)
2. Tracking, which limits access to academic courses and justifies learning environments that do not foster academic development and socialization (Noguera, 1999; Oakes, 1990) or perception of the self as a competent learner and language user
3. A lack of opportunities to engage in developmentally and culturally appropriate learning in ways other than by teacher-led instruction (García, 1999; Ladson-Billings & Tate, 1995)

RESPONSIVE LEARNING COMMUNITIES

The learning environments that we consider essential to the development of a responsive pedagogy are those that produce "high performance" learning communities (Berman, 1996). The focus on the social, cultural, and linguistic diversity represented by students in today's public schools further challenges us to consider the theoretical and practical concerns needed to ensure educational success for diverse students. That is, responsive learning communities must necessarily address issues of diversity in order to maximize their potential and sustain educational improvement over time. The following is a summary of the conceptual dimensions of addressing cultural and linguistic diversity in responsive learning communities:

Schoolwide Practices

- A vision defined by the acceptance and valuing of diversity
- Treatment of classroom practitioners as professionals in school development decisions
- Instruction characterized by collaboration, flexibility, and enhanced professional development
- Elimination (gradual or immediate) of policies that seek to categorize diverse students, thereby rendering their educational experiences as inferior or limiting for further academic learning

- Reflection of and connection to the surrounding community, particularly with the families of the students attending the school

Teacher/Instructional Practices

- Bilingual/bicultural skills and awareness
- High expectations of diverse students
- Treatment of diversity as an asset to the classroom
- Ongoing professional development on issues of cultural and linguistic diversity and practices that are most effective
- Basis of curriculum development to address cultural and linguistic diversity:
  1. Attention to and integration of home culture/practices
  2. Focus on maximizing student interactions across categories of English proficiency, academic performance, and schooling prior to immigration to the United States
  3. Regular and consistent attempts to elicit ideas from students for planning units, themes, and activities
  4. Thematic approachs to learning activities—with the integration of various skills, events, and learning opportunities
  5. Focus on language development through meaningful interactions and communications rather than on grammatical skill building that is removed from its appropriate context

August and Hakuta (1997) provide the most comprehensive review of theoretical and empirical work related to the education of bilingual students in the United States. That work—generated at the National Research Council (NRC), an independent arm of the National Academy of Science—was based in the analyses of research and theory by a highly regarded panel of scholars. The panel concluded their review by enunciating the need to tie education interventions for bilingual students more strongly to education research by extending scientific-based research into this arena. The concern centered around the lack of evidenced-based research and scholarship that could lead the nation to better educational attainment for its bilingual students.

A recent contribution to this discussion is another NRC report, *Scientific Research in Education* (Shavelson & Towne, 2002), which recognizes that the purposes and goals of public education in the United States have changed dramatically over the last two decades. Shifting demographics have fundamentally altered the face of education. Moreover, Shavelson and Towne conclude that scientifically based research and evaluation in education are needed to shed light on an increasingly complex, performance-driven system.

The report concedes:

> At its core, scientific inquiry is the same in all fields. Scientific research, whether in education, physics, anthropology, or economics, is a process of building understandings in the form of models that are tested empirically. These empirical tests lead to refinements in models and theories and also to refined and new scientific methods for future empirical tests. The essence of science is this dynamic interplay between methods, theories, and empirical findings, not the mechanistic application of a particular scientific method to a static set of questions. (Shavelson & Towne, 2002, p. 2)

However, the report does conclude that education has its own set of features, not individually unique from other professional and disciplinary fields of study, but special in their combination. As the report (Shavelson & Towne, 2002) cautions:

> Education is *complex* in many dimensions. It is multilayered, unstable, and occurs within an interaction among institutions (e.g., schools and universities), communities, and families. It is highly value laden and involves an array of political forces that significantly shape its character. A key implication of this complexity is that education research must attend to important conditions of *contextualization*. The physical, social, cultural, and historical attributes of the particular aspects of education being studied are particularly critical for allowing the future replication of findings and for understanding the extent to which individual study findings generalize to other times and places. Finally, education research depends on its *relationships* with practice. These links exist along a spectrum; some types of research require only a weak connection (e.g., analyzing state assessment data requires that at some point parents and schools agreed to a test administration) while others require full partnerships with schools or other entities (e.g., studying the mechanisms by which interventions increase student achievement over time often requires that long-term partnerships be forged that enrich both research and practice). (p. 16)

The design study as a form of scientifically based educational research has evolved from the cognitive development literature. The research is still emerging in both conceptual and methodological aspects (Brown, 1992, 1994,; Collins, 1999; Lehrer, Carpenter, Schauble, & Putz, 2000). Design studies emphasize children's learning through articulated, theoretically driven hypotheses testing instructional interventions that include rigorous measures of the interventions themselves and student achievement both narrowly (pre–post testing) and broadly defined (measures of student participation). This research exemplifies the principles of scientific research in education that is very directly use-inspired and addresses important, complex, multidimensional issues in student teaching and learning in the context of schooling.

In general, design studies share some common features. Using theoretically grounded pedagogy, these efforts are based on a constructivist theory of teaching and learning. With instructional scaffolding, children engage in collaborative activities in which they learn to think, act, and talk as members of a learning community. Through these activities, children also come to a deeper understanding of the concepts, powerful ideas, and epistemology of the subject matter. Design studies are particularly interested in the developmental trajectories of children's abilities in carefully designed learning environments that promote ever-increasing levels of knowledge (Lehrer, Carpenter, Schauble & Putz, 2000).

In summary, design experiments indicate that effective instruction is essential to fostering elementary students' learning. Researchers design learning environments that promote student learning and carefully document interventions and learning. They rely on design principles that are derived from a specific theoretical/conceptual framework. Lehrer and colleagues (2000) argue that working with teachers in complex instructional settings adds greatly to both our pure and applied knowledge bases:

> Sustaining and elaborating these initial efforts, however, requires attention to some important design features that are seldom articulated, features that teachers can orchestrate to help children build a chain of learning rather than a succession of fleeting interests. (p. 96)

THE DESIGN STUDY—A RESPONSIVE BILINGUAL LEARNING COMMUNITY: SITES, TEACHERS, AND INTERVENTION

It has become important to focus on the process of guiding our instruction, organizing our curriculum, teaching the children in a way that is more appropriate for them.
(Juliana, Teacher, Chang Ching School)

This initial discussion of this design study addresses the professional planning and development component of the Authentic Literacy Assessment System (ALAS). The ALAS, a collaborative project of the San Francisco Unified School District (SFUSD), university researchers, and teachers in two urban, linguistically diverse elementary schools (Sierra Madre Elementary School and Chang Ching Elementary School), reformed schoolwide writing instruction for linguistically and culturally diverse students. Since the summer of 1997, teachers at these schools, an SFUSD literacy coach, and researchers from the University of California, Berkeley, worked together to develop and implement research-based ways of teaching and assessing writing to diverse elementary school students.

Teacher involvement has been a central component of this longitudinal project. In the two participating elementary schools, teachers have been engaged in intensive, ongoing planning, implementation, and training aimed at reforming writing instruction and classroom assessment practices. Reform has been evident in four schoolwide activities: (1) development and yearly administration of ongoing ALAS writing events for all students in each language of instruction; (2) creation and revision of writing rubrics, including alignment of rubrics with district writing standards and selection of writing exemplars, or "anchor papers," for all rubric scores; (3) frequent scoring of students' writing samples; and (4) linking ALAS data to biliteracy instruction.

Using qualitative data consisting of field notes, teachers' written assessments of meetings, and four in-depth interviews, this aspect of the research explores ways in which individual teachers have integrated the notion of linking authentic assessment to existing language arts instruction. They address these issues in the core curriculum areas within multilingual, multicultural contexts.

The Sites

Sierra Madre Elementary School serves students in kindergarten through fifth grade and is located in a residential, middle- to upper-middle-class neighborhood of San Francisco. The school offers kindergarten through fifth-grade Spanish/English bilingual education, English-language development (ELD), and special education classrooms (one for learning difficulties and one for developmental delays). Approximately 80% of the nearly 345 students receive free or reduced-price lunches. About 35% of students are language-minority students classified by the school district as limited or non-English proficient. Students who are U.S.-born, Mexican American, or of Central American Latino backgrounds constitute the largest ethnic groups in the school. The demographic profile of Sierra Madre Elementary is shown in Figures 6.1 and 6.2.

Chang Ching Elementary School, serving students in prekindergarten through fifth grade, is located in a vibrant working-class Latino community in the heart of San Francisco. School staff maintain close ties with the surrounding community and with parents. The school offers a prekindergarten program as well as kindergarten through fifth-grade Spanish/English and Chinese/English bilingual, ELD, deaf education, and special education (learning disabilities) classrooms. Approximately 80% of the nearly 470 students receive free or reduced-price lunches. Of the students 76% are language-minority students classified by the school district as limited or non-English

Figure 6.1. Sierra Madre Student Profile

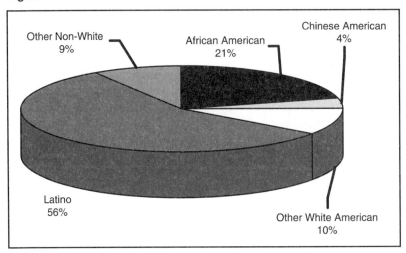

proficient. Latino students of U.S.-born, Mexican American, and Central American backgrounds constitute the largest ethnic groups in the school. U.S.- and foreign-born Chinese-background students constitute the second-largest ethnic community. The demographic profile of Chang Ching Elementary is shown in Figures 6.3 and 6.4.

Professional Planning and Development

The traditional terms *professional development* and *teacher training* can give the false impression that in this project, learning has been unidirectional, with teachers simply receiving knowledge from an external source (such as a university or a teacher coach), then implementing it in their classrooms. However, teachers, principals, and researchers have shared decision making in the design and implementation of this bilingual, authentic writing assessment since it was implemented in 1997. Teacher workshops, where teachers take a more formal "learner" role, do take place. However, these generally occur at the request of the teachers themselves. For instance, teachers occasionally express the need to learn more about teaching a certain aspect of writing, and we work with the school's professional development committee or with the principal to set up workshops on areas identified by teachers. As a result of this co-development, the ALAS has taken shape differently at each of the two schools, depending on local circumstances and on site-based decisions made by teachers and administrators. Still, the ALAS at

Figure 6.2. Sierra Madre Home-Language Profile

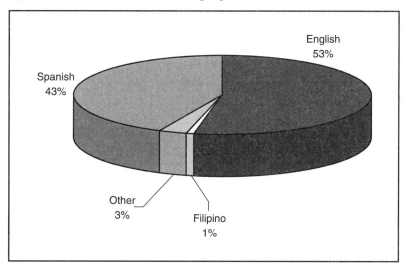

both schools share the same general implementation characteristics that are described next.

Development of the ALAS

In July and September of 1997, University of California researchers met with teachers and principals from Chang Ching and Sierra Madre under the auspices of the SFUSD's Bilingual Education Language Academy. Together, school staff and researchers worked through a data examination process, scrutinizing students' standardized scores and attempting to identify areas of instructional need. Teachers at both schools confirmed what they already knew to be true: As measured by standardized assessments, first- through fifth-grade students demonstrated language and literacy skills that were well below grade-level expectations.

However, while teachers were able to make such general data statements, they found that the standardized testing information did not provide specific information about students' academic knowledge in a way that was immediately relevant to classroom instruction. The statewide, external assessments were not aligned with the California or the SFUSD language arts standards and were not embedded in daily classroom practices. Additionally, standardized test results were not made available in a time frame that allowed teachers to improve their instruction before students completed the academic year.

Figure 6.3. Chang Ching Student Profile

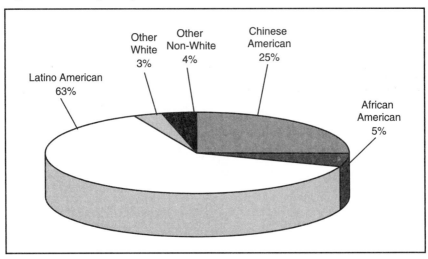

Figure 6.4. Chang Ching Home-Language Profile

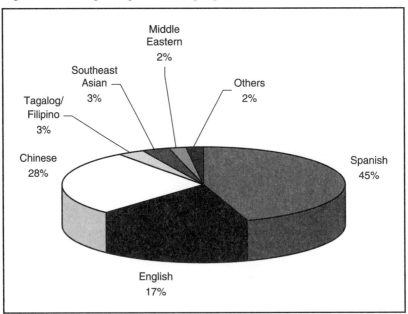

Teachers expressed an urgent need to have an assessment that would provide specific data about their students' literacy on an ongoing basis throughout the schoolyear and in all the languages of instruction. Teachers could use this type of data to tailor their instruction to the specific strengths and needs of the students in their classrooms. Later, in an interview, Juliana, the Chang Ching teacher quoted earlier in this chapter, expressed this idea:

> [If] I want to see how effective my instruction is, I would like to have a baseline to say, "OK, they arrived to me like this, and this is what they are doing now. And so, what is going to be the goal?"

Teachers and researchers noted that the school district's Integrated Writing Assessment (IWA), which was administered once a year in English to fourth graders, contained elements that, if modified substantially, would have the potential to inform instruction. This existing assessment was aligned with SFUSD's language arts standards. It was based on process writing theories and direct assessment of children's writing.

The collaborative team of researcher and school personnel noted that if such an assessment (1) were altered to suit students at different grade levels, (2) took place several times a year, and (3) took place in all the languages of instruction, it would yield data that would be useful to teachers working to tailor language arts instruction to their students. So, while initially inspired by the SFUSD's IWA, the ALAS can be distinguished from the districtwide assessment in that it is developed specifically for the student body at the schools, it is offered to students at every grade level, it is ongoing, and it is bilingual. Additionally, it includes a substantial amount of teacher involvement and development, through which instructional reform happens. At the end of this planning a set of design and implementation principles were articulated:

1. The assessment process and instrument must be aligned with instructional activity that exists in the classroom, including the language in which instruction is taking place.
2. The assessment must maximize students' experience and ability to demonstrate literacy competencies in several domains.
3. The assessment must be ongoing and able to demonstrate development/learning over the entire academic year.
4. The assessment must be tied to a theoretical and empirical knowledge base and coupled with teacher practice expertise.
5. The results and analysis of the assessment must be usable by teachers to inform, adapt, and maximize literacy instruction schoolwide.
6. Wherever possible, students should be able to participate in the development and utilization of the assessment process.

Using these design principles and with the guided assistance of the Bilingual Education Language Academy's literacy coach, during the 1997–1998 schoolyear we developed and piloted several authentic writing assessment events in the different languages of instruction at all grade levels. This process began with an experiential workshop, where teachers themselves "sat"(or participated in) the district's fourth-grade assessment, then reflected on ways in which it could be modified for their particular students. For instance, at Sierra Madre School, teachers brainstormed different types of prewriting exercises they could use with their classes. The list included sequencing events in the story with sentence strips and through small-group dramatic enactment, and detailing characteristics of the protagonist's personality and decisions in the story. After this initial workshop, teachers, researchers, and the coach worked together to develop grade-specific assessments. Teachers felt that the instructional practices embedded in the ALAS procedures were authentic in that they mirrored the elementary-level writing curriculum. However, they recognized that some of the authenticity of the assessment would be lost by standardizing the administration procedures across same-grade classrooms. Still, they agreed that similar procedures should be followed in different classrooms in order to have data that could be used on a schoolwide basis.

Since the beginning of the project, we have worked through initial implementation issues regarding administration procedures, including (1) whether to standardize same-grade prewriting activities, (2) whether to elicit students' writing in the same genre during each year's multiple assessments, (3) how frequently to administer the assessment, and (4) how to develop multiple quality assessments for each grade level in each language of instruction.

During the 1997 pilot year, teachers maintained uniform administration procedures for the writing segment of the assessment. However, they varied in the prewriting activities they presented to students prior to the written response. For instance, one teacher may do all the prewriting activities in 1 day, while another may do a variety of activities over the course of 3 days. Teachers saw the value in this individual approach to prewriting for day-to-day instruction. However, by the end of the pilot year, teachers agreed that, in order to have data that were comparable across the school at the time of the assessment, all teachers should follow the same procedures. Ongoing grade-level discussions among teachers ensure that the ALAS continues to address the realities of the culturally and linguistically diverse students at the school.

We learned that in order to get the greatest benefit from the frequent administrations of writing assessments, prompts should elicit student writings in roughly the same genre each time. That is, we found that it was difficult to assess three writings done by an individual student when two pieces had been written for narrative purposes and one for persuasive purposes. While teachers continued to provide opportunities for students to write in varied genres, they held that students should not be required to write in widely ranging styles for the three ALAS administrations.

The issue of the frequency of the ALAS administrations was one that needed refining as well. During the pilot year, we attempted to administer the ALAS bimonthly in both languages of instruction. Preparation for such frequent administration proved to be extremely impractical and did not leave teachers with sufficient time to alter their instruction between the scoring of papers. This was especially true of bilingual classrooms, where assessments were administered in two languages. In 1998–1999 we administered the ALAS quarterly. While the frequent paper-scoring meetings enabled teachers to become experts in analyzing their students' writing, they did not leave time for teachers to develop ways of modifying their instruction to accommodate individual students' literacy needs and strengths. In 1999–2000 and again in 2000–2001, the ALAS was administered three times: once in the fall (at the beginning of the schoolyear), once in the winter, and once in the spring. This schedule has allowed teachers and researchers to analyze data more fully and to spend more time developing instructional strategies to improve students' writing.

One issue that continued to generate concern was the creation of high-quality ALAS activities for each grade level and in each language of instruction. Quality literature had to be identified, appropriate prewriting activities developed, and good writing prompts (in similar genres) created. The district-adopted language arts series had quality literature for primary grades in English and Spanish. After the first year, fourth- and fifth-grade teachers decided that the lengthy texts of the adopted series were inappropriate for the purposes of the ALAS. They began to select other high-interest, grade-level literature for the ALAS. Chinese/English bilingual teachers have struggled to find interesting and appropriate literature in Chinese, but the small team of teachers has worked together to develop grade-level appropriate prewriting activities and prompts to compensate for the paucity in literature.

Needless to say, developing quality ALAS activities is time consuming and challenging and could not easily be done during the schoolyear. After a trying first year of preparing assessments during the academic year, the summer 1999 team of teachers at Sierra Madre Elementary worked to develop a full packet of K–5 ALAS activities in English and Spanish. These were given to teachers at the beginning of the following schoolyear.

In sum, the implementation challenges led teachers and researchers to continue altering the way in which the assessments were administered. Even as these challenges took place, the coach worked with teachers in a workshop setting to analyze student writing and to create school-specific writing rubrics to use for scoring the student writings. Like other rubrics, this one identified key observable attributes of a student product—in this case, a writing sample.

The rubric, through numeric values assigned to the articulated attributes, allowed teachers a common tool to evaluate the student product. The next section of this chapter describes this aspect of the teachers' work.

ANALYSIS OF WRITING, CREATING, AND REVISING WRITING RUBRICS

In late 1997, the literacy coach met with the staff at the two schools to examine student writings and to begin developing a common language for discussing students' work. The teachers examined varied writing rubrics, or scoring guides. In particular, they looked at holistic and analytic rubrics. The holistic rubrics described general features of student writing at different levels of proficiency, while analytic rubrics studied different elements of writing in relation to each other (e.g., topic, organization, style/voice, conventions). At both schools, teachers saw that while holistic rubrics provided good general pictures of how written work was done, analytic rubrics provided more specific information that could provide details on classroom instruction. They opted to generate analytic rubrics using the four categories described earlier.

In the spring of 1998, the literacy coach led the two groups of teachers in creating first drafts of 6-point analytic rubrics they would use to score student papers. The score of 4 would be the benchmark score for the grade level, and teachers' instructional goals would include getting students to score at least 4 in the different categories (topic, organization, style/voice, conventions).

Site-specific decisions in how the ALAS scoring would develop began to emerge as the schoolwide rubrics were being created. The general rubric development procedures are described here, with attention to the two school's varying approaches. As an example, a rubric from Sierra Madre is presented in Table 6.1.[1]

At both sites, teachers worked in grade-level teams examining other writing rubrics and selecting student writing examples that made sense to them. At Sierra Madre School, teachers developed three rubrics for grades K–1, 2–3, and 4–5. Since at that time many classrooms at Chang Ching School were multiage, teachers opted for two rubrics: Grades pre-K–2 and 3–5. The rubric-creation exercises were the first of many opportunities that teachers had to develop a schoolwide language for discussing their students' literacy learning. Once complete, the first drafts of the rubrics were used to begin scoring student work. Teachers also worked with the coach to begin selecting the best exemplars, or "anchor papers," for each score on the rubric.

At both schools, the teachers began by developing English rubrics as a whole staff. Later, bilingual teachers developed rubrics in Spanish and, at Chang Ching School, in Chinese as well. The Spanish and Chinese rubrics

Table 6.1. K–1 Grade Writing Rubric, Sierra Madre Elementary

	Topic	Organization	Style/Voice	Conventions
6	☐ Expands on topic with some details, mostly relevant ☐ Develops topic with 3 or more sentences	☐ Combines at least three sentences to develop one topic in a paragraph ☐ Shows some evidence of organizational plan (beginning, middle, and end)	☐ May move beyond simple sentence structure ☐ Writes detailed descriptions of familiar persons, places, or objects	☐ Demonstrates exceptional command of *spacing* between words, sentences ☐ Uses conventional *spelling* for most high-frequency words ☐ Applies varied strategies to *spell* some irregular words ☐ Few errors in *capitalization* (beginning sentence, proper nouns) ☐ *Punctuation:* few errors in the use of (? . !) at the end of sentences ☐ *Punctuation:* may use commas in a series and in dates ☐ *Grammar:* pays some attention to proper use of nouns, pronouns, adjectives ☐ Few run on sentences, due to content ☐ Indents paragraphs
5	☐ Expands on topic with few details ☐ Develops topic with a few sentences	☐ Writes at least one topic sentence and two supporting sentences ☐ May demonstrate a logical sequence	☐ May use varied sentence structure ☐ Uses a variety of adjectives ☐ Integrates personal interests and experiences ☐ Illustrations extend writing	☐ Almost always uses *spaces* between words, sentences ☐ Uses conventional *spelling* for most high-frequency words and words with regular spelling patterns ☐ Uses common phonics rules to attempt *spelling* of irregular words ☐ Few significant errors in the use of *capitalization* at beginning of sentences, proper nouns ☐ *Punctuation:* uses (? . !) at the end of a sentence with few errors ☐ Some run on sentences, due to content

Table 6.1. (cont'd)

4	☐ Expands on topic with a couple of details ☐ Communicates main idea in a sentence	☐ Organizes ideas around one topic ☐ Produces more than one sentence about main idea, line of thought may wander ☐ Uses some supporting details	☐ Uses simple sentence structure ☐ May use adjectives ☐ Uses simple language (nouns, verbs) ☐ Uses repetitious, pattern like vocabulary ☐ May integrate personal interests and experiences ☐ Illustrations extend writing	☐ Uses *spaces* between most words ☐ Uses conventional *spelling* for some high-frequency words and words with regular spelling patterns ☐ Uses common phonics rules to attempt *spelling* of some irregular words ☐ Few significant errors in the use of *capitalization* (beginning of sentences, proper nouns) ☐ *Punctuation*: uses (? !) at the end of a sentence ☐ *Punctuation*: uses a period at the end of a sentence ☐ *Grammar* : uses verb tense, plurals, s/v agreement
3	☐ Writes about topic in a phrase or simple sentence ☐ Illustrates about topic	☐ Writes a phrase or simple sentence	☐ Uses simple language (nouns, verbs) ☐ May use simple sentence structure ☐ May express feelings and personal style through writing and illustrations	☐ May use *spaces* between words ☐ *Spells* some familiar words with regular spelling patterns ☐ Uses beginning sounds and uses some medial and final sounds (letter/sound correspondence) ☐ May use temporary *spelling* ☐ May use *capitalization* (beginning of sentences, proper nouns) but still may use a combination of upper case and lower case letters ☐ *Punctuation*: may use a period at the end of a sentence
2	☐ Lists words related to topic ☐ Illustrates about topic	☐ Lists words (approximates sentence structure)	☐ Expresses personal interests or experiences through writing and illustrations ☐ Illustration/text match	☐ Uses *temporary spelling* ☐ Uses beginning consonant sounds (letter/sound correspondence) ☐ Demonstrates the *alphabetic principle* ☐ Writes upper and lower case letters independently, attending to form and spatial development
1	☐ Illustrates about topic	☐ Illustration suggests main idea	☐ Communicates with pictures and letters	☐ Writes strings of letters (may include numbers) ☐ May write random letters ☐ Copies environmental print

began as direct translations of the English rubrics that had been agreed upon by the whole staff. This is because (1) teachers wanted the rubrics in different languages to relate to one another and (2) there were few resources for the creation of rubrics in Spanish, and especially in Chinese. After rubrics were translated into Spanish and Chinese, bilingual teachers began the difficult work of tailoring the rubrics to the specifics of teaching and learning writing in the specific languages.

Teams of teachers from both schools worked with researchers to revise the rubrics and to align them with the SFUSD's language arts standards. Teachers looked critically at the first drafts of the rubrics, then moved and rephrased descriptors. They also examined the language arts standards and made sure that the school's expectations were not below those of the school district. At both schools, teachers tried to set higher expectations for students. While the revision of the Sierra Madre rubrics was straightforward, the revision of the Chang Ching rubrics presented some problems. As teachers from Chang Ching tackled the rubric-revision process, they found that in their attempt to have two rubrics spanning three to four grades (pre-K–2 and 3–5), they had created two rubrics that displayed no continuity in what was expected of students in primary and upper elementary grades. Additionally, since there would be few multiage classrooms in the upcoming schoolyear, there was a need for three rubrics that would be used to assess students at the K–1, 2–3, and 4–5 grade levels. Finally, teachers noted that the existing writing descriptors for kindergarten did not describe features of the earliest emergent writing, such as curls and lines.

The team of teachers modified the existing rubrics in the following ways. First, they added two scores to the bottom of the primary-level rubric for emergent, or what they termed prekindergarten, writing. Second, they expanded the two rubrics into three rubrics. In order to ensure that these three rubrics were related, teachers decided to overlap the descriptors so that the top two scores of the K–1 rubric (scores 5 and 6) became the bottom two scores of the 2–3 rubric (scores 1 and 2). Similarly, the top two scores of the 2–3 rubric became the bottom two scores of the 4–5 rubric. The teachers felt strongly that this continuum should be reflected in the numbering of the scores of the rubric. They decided that, instead of having three rubrics numbered 1–6, the schoolwide rubric should have a single numbering system, as follows: (1) Scores 1 to 2 should be assigned to pre-K; (2) the following six scores (scores 3–8) should be assigned to K–1; (3) the six scores 5–10 should be assigned to grades 2–3; and (4) the six scores 9–14 should be assigned to grades 4–5.

The Sierra Madre team of teachers opted for a more simple approach, keeping the three rubrics separate with scores from 1 to 6. At the 1998 summer work sessions, Sierra Madre teachers were also able to revise the Spanish rubric. Chang Ching teachers did so only at the beginning of the 1998–1999 schoolyear. This delay caused some logistical difficulties in the implementation of the ALAS that fall. The revised rubrics and their accompanying anchor papers were used to score the students' samples during the schoolyear.

Finally, using the new rubrics, the teams of teachers from both schools scored student papers in order to identify anchor papers for every score. By the end of the summer's work meetings, student papers that met specific numerical scores had been selected for every score of the English rubrics. These papers were identified as anchors because teachers used them as guides to anchor their evaluations of student ALAS writing. At Sierra Madre, Spanish anchor papers were also identified. Once teachers identified anchor papers, researchers wrote narrative descriptions of the selected student samples, and these, along with the anchor papers, were used as references for scoring by the staff during the following schoolyear.

At both schools, the rubrics are considered to be works in progress. As teachers gain familiarity with the rubrics through scoring (described in the following section), they identify inconsistencies in the rubrics. Therefore, revision of the rubrics is an ongoing goal.

The Scoring of Student Writings

As discussed above, the scoring of student writings is interrelated with the creation and revision of the rubrics. In order to learn to score papers, teachers first dialogued with each other and with the coach to come to agreement about strengths and weaknesses of different student samples and about the relationship among standards, rubrics, teaching, and learning. Once the rubrics were ready, teachers used them to score students' papers in grade-level groups. As teachers worked in these groups, they learned to identify features of students' writings according to the rubric descriptors. Initially, both schools scored papers fairly similarly. Developing scoring procedures that worked with both teachers and researchers was difficult. Teachers insisted that they should score their own students' papers in order to understand their strengths and needs. Researchers wanted to ensure that teachers were scoring in equivalent ways schoolwide and that preference was not given to individual students. Individual teachers expressed these concerns as well, and over time we developed scoring procedures that included external checks on individual teachers' scoring. At both schools, teachers were asked to use the anchor papers to guide their scoring in order to provide a common reference.

At Sierra Madre, teachers and the principal developed the following procedures. Individual teachers score one-third of their own students' papers and one-third of two other teachers' papers. At Chang Ching, teachers first score one paper all together and discuss any differences in the scores. When the scoring begins, teachers exchange 10% of their papers with another teacher. The scoring that new teachers do is overseen by returning teachers. Additionally, the types of scores given by the two schools are different. At Chang Ching, teachers give papers scores for each category on the rubric as well as a holistic score. This procedure allows teachers to first look at the specific areas where the curriculum needs modification. After the analytic scoring, teachers look at each piece as a whole after having scored it for topic, organization, style/voice, and conventions. Since this is not a standardized assessment, teachers are trained not to let the holistic score be a mathematical average of the scores in the four categories; rather, the writing samples should bear a resemblance to the anchor paper for each score.

At Sierra Madre, the staff found that the holistic scores are not as useful to their instruction as the analytic scores. First, the analytic scores are the ones that provide clues to further instruction. Second, the holistic scores may conceal students' areas of weakness. For these reasons, at Sierra Madre, only analytic scores are given.

The scoring of student work has been the most difficult and time-consuming element of ALAS for teachers. This is particularly true for upper-grade teachers whose students write two- to three-page pieces. At both schools, teachers record their individual students' scores in ways that inform them, their students, and parents. First, scores for each student's ALAS writings are recorded in graphic form on one 6-point rubric. Scores for the first sample are marked in one color, scores for the second sample are marked in a second color, and scores for the third sample are marked in a third color. The result is a graph indicating how the student has progressed in topic, organization, style/voice, and conventions during the year. Students and parents can look at this graph and at the three samples to understand the ALAS process. Second, all teachers keep score sheets with all their students' scores in each category. This spreadsheet serves as a database as teachers tailor their instruction to suit students' strengths and needs. The next section describes the ways in which the authentic writing assessment links to instruction.

Linking ALAS Data to Instruction

In the spring of 1998, we asked teachers to write a response to the following question: "What role do you see that rubrics might have in informing your writing instruction?" Their responses highlight some of the key ways in which this assessment can be used as a tool to tailor classroom instruction to individual students and to unify instructional goals schoolwide.

Rubrics set one standard for our instruction. They set the goals for levels that the students need to achieve in their grade levels.

[Rubrics] help direct your attention to just where each child is, what needs to be worked on [individual assessment].

Rubrics give the teacher clear expectations for students' writing. The rubrics we are developing indicate the range of students' writing within a grade level. I . . . look at what skills [on the rubric] my students have not yet developed, and focus on these skills during mini-lessons.

I'd use [rubrics] at the start of the schoolyear to help me with [student] grouping and planning. During the year, I'd use them as guidelines [for instruction]. At the end of the year I'd use them to evaluate the child's progress and to inform the following teacher.

I think that rubrics can really help a writing program. It would fit well with portfolios. This would be a great way for me to really know where a student stands and what they need. It would also help me organize instruction.

I think it will not only help my instruction, but it will help students be aware of their own writing goals and where they need improvement.

Throughout, teachers have used the ALAS data individually, and to varying degrees, to inform their language arts instruction. For instance, at the scoring meetings for the English ALAS at Chang Ching School, upper-grade Spanish/English bilingual teachers noticed that virtually all the students in the Chinese/English bilingual classrooms were using paragraphs. They asked, "How did you do that?" And the Chinese/English bilingual teachers discussed the instruction that they were using to teach paragraphing. This type of informal dialogue and schoolwide collaboration in instructional re-form has been a healthy by-product of the ALAS project. Still, it has been the goal of the staff and principals to make the link between the ALAS data and instruction more explicit and formal. Starting in 1998–1999, we have worked to provide teachers with time to meet, analyze their students' scores, and identify next steps for their writing instruction.

As the ALAS administration and scoring processes became embedded in the schools' practices, more physical and conceptual time was made avail-able for schoolwide "links to instruction" meetings. At these meetings, staff met with the coach or with researchers to group students with different in-structional needs and to develop lessons. Teachers used their class score sheets, circling groups of similar scores and using these scores to create flexible stu-dent groupings for mini-lessons depending on individuals' needs. For instance, some students may benefit from a mini-lesson on topic development, while others may benefit from a mini-lesson on punctuation.

Through collegial conversations at the scoring sessions and "links to instruction" meetings, teachers have discussed the various ways in which students were becoming competent writers and reaching the benchmarks. Teachers used the rubric partly as an indicator of students' writing development. However, because of the nature of the analytic rubric, the definition of *development* took on a multifaceted quality—the same student who showed strengths in the conventions of writing may show difficulty in developing a topic. The same student who showed a complex understanding of writing voice in a given genre may have difficulties with verb-tense agreement. Rather than viewing the rubric as a set of linear stages that students invariably pass through to become competent writers, we saw that rubrics were being considered as providing multiple pathways toward writing competence in the languages of instruction. Evidence was found that they were being used by teachers not only as indicators of student progress but also as guidelines for instruction.

Local circumstances at the two schools caused different levels of involvement in linking ALAS data to instruction. At Chang Ching, a sudden turnover in leadership in the 1998–1999 schoolyear disrupted every aspect of the school's operations, including the ALAS work. Over the following 2 years, the school would have three different principals. Juliana describes the ALAS project as a unifying factor during these difficult times for the school:

> There are certain things that I'm glad we agreed on before [the principal changed]. Like, for example, the ALAS: That's one thing that I think has given us cohesion, as a whole staff—we needed to have something that is part of our program. This is part of our program, and we're not going to [give it up if the new principal wants to change it] because we discussed it a long time ago, and we agreed that that was good.

While the ALAS served to continue the cross-grade articulation of instruction and assessment during the organizational upheavals at Chang Ching, the process of formalizing the assessment's links to instruction was interrupted.

Conversely, at Sierra Madre, there has only been one principal, which has added stability to the ALAS process. The principal, who is deeply committed to raising students' overall achievement, has expanded the schoolwide articulation of instructional goals to include mathematics, and with the support of university researchers, a federal grant, additional administrative staff, and other outside resources have created a database of student scores that is used to inform instruction. Also created as a part of a "cycle of inquiry" is an Authentic Mathematics Assessment System (AMAS). The AMAS is an independent project of Sierra Madre School and receives minimal technical assistance from university researchers. Additionally, the ALAS work has been expanded to include student–teacher conferences where students and teachers look at ALAS samples together and decide on goals for the next ALAS.

CONCLUSION

In summary, a responsive bilingual learning community recognizes that academic learning has its roots in both out-of-school and in-school processes. A focus on responsive instructional engagement encourages students to construct and reconstruct meaning and to seek reinterpretations and augmentations to past knowledge within compatible and nurturing schooling contexts. Diversity is perceived and acted on as a resource for teaching and learning instead of a problem. A focus on what students bring to the schooling process generates a more asset/resource-oriented approach versus a deficit/needs assessment approach (Cole, 1996; Garcia, 2001a; Tharp & Gallimore, 1988).

The above description of the design study activities, the principles they generated, and the implementation strategies give a first-hand look at the ways in which participants worked together to develop a site-based intervention process utilizing multilingual assessments, the ALAS. These design research colleagues, within the context of a standards-based reform effort, brought their expertise to the enterprise of assessing and instructing their students.

The next chapter will provide specific data that help us understand the effects of this reform and design study on the academic achievement of participating students and how teachers went about that work.

NOTE

1. Rubrics for other grades and in Spanish and Cantonese are available from the author.

CHAPTER 7

Bilingual Student Achievement in a Reform Context

In the previous chapter, I described the sites, individuals, and processes that moved two schools instructionally in response to articulated goals in multiple languages with regard to students' literacy development. This included defining those goals by grade level. In school reform language, identification of the standards was the beginning of the reform process. Beyond identifying the standards, the schools moved to "authentically" assess student achievement with the Authentic Literacy Assessment System (ALAS), to formalize ways in which to organize that measured information regarding literacy achievement, and to act on the basis of that information to modify instruction. This cycle was repeated several times a year and over a period of years for all students in the school. Bilingual students received instruction in their non-English native languages (Spanish and Chinese—Cantonese) and English. Most native English-speaking students received instruction in English and in Spanish or Chinese, or, if parents requested, only in English.

This chapter presents the empirical results related to student performance of this design study. It features student performance data over a period of 3 years for the ALAS. For scores derived from the ALAS, it is important to note that interrater reliability on the reported scores was determined to be in the range of above 80% agreement for scores in first and second grade and 70% or greater on scores for third grade. Standardized test data for these same students in English and Spanish, where such data are available and appropriate, are also reported. Unfortunately, no such data are available for Chinese.

In essence, this chapter attempts to provide an empirical test of the longitudinal intervention meant to enhance instruction for students in a diverse bilingual context. It is a "design" test of U.S. school reform for schools that serve a highly linguistically and culturally diverse student population. Taken together, this chapter and the previous one form a conceptual and empirical exemplar of what can be done to ensure high academic achievement in literacy domains for bilingual students in the United States.

SIERRA MADRE FINDINGS

The data collected for the first- to third-grade cohort included scores for the four domains of the rubric (topic, organization, style/voice, conventions) and analysis of the students' performance in Spanish and English. Students were given a score between 1 and 6 on each domain according to the level of development demonstrated in their writing samples. Scores for students in the first-grade cohort (1998–1999 schoolyear) were analyzed, as were their scores the following 2 years when they entered the second and third grades (1999–2000 and 2000–2001 schoolyears) using the second/third-grade rubric. Data from two student cohorts are presented for Sierra Madre. This is necessary because the longitudinal student sample was disrupted with mobility. That is, less than 30% of the students who began the school in the study group in first grade remained at the end of the third grade. Therefore, data are presented for the longitudinal cohort group (students that remained in the school for the entire study period) and a yearly cohort group (students that were in the school and grade for any particular year of the study). The Appendix at the end of this chapter presents ALAS scores for these two groups of students. These figures present data for Spanish/English Bilingual students and ALAS writing scores over the 3 years in English (Figures A.1 and A.2) and Spanish (Figures A.3 and A.4). Similar data are presented for ALAS English writing for English-only students (Figures A.5 and A.6).

The rubrics' alignment with the school district's standards facilitated establishing benchmark scores representing grade-level performance. For example, when students were in the second grade, they were measured against a score of 3 within each domain, the benchmark goal. When these students entered the third grade, they were measured against a score of 4 on the 6-point rubric. The following results are organized around one central related question: *Is there equivalent literacy development in Spanish and English when students are taught in both languages?*

The longitudinal data collected on these cohort student groups over the course of 3 years show significant growth in writing for all students. Of particular interest is the parallel development of Spanish and English writing for the bilingual education students. This is evident when we compare the initial ALAS scores attained by students during the 1998–1999 schoolyear to the final scores recorded at the end of the third year (2000–2001). Students' writing maturity in both languages became apparent when we analyzed their performance in each individual domain for both Spanish and English.

Topic

The *topic* category in the ALAS rubric deals with the student's ability to address and support the writing prompt given. The prompt is directly related to the piece of literature read by or to students the previous day.

At the time of the initial Spanish and English ALAS administration during the 1998–1999 schoolyear, the bilingual students were able to expand their writing by providing several details related to and in support of the topic in their Spanish and English writing. These characteristics drew a score of 1 on the 6-point rubric scale for Spanish and English ALAS. (See Figures A.1–A.4 in Appendix.)

An increase was noted by the second and final ALAS administration in both languages, where students demonstrated the ability to expand on the topic of the writing with more than two details as well as to communicate the main idea with more than one sentence. A similar trend in development of topic emerged the following years (1999–2000 and 2000–2001) as ALAS scores were collected. Scores in both Spanish and English made steady gains throughout the years, culminating with significantly higher scores.

At the end of third grade, students were able to strengthen their use of details in support of the topic in both Spanish and English. This was evident by the benchmark score in English and a similar score in Spanish, which approached the benchmark score. The final ALAS administration further revealed the students' ability to deal with the topic in both languages. The longitudinal data presented delineates this biliteracy development.

Organization

The second category in the ALAS rubric outlines specific criteria that gauges the organization of the students' writing. The criteria include a logical sequence to the paper, a topic sentence at the beginning of the paper, a concluding sentence toward the end of the paper, and presentation of ideas in paragraph form with internal organization. The average English and Spanish scores for the students during the 1998–1999 schoolyear were relatively low.

Students' writing increased by ALAS #2 Spanish and ALAS #3. A similar trend was visible during the 1999–2000 and 2000–2001 schoolyears when the students completed the third grade. Scores went from an initial English score of 2.06 and Spanish score of 2.26 to an English ALAS #3 score of 3.71 and Spanish ALAS #3 score of 3. These scores made clear that from grade 2 to grade 3, students were developing an understanding of the need to pay particular attention to the organization of their writing. When students wrote in English, the organization score hovered near the benchmark score in the third grade with a score of 3.71 followed close behind by a Spanish organization score of 3.61.

These growths in scores reflect a substantial gain in writing ability. In first grade, an achieved score of 2.0–2.5 indicates that students were minimally attending to the topic of their writing. By third grade, the achieved score of 3.6–3.7 indicates a consistent and even expanded attention to the topic students were asked to address. In short, students gained the skill of adapting their writing to the topic they were asked to write about.

Style/Voice

This domain of the rubric is shaped with three characteristics in mind: (1) sentence structure (varied versus simple), (2) detailed descriptions of familiar persons, places, or objects, and (3) incorporation of a sense of audience. Initial scores revealed a lack of control over this domain with an equivalent ALAS #1 score of 1 in both English and Spanish. This average score of 1 meant their sentence structure was simple, using simple language (e.g., mostly nouns and verbs). Scores in both languages with respect to this domain followed a similar developmental pattern with ALAS #2 scores for English and for Spanish.

The students displayed heightened awareness of varying their sentence structure when describing their experiences in their writing by the final ALAS administration in the second grade in English and Spanish. ALAS scores for these cohorts of students, collected the following year, decreased from their scores the previous year. Recall that student papers are scored on the same rubric. Students quickly rebounded by exhibiting their developing command of the style and voice domain when writing in both languages. Their writing came to reflect their own interpretations of the topics they were asked to address. Phrases and sentences were more engagingly extended and combined to provide richer meaning.

Conventions

The skills in the conventions domain clearly were the most difficult for students to fully grasp. The characteristics of the conventions domain include (1) spelling, (2) grammar, and (3) punctuation. Students' ALAS #1 score of 1 in both languages reflected their difficulties with these three elements.

Students made consistent gains in succeeding ALAS administrations, posting gains in Spanish. Subsequent ALAS scores demonstrate a parallel development in English. These gains demonstrated the students' slow but progressive understanding of the spelling, grammar, punctuation, and conventions.

The improved scores over subsequent data periods illustrate the students' better understanding of the various spelling strategies, orthographic patterns, contractions, compounds, homophones, and the role of correct punctuation to make their writing more cohesive. The conventions domain fell short of the benchmark scores when we measured the final ALAS, administered in the third grade, against the benchmark.

These findings reveal that, in both languages, students demonstrated a stronger grasp of the topic and organization domains than the style/voice and conventions categories, but significant growth toward the benchmark standard was observable in each language.

CHANG CHING FINDINGS

Similar data are presented for Chang Ching longitudinal cohort group students. The loss of students in this cohort was much smaller than at Sierra Madre. At Chang Ching, some 63% of the study group students beginning at first grade remained at the end of the third grade. Therefore, only longitudinal cohort study group data are presented. Figures A.7 through A.11 present these data for bilingual Chinese/English students in English and Chinese, bilingual Spanish/English students in English and Spanish, and English-only students, in English.

The 1998–2000 ALAS performance score analysis indicates the following:

1. Consistent parallel writing progression in both English and Chinese was evident in all the writing domains (topic, organization, style/voice, and conventions).
2. Writing scores in both languages equaled or were slightly above grade-level writing benchmarks.
3. Limited-English-speaking students in the two cohorts acquired English writing proficiency at grade level, as did their English-only peers, while at the same time developing and maintaining proficiency in their native language.

Student Writing Samples

The best way to look at the quality of the writing over time is to look at individual writing samples closely. We will examine two ALAS Chinese and two ALAS English writing samples of the same student (we will call him Kai) who was part of this second- and third-grade cohort.

Kai was born in San Francisco. His primary language is Cantonese. He was 8 years and 8 months old at the start of the study in the fall of 1998. He entered Chang Ching Elementary School in kindergarten and was designated non-English-proficient (NEP) based on his low oral (level one) and reading skills. Evaluation of primary language at entering kindergarten showed Kai to be fluent in oral Chinese and limited in reading and nonproficient in writing.

Kai's two Chinese writing samples

Chinese ALAS #2 (Second Grade) Writing Prompt: Please write a story about a pet. Describe what you and your pet like to do together and how it makes you feel. [See Figure 7.1 for Kai's response.]

I have a little red kitten. Her name is "Siu Ying". Already 5 years old. No sharp teeth. I read books to her [drawing of cat]. I draw books for her to read. She and I are very happy. [English translation]

This writing sample was produced in December 1998, Kai's first Chinese ALAS. Topic was scored at 6, organization at 6, style/voice at 6, conventions at 6, and overall holistic at 6. This puts Kai's overall writing for this piece at first-grade level (benchmark of 6). This piece contains 7 sentences and 36 words. Kai addresses the topic directly and gives good descriptions of the pet (i.e., red, little, sharp teeth, 5 years old) as well as the activities he and Siu Ying do together. Kai also expresses his personal feelings. This piece is well organized with a clear beginning, middle, and end. Some phrasing and sentence structure are not conventional, but they do not interfere with the overall meaning.

Chinese ALAS (Third Grade) Writing Prompt: Please write a story on how you solve a problem. What was the problem and who was involved? How did you go about solving the problem? After you solve the problem, how did you feel? [See Figure 7.2 for Kai's response.]

My Sister Fell Down

During recess, I took a ball out to play. I called out to my sister to play ball and she came to play. I gave her the ball. She [drawing of a ball] to play [drawing of four square]. She did not enter. Then she gave the ball to me. She [drawing of figure eights and circles]. Then I was careless and tripped her hand. My sister's hand was bleeding. I helped her up. I took her to get bandage. Then I took her back. [English translation]

This writing sample was produced in May 2000. Topic was scored at 9, organization at 8, style/voice at 6, conventions at 7, and holistic score at 8, which puts Kai's overall writing for this piece at third-grade level (benchmark of 8). This piece contains 12 sentences and a total of 71 words, which is almost three times as much as the last piece. Kai gives his story a title, addresses the topic directly, and answers the questions of what, who, how, and when. When he lacks the words, he draws them and some of the drawings such as

Figure 7.1. Kai's 12/98 Chinese ALAS

Sample 1. Chinese ALAS #2 (Second Grade) 12/10/98

[English translation] I have a little red kitten. Her name is "Siu Ying." Already 5 years old. No sharp teeth. I read books to her [drawing of cat]. I draw books for her to read. She and I are very happy.

Figure 7.2. Kai's 5/2000 Chinese ALAS

Sample 2. Chinese ALAS #3 (Third Grade) 5/1/00

the picture of four square provide meaning. The only question not addressed was how he felt afterward. There is a clear beginning, middle, and end, with the use of transitional words. Kai shows his knowledge of storytelling and describes parallel actions between two characters. Sentences are short, but the word choices are conventional with few grammatical and punctuation errors.

In the two Chinese compositions written over the course of 3 years, Kai consistently demonstrates that he is a thoughtful and attentive writer who addresses the topic and provides personal examples. He also shows strengths in his story organization and in creating parallel actions. Kai shows his growing ability to describe a scene with careful attention to details of characters, action, setting, and mood. As Kai composes more Chinese narratives and essays, the areas that seem to be the most challenging for him are in making smoother transitions between sentences, developing paragraphs, using more dialogues and conventional sentence structure and phrasing as well as a variety of punctuation marks besides periods. Promoting his writing through grade-level literature and writing practices in different genres seems to be useful instructional support to promote and maintain Kai's Chinese writing proficiency. Comparing Kai's earlier Chinese writing samples to the later ones provides us with a very vivid picture of his development in Chinese writing proficiency.

Kai's two English writing samples

English ALAS (Second Grade) Writing Prompt: Who is your best friend? What do you like to do together? Draw a picture and write about it. [See Figure 7.3 for Kai's response.]

This writing sample was completed in September 1998. Across all the categories (topic, organization, style/voice, conventions, holistic), Kai was given the score of 5, which puts his writing competence below first-grade level (benchmark of 6). There are three sentences and 18 words in this composition. Kai is able to address the topic briefly but with little development of his ideas. For organization, he is able to produce short sentences, but they are mainly a list without transitional words to connect the ideas. In conventions, he has difficulty with grammatical structure and punctuation.

English ALAS (Third Grade) Writing Prompt: Write a first person narrative about a big event that has happened to you. [See Figure 7.4 for Kai's response.]

This writing sample was produced in May 2000. The rubric domain topic was scored at 9, organization at 9, style/voice at 8, conventions at 8, and holistic score at 9, which puts Kai's overall writing at the third-grade level

Figure 7.3. Kai's 9/98 English ALAS

Benjamin - I Play basket ball - - - - - - -

I read book with best friend's - - -

My best friend's at my house to clean up

Sample 3. English ALAS #1 (Second Grade) 9/17/98

Figure 7.4. Kai's 5/2000 English ALAS Third Grade

Once upon a time my dad took me and my Sister to the park. We bring my bake. My sister bring a bike too. But my dad is not bring it My dad play with me too.

My dad sometime play my brke too. But he can't sit on it. Pie is so strong. He is not playing anymore. He try my blue bike.

I had bring my basketball We are playing over there. my dad can use one hand to throw on the basket. My basketball is little but we can't My sister hand is small and me too. We use two hand to throw on the basket. My sister can't throw on it. because she is little.

Sample 4. English ALAS #3 (Third Grade) 5/4/00

(benchmark of 9). This composition contains twice as many words and sentence as the last one (255 words with 38 sentences ranging from 4 to 15 words). There is a main topic sentence as well as four supporting paragraphs containing details of who, where, what, and how. There is a clear beginning, middle, and end, but they are not well developed. Kai is using more pronouns, verbs, prepositions, and a few adjectives to describe the scene and action. There is a marked progress in correct sentence structure but still some difficulties with correct verb tenses and syntax—but they do not interfere with the overall meaning. In spelling, he is using mostly conventional spelling and attempting to spell more difficult words by sounding them out (i.e., "shek" for *shake*, "swills" for *swings*).

In this particular writing sample, it is interesting to point out that a teacher rating this paper might question why a day in the park would be considered a "big" event and whether the student is "off topic," since all the activities described can be considered "typical" things one does at the park. This example illustrates how critical it is for a teacher to understand the student's background and social environment. For example, going to the park and spending time with family is a "big" deal for some of the students who are from low-SES households. They live in a world where going to a safe park in the neighborhood and spending time with your parents are not things a youngster can take for granted due to many economic pressures on the parents. It is in this context that we understand how a day in the park with family was chosen as the big event in Kai's world.

Kai's final English ALAS of May 2000 is his most expressive and thorough. He is mastering the conventions of English writing, producing high levels of capitalization, punctuation, and paragraphing. None of these conventions are required in Chinese writing. In short, Kai has mastered at grade level, writing in two very distinct languages, Chinese and English. (Compare Figures 7.2 and 7.5 for this stark contrast.)

In comparing this piece to Kai's composition produced at the first and second grade (9/98), there is an impressive development. The early piece consists of three short sentences with underdeveloped ideas and incorrect syntax and punctuation. Later pieces exemplify writing personal narratives where there is a clear focus following a line of thought and paragraphs containing rich details, personal voice, and mostly conventional sentence structure and spelling. The author shows his growing ability to describe a scene with careful attention to details of characters, action, setting, and mood.

As Kai composes more narratives and essays, the areas that seem to be the most challenging for him are in making smoother transitions between sentences and paragraphs, paying more attention to audience, and developing the middle and ending of a piece. Another area is in creating dialogues between characters to develop the story, and, finally, attention to verb-tense agreement and correct syntax, punctuation, and using more conventional spelling.

Figure 7.5. Kai's 5/2000 English ALAS Third Grade Continued

We are playing swills. My dad teach me hand to Play. He push me first. And then I shek me feet. He help My sister too. My dad Push my sister too. And than she Shek her feet. I had little bit hid.

I play slid will My sister. The sled is long. Sometime My sister Push me down. And then I hit on the floor. My legs are hurt. I can Climb up to the slid.

Sometimes the slid had So much Sand We are put it back on the floor. The sand some had hard. I throw it on the wall. The sand is break. The slid had Water because the sand is wet. Than we go home.

The
End

Sample 4 (contd.). English ALAS #3 (Third Grade) 5/4/00

Promoting Kai's writing and building his vocabulary through literature-based reading and writing practices in many different genres seem to be useful instructional supports for Kai's English writing development. Comparing Kai's earlier English writing samples to the later ones provides us with a very vivid picture of development in English writing proficiency.

Longitudinal examples of other individual students with varied primacy languages are available directly from the author. This individual student data, much like the quantitative data, affirms that instruction in two languages can produce high levels of literacy achievement in the languages that are taught. It is from such ongoing individual assessment that we understand what the student can do and also where the difficulties are. While it is useful to look at cohort trends in this study, the effectiveness of authentic literacy assessment lies in teachers being able to evaluate individual level consistently. Furthermore, the assessment should not be restricted to just the text itself. It is very important for the teacher to have ongoing writing conferences with each student. This interactive assessment of writing allows teachers to understand the context of a student's writing as well as to identify with greater accuracy where the strengths and needs are for each particular student.

STANDARDIZED TEST ACHIEVEMENT MEASURES

In the United States, assessment of achievement via a set of standardized tests is the norm. Therefore, we obtained measures of this form of achievement for the students in this design study. Students at each school were tested by the district at the completion of second and third grades. In particular, the Stanford Achievement Test 9 (SAT-9) scores for those students in the sample who were defined as competent in English by the school district are presented for Sierra Madre students (Figure 7.1) and for Chang Ching students (Figure 7.3). These students come from English-only classrooms, bilingual Spanish/English classrooms at both schools, and bilingual Chinese/English classrooms at Chang Ching. Spanish achievement is presented for Spanish/English bilingual students at Sierra Madre (Figures 7.6 and 7.7) and at Chang Ching (Figures 7.8 and 7.9). (Recall that no standardized testing was available in Chinese.)

These data make it clear that on measures of standardized achievement in both English and Spanish, students in these schools were scoring at or above the national norm on measures of reading, language arts, and mathematics. The data are presented here to counter any concerns that the robust measures provided by the ALAS only in the domain of writing are not related to other measures of academic achievement. Although we are not able to perform a statistical test of this relationship, this parallel achievement data from

Figure 7.6. Sierra Madre SAT-9 Grade 2–3 English-Only NCE Mean Score

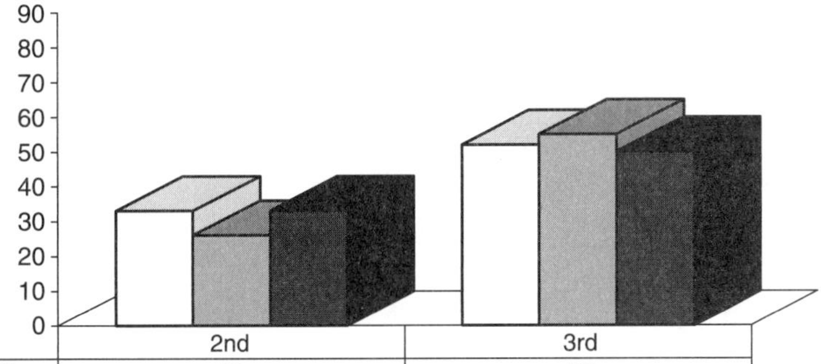

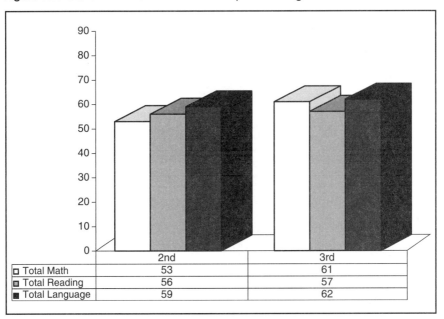

	2nd	3rd
▫ Total Reading	33	52
▣ Total Language	26	55
▪ Total Math	33	50

Figure 7.7. Sierra Madre SABE Grade 2–3 Spanish Bilingual NCE Mean Scores

	2nd	3rd
▫ Total Math	53	61
▣ Total Reading	56	57
▪ Total Language	59	62

Figure 7.8. Chang Ching SAT-9 Grade 2–3 English-Only NCE Mean Scores

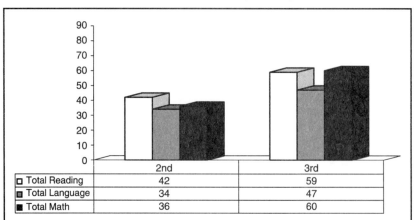

	2nd	3rd
☐ Total Reading	42	59
▦ Total Language	34	47
■ Total Math	36	60

Figure 7.9. Chang Ching SABE Grade 2–3 Spanish Bilingual NCE Mean Scores

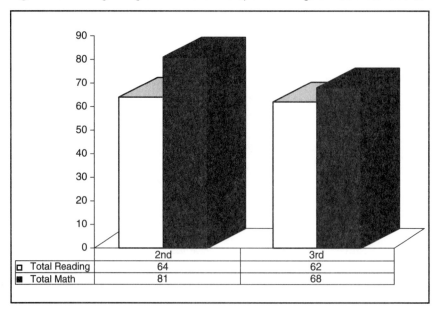

	2nd	3rd
☐ Total Reading	64	62
■ Total Math	81	68

the ALAS and related standardized achievement tests strongly indicates the existence of such a relationship.

TEACHERS' PERCEPTIONS OF THEIR WORK, ALAS, AND INSTRUCTION

Over the past 4 academic years, we have had nearly staffwide participation in the different components of the ALAS professional development. The degree to which the ALAS has impacted teachers has differed, depending on site-based factors such as school organization and on individual teachers' professional experience and initiative. In the spring of 2000, we interviewed four teachers (two from each school—early elementary and late elementary), and included here are excerpts of their reflections on their classroom practice, assessment, and the role of ALAS in their teaching lives. The selections here are provided as narratives to give an idea of the multiple interconnected factors influencing how teachers use ALAS in their classrooms.

At Sierra Madre School, we interviewed two Spanish/English bilingual teachers (first and fourth grades). The first-grade teacher, Eva, is a veteran bilingual educator and teacher trainer, having taught in bilingual classrooms across the country for 25 years. Lucia, the fourth-grade teacher, has been teaching for 4 years. At Chang Ching School, we interviewed one Spanish/ English bilingual teacher and one Chinese/English bilingual teacher. Juliana has taught for eight years, and at the time of the interview she had been teaching the bilingual third-, fourth-, and fifth-grade special education classes for students with identified learning disabilities. Guillermo has taught for 6 years, and at the time of the interview he was teaching a second-grade class.

Eva (Sierra Madre Elementary School). In her interview, Eva expressed support for the ALAS insofar as it supported practices she had already developed to assess students' learning in the classroom. She saw its value as a way of unifying the staff's approaches to instruction, and she was a member of the planning and training team along with the principal.

What do you do to provide your students with strong academic support?
What is your goal for those students who are learning in two languages?
E: I treat them equally. [We need to] get rid of that word *LEP* [limited English proficient]. I don't know where that word comes from, but my [native English-speaking] kids are limited Spanish speakers, and no one ever asks me about my LSPs. So, [I] get rid of that and let them know that I'm holding them accountable to the same level that

everybody is [held to]. My goals are for students to meet the content standards of the district. To be readers and writers. To feel like, "I have a voice, I'm somebody important in this world. This world isn't going to go as far as it possibly could if I'm not there."

What is your opinion about different forms of assessment?

E: Well, I always say that's why I teach first grade—because I don't have to use standardized measures (ha, ha). Why? What does it tell you? One picture—ping. Photograph. Done. This is what [the student] cannot do. [I] don't like that. I am more interested in the other side of assessment: . . . lots and lots of pictures over time, multiple pictures, drawings, writings, whatever we have [to show growth] over time. . . . Of course, of course [kids] should be [assessed]. I have no problem with the right type of test.

How do different kinds of assessment, such as standardized versus perfor-mance/authentic, provide useful or accurate information about linguisti-cally and culturally diverse students?

E: Well, standardized, first of all, I'm going to say what everybody else says. There isn't a fair test for those kids. When I look at authentic measures [I assess] what I'm teaching. If I'm not teaching very much, my kids aren't going to [produce] very much. It is authentic. It is what [I] do every single day so [I] get better at it.

Is ALAS one of the tools you use to measure and follow students' progress? How does ALAS relate to other ways in which you monitor student progress?

E: Sure, absolutely. And if you saw our school portfolio collections, every grade level has ALAS at least three times to four times listed as one of the things to show the content and the performance standards. So we're actually saying, "with ALAS I'm showing that my kid has five performance standards that they [met]."

*Lucia (**Sierra Madre Elementary School**).* Like Eva, Lucia also participated fully in the ALAS implementation but felt somewhat disenfranchised from the process. She described ways in which the ALAS work could be utilized more fully by the school.

What do you do to provide your students with strong academic sup-port? What is your goal for those students who are learning in two languages?

L: To provide them with strong academic support, I break up my class into different structures. Sometimes it's the whole group, but not that much. Often, I'm teaching something, and students are working in pairs or in small groups. A lot of times they work in centers where they're either doing something independently and I can give some individual attention to one person, or to a group of kids that are the same place. I think the more individual attention or small-group attention they can have the better. . . . For learning in two languages, each goal is different. Like Joshua who is an EO [English-only student], his personal New Year's goal was to learn to read and write better in Spanish. So I have paired him with a reading buddy occasionally during DEAR [drop everything and read] time, and they'll read in Spanish. But I think I have to give a different answer to that question for my EOs and for my Spanish speakers. I have to push [my Spanish speakers] in English just as much. . . . A fourth-grade literacy goal is to be able to write a good paragraph in English and in Spanish. So, I push all my kids towards that minimal goal, but some kids will exceed that.

What is your opinion about different forms of assessment?

L: [Standardized] testing, it's not really reflective of what kids [are learning] . . . it makes kids anxious. . . . [The district] adopts a curriculum like Math Land, which builds really open and analytical thinking. And then suddenly, you're assessing the kids on all this other stuff. Standardized assessments are also inherently unnatural, and they promote divisiveness.

    . . . We have school portfolios [that we use to assess kids]. . . . I tend to look more at the progress that's on the walls. For example, with our [journal] writing samples. I have students reflect on their writing quarterly. I ask them what their best journal piece was, why, and how their writing is progressing.

Is ALAS one of the tools you use to measure and follow students' progress? How does ALAS relate to other ways in which you monitor student progress?

L: I have found the ALAS student conferences, and the time with students, to be effective if they're done in the right way and immediately after the writing. And I have found ALAS to be effective when we [the staff] have spent time on it. It helps us all understand what is expected at each grade level and how students are doing in comparison to those expectations—the standards in the language(s) of instruction. We never had that before at this school.

Guillermo (*Chang Ching Elementary School*). Guillermo was an enthusiastic participant in the ALAS work and relied on ALAS to give shape to his in-class assessments.

What do you do to provide your students with strong academic support? What is your goal for those students who are learning in two languages?

G: I try to develop a love for reading, because that makes students independent learners. I show them how to access information in books, how to find pleasure in books. They are very good at finding and using resources in the classroom, and I encourage them. I also like to get people involved. People come to my classroom and read to them. I like to connect them with the rest of the school so they can use what they're learning.

What is your opinion about different forms of assessment?

G: I think we're doing too much standardized testing, especially at the levels that I teach. I think it's not very helpful to teaching. Because by the time we get the results, the kids are no longer your students.

Is ALAS one of the tools you use to measure and follow students' progress?

G: Definitely!

How does ALAS relate to other ways in which you monitor student progress?

G: Well [it relates] to the portfolios and also to setting goals. If I see a child is not using capital letters, let's say, then I work on that with the child, give her a mini-lesson. With the rubrics we developed with ALAS, it's easier for me to set goals for the students and for [students to set goals for] themselves.

So students are involved in their own assessment and goal setting?

G: Yes, definitely.

Juliana (Chang Ching Elementary School). As a special education teacher, Juliana was well versed in different kinds of assessments that children could be given, and this knowledge enhanced her use of the principle of linking assessment to instruction in her own practice. She described her excitement about the ALAS work and described how she used elements of the ALAS work in other aspects of her instruction.

What do you do to provide your students with strong academic support?

What is your goal for those students who are learning in two languages?

J: Vocabulary is very important. There are some things that you just need to memorize—see them a thousand times, so they stick. So, a lot of vocabulary. A print-rich environment—I don't use that many auditory-processing strategies, because many of my kids have problems with that [Juliana teaches a special day class for kids with learning difficulties]. So I use a lot of visual strategies.

What is your opinion about different forms of assessment?

J: I really like assessments. That's something that I love to do. It depends, though, what you are assessing. The [standardized and authentic] assessments measure different things. So as a teacher you need to be very clear about what you are assessing. What the SAT 9 assesses is very different from what portfolios would assess. What the ALAS assesses is very different from what the SAT-9 assesses. So you need to be clear what you're assessing. Are you assessing if you taught all the standards? Then you need to use something. If you were trying to assess writing process development, then you should use the ALAS. The real issue is what are you going to do with the data of the assessments? Is that data going to inform your instruction? Or is that data just going to go to a graph? Is that data going to be a number, or is it really going to make a change in your classroom? And maybe sometimes the accumulation of numbers, of graphs, will make a change in something, but I don't know. It really depends on what you are looking for and why you are using that information. I think assessment is very important because it keeps the children, the teachers, and the principal accountable. The ALAS worked for me in this way.

CONCLUSION

In this chapter, I have described the importance of developing and implementing a more responsive pedagogy and establishing a learning community with particular attention to authentic assessment of literacy for multilingual and multicultural students. From this work, we have demonstrated that the language of the student can be developed and assessed using a set of important principles to guide this effort. The assessment process and instrument must be aligned with instructional activity that exists in the classroom, including the language in which instruction is taking place.

In the schools in which we are working, we found little student assessment in the primary languages of the students, even though instruction in the primary language was an important part of the instructional program. For example, we found no informal or formal student assessments in Chinese in a program that was very clear about instructing and achieving literacy goals in that language. Moreover, the only Spanish student assessments that took place used a standardized test in math and reading given to students in the spring of each year. Results of that test were not distributed or discussed until the following fall. Discussion of this test by instructional staff was often problematic, since they were unfamiliar with the test terminology National Curve Equivalent (NCEs) and indicated a concern that the test did not measure what they were teaching.

Student assessments that were available also suffered from standardized approaches to the materials that were included in the actual assessment. For example, students were asked to write about vacations or travel, although many of the students in these urban and poor schools were not likely to vacation or travel. Therefore, in the ALAS integrated assessment, teachers discussed and chose reading material and prompts that they felt would be more intrinsically interesting, motivating, and likely to maximize common experiences for the students. In addition, the rubrics that were developed took into consideration four distinct but interlocking areas of literacy. In doing so, teachers recognized that a writer must be able to make clear statements and keep to the topic, organize his or her writing, develop a sense of audience or style/voice, and attend to proper writing conventions. The multiple "skilled" assessment recognizes the complexity of the domains of literacy. The scoring of the assessment produces a score for each domain as well as a holistic score.

If student assessment is to benefit instruction, it is imperative that such assessment occur at strategic times during the year. In the present work, the ALAS was/will be given to students once every 2 months. By doing so, teachers have access to information regarding students literacy on a continuous basis. Moreover, instructional modification can be aligned to what this assessment, coupled with other students' generated information, makes available. Of significance as well is the development and growth information that becomes available. The rubrics were constructed in a way that reflects our theoretical and empirical understanding of literacy development. Such an understanding makes clear that such development is not linear, can be unique to each student, and is related to the opportunity structure created by literacy instruction. Therefore, for example, in the development of writing conventions, we would expect that the development of these conventions would be directly related to the types of conventions that have been emphasized during instruction. Growth and development can be linked directly to those instructional opportunities. If we see that students are not developing these conventions, we do not look to the student as a primary source of nondevelopment—we look to the instructional opportunities.

The uses of authentic assessments strategies and their promise are not new to education (Garcia, 1999). In most cases, the promise has been more than the realized product. For these reasons, as authentic literacy assessments were emerging in these schools, it was important to recognize previous work in the field and build on that work while at the same time recognizing the expertise of the individual teachers who were using ALA. Moreover, the school district and state were in the process of articulating a set of language arts standards in English, Spanish, and Chinese (only at the district level). The intent of these standards was to make clear the expectations for students' skill level at each grade. Therefore, the rubrics developed for the ALA reflected and were aligned with these standards. They also went one step further, indicating grade-level benchmarks. That is, these levels were identified as a minimum level of development expected by that particular grade level associated with the benchmark.

We learned that the results and analyses of the assessment must be usable by teachers to inform, adapt, and maximize literacy instruction. In what became to be known as "literacy digs," teachers worked in groups with scoring sheets and actual student writing products from the ALAS to do the following:

1. Verify the writing they were seeing on the ALAS and what they might know of the students' writing on other writing activities
2. Explore particular trends in the ALAS artifacts in single students and groups of students
3. Identify specific instructional strategies that might help students to develop in areas that were identified as weaknesses and, likewise, to share instructional strategies that may have led to the observed strengths

These "digs" and related efforts attempted to use assessment results to understand how instruction might be influencing literacy development as well as what new strategies might be beneficial.

The present study of schooling in multilingual/multicultural sites is based on a conceptual framework we have identified as a *bilingual responsive learning community*. The framework recognizes the primary linguistic assets that each child brings to the schooling process and uses those assets to construct instruction. Moreover, it provides for the authentic assessment of the effects of that measure within well-articulated primary and English literacy standards and utilizes those assessments on an ongoing basis to modify instruction to benefit student learning. Through establishment of a responsive learning community, particularly utilizing an authentic assessment cycle, a high level of student writing achievement is evident.

The data in this study make clear that students from distinct primary-language experiences in Spanish and Chinese can develop sophisticated literacy expertise in their primary language and in English. The framework of the study, its principles, and its implementation at two specific schools add an important ingredient to our continuing challenge of effectively serving bilingual students to reform efforts within U.S. schools.

Figure A.1. Sierra Madre 1998–2001 Yearly Cohort Spanish Bilingual Ed. Domain Scores—English Writing Grades 1–3 [1998–1999; *n* = 19] [1999–2000; *n* = 20] [2000–2001; *n* = 23]

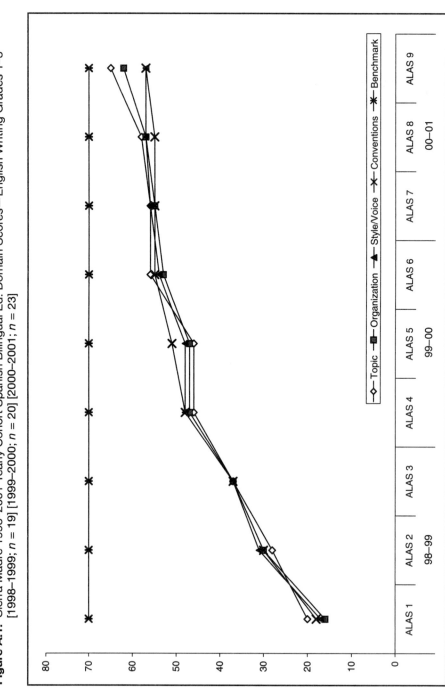

Figure A.2. Sierra Madre 1998–2001 Longitudinal Cohort Spanish Bilingual Ed. Domain Scores—English Writing (Grades 1–3; *n* = 10)

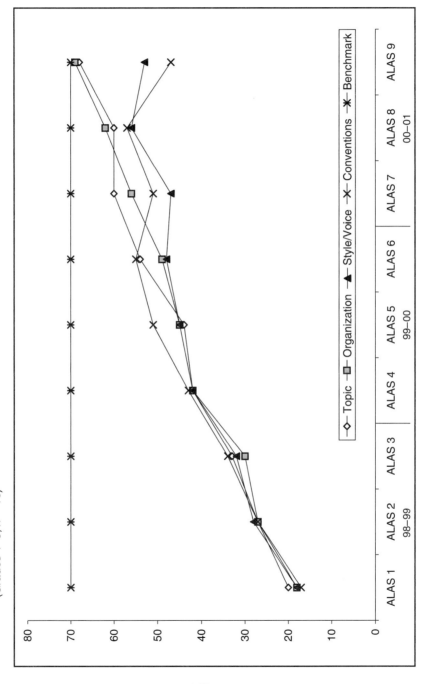

Figure A.3. Sierra Madre 1998–2001 Yearly Cohort Spanish Bilingual Ed. Domain Scores—Spanish Writing (Grades 1–3 [1998–1999; $n = 19$] [1999–2000; $n = 20$] [2000–2001; $n = 23$])

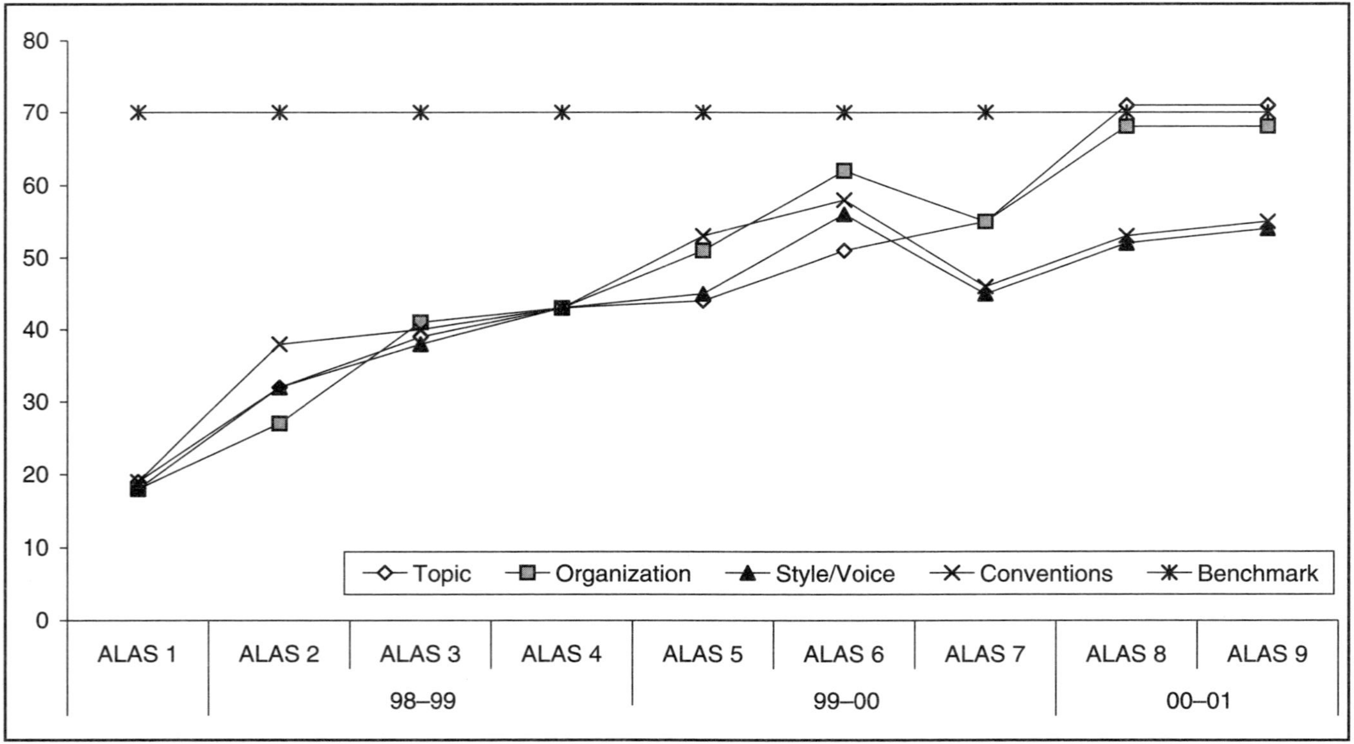

Figure A.4. Sierra Madre 1998–2001 Longitudinal Spanish Bilingual Ed. Domain Scores—Spanish Writing (Grades 1–3; *n* = 10)

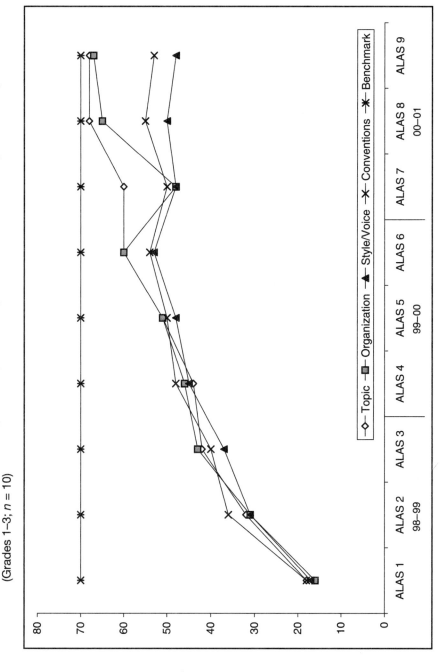

Figure A.5. Sierra Madre 1998–2001 Yearly Cohort General Ed. Domain Scores—English Writing Grades 1–3
[1998–1999; *n* = 17] [1999–2000; *n* = 14] [2000–2001; *n* = 11]

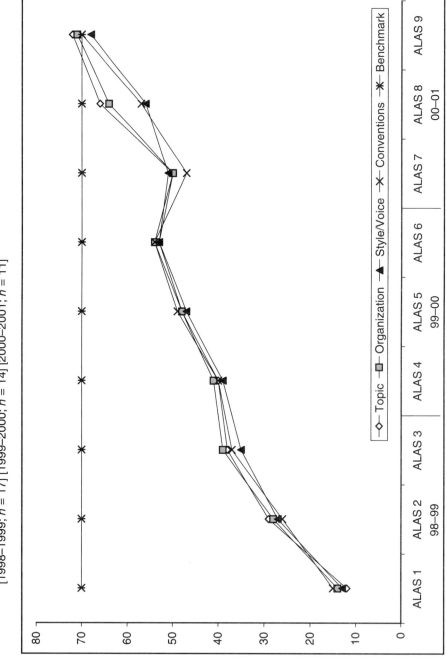

Figure A.6. Sierra Madre 1998-2001 Longitudinal ELD Domain Scores—English Writing (Grades 1-3; $n = 6$)

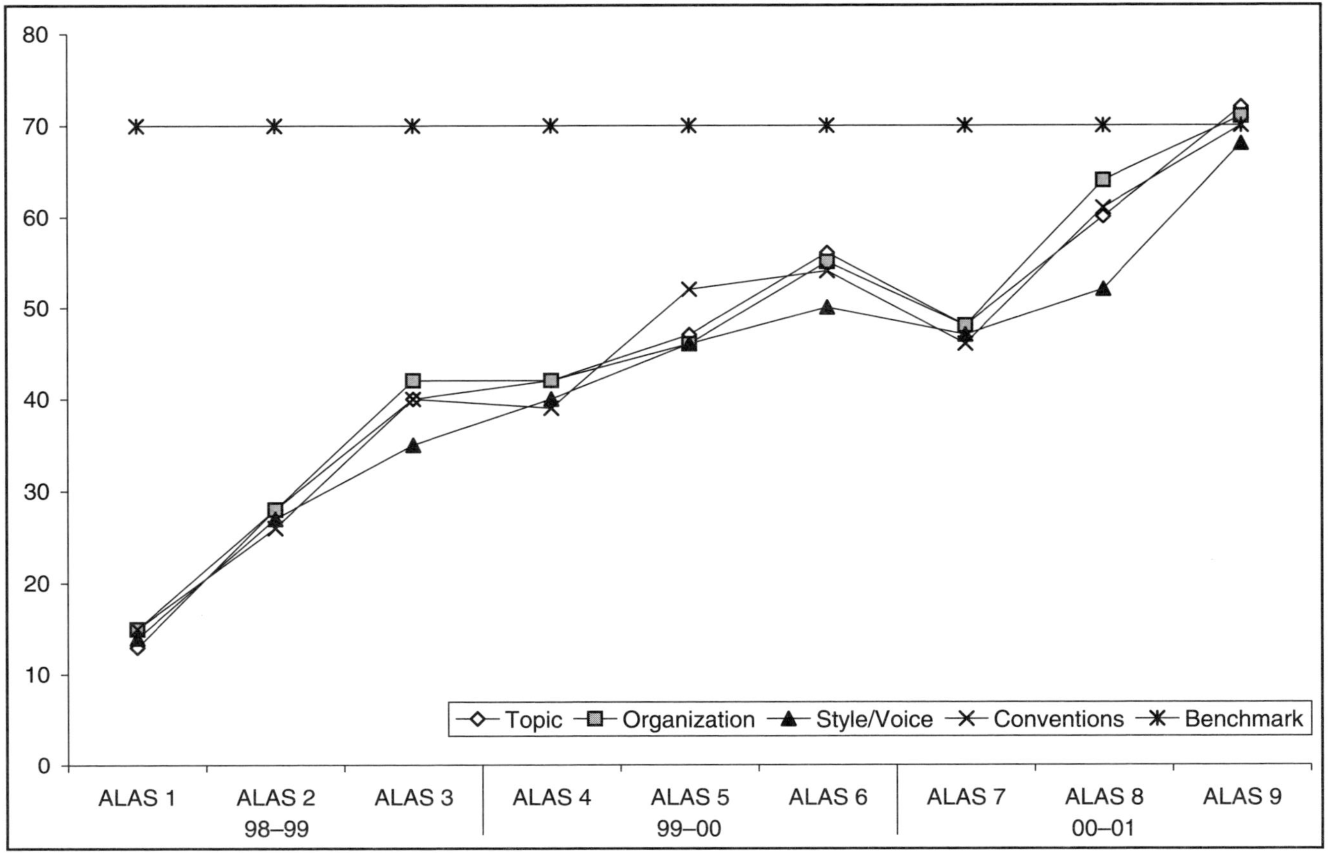

Figure A.7. Chang Ching 1998–2001 Longitudinal Cohort Chinese Bilingual Ed. Domain Scores—English Writing (Grades 1–3; $n = 14$)

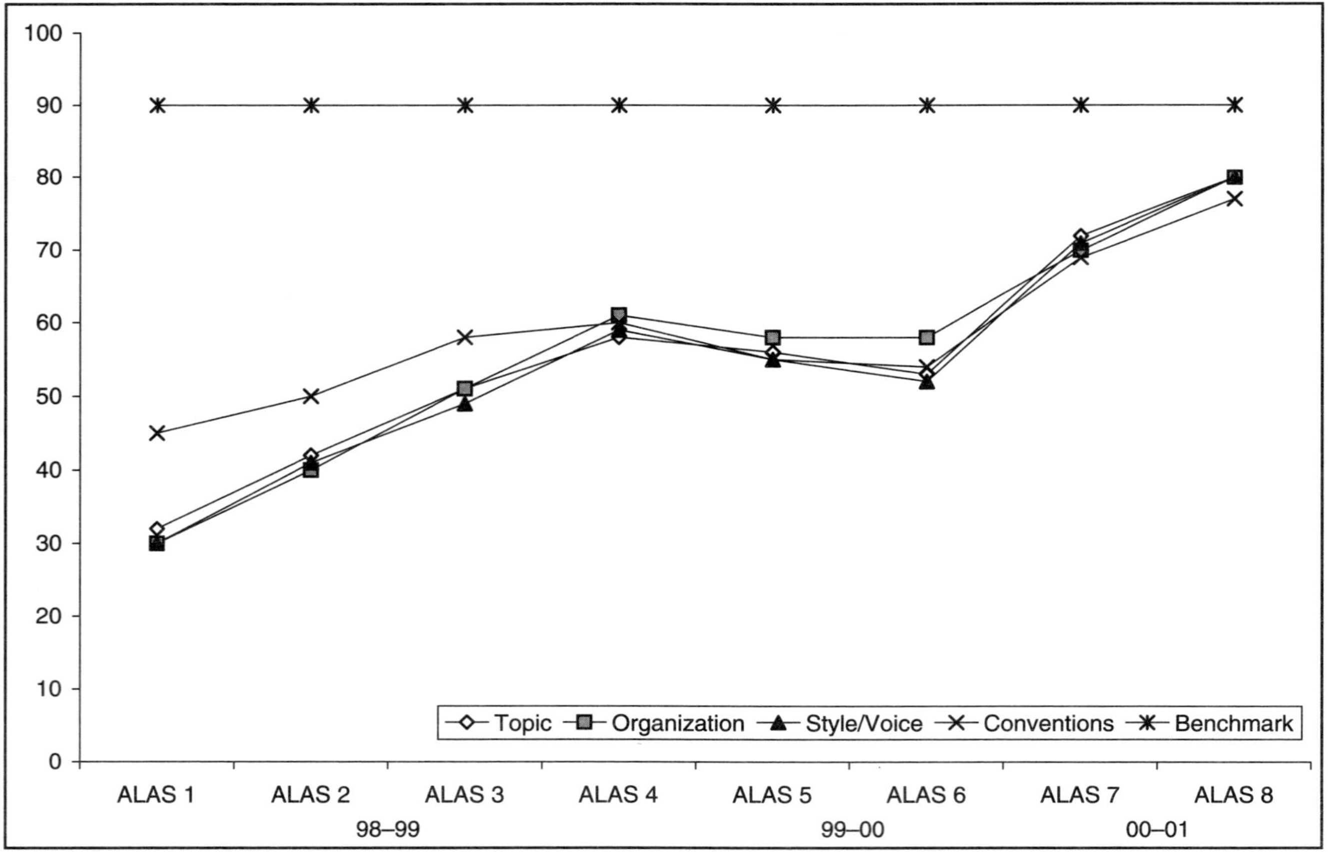
100
90
80
70
60
50
40
30
20
10
0
Topic
Organization
Style/Voice
Conventions
Benchmark
ALAS 1
ALAS 2
ALAS 3
ALAS 4
ALAS 5
ALAS 6
ALAS 7
ALAS 8
98–99
99–00
00–01

Figure A.8. Chang Ching 1998-2001 Longitudinal Cohort Chinese Bilingual Ed. Domain Scores—Chinese Writing (Grades 1–3; *n* = 14)

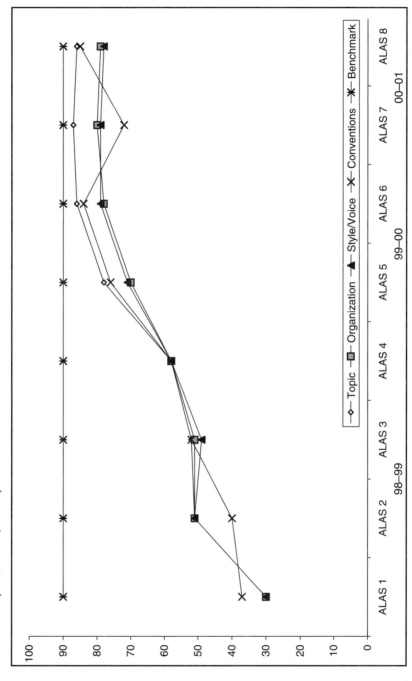

Figure A.9. Chang Ching 1998–2001 Longitudinal Cohort Spanish Bilingual Ed. Domain Scores—English Writing (Grades 1–3; *n* = 29)

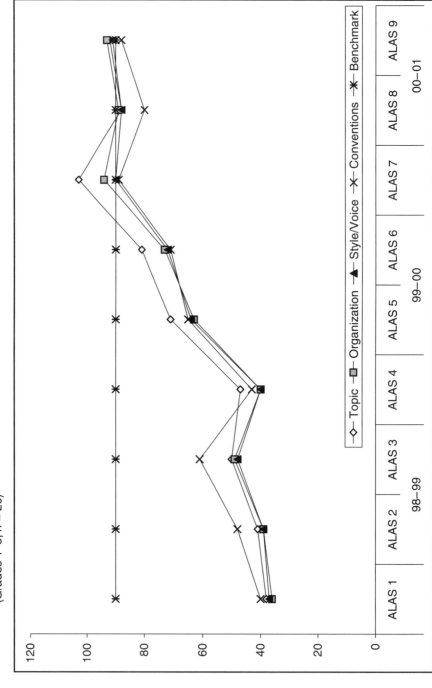

Figure A.10. Chang Ching 1998–2001 Longitudinal Cohort Spanish Bilingual Ed. Domain Scores—Spanish Writing (Grades 1–3; *n* = 29)

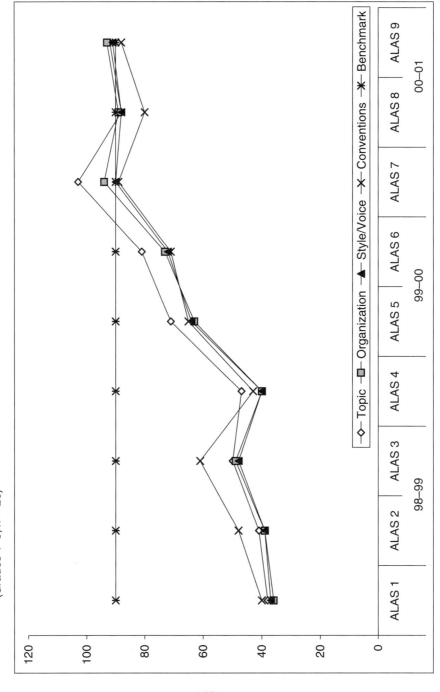

Figure A.11. Chang Ching 1998–2001 Longitudinal Cohort Spanish General Ed. Domain Scores—English Writing (Grades 1–3; *n* = 21)

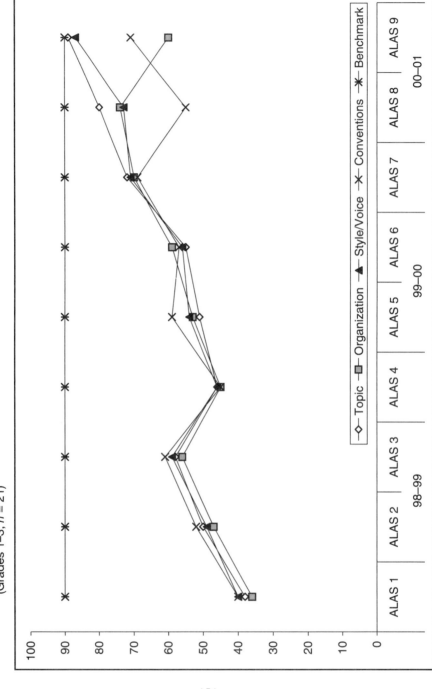

CHAPTER 8

Final Thoughts Regarding Theory, Practice, and Policy Relevant to U.S. Bilingual Students

For bilinguals, the significant uses they have for their languages are grounded in their daily practice. In the United States, millions of children come to school with languages that are different from the schooling language. This set of circumstances immediately generates language contact between those who do and do not speak English. The result is a population of bilingual students, speaking a non-English language and learning English in school.

There are several educational implications of these circumstances. In a nation with a large culturally and linguistically diverse population, it is problematic when schools fail to recognize the diverse contributions that each of these languages and cultures can make in teaching and learning. Children come to school with a complex set of histories as members of diverse families and communities (Garcia, 2001a), including distinct and diverse histories of literacy. As teachers, we come to know our students through the interactive spaces that are created in our classrooms (Dyson, 1993). Too often, however, we deny them, and ourselves, the benefit of the diverse languages/literacies.

In referring to family intervention programs for families of Mexican origin, Valdes (1996) suggests, for example, that programs "must be based on an understanding, appreciation and respect for the internal dynamics of families and for the legitimacy of their language, values and beliefs" (p. 203). Too often parents are coerced into believing that "success" entails giving up many of their beliefs, values, and language practices. Worse yet, as in the case of diverse literacy practices, schools perceive these children as devoid of any school-related literacy experiences.

From these observations, it seems evident that the uses and functions that languages and literacies may have for people are much more than diverse ways of being in the world, as suggested by Hornberger and Skilton-Sylvester (2000). Just as I am using this book on bilingualism as a way of being in the social world, so, too, is our developing curriculum fulfilling the same function for the practitioners that will use it.

It is important to affirm that there is an indelible link between under-standing a conversation or text in a schooling setting and understanding a place for us in the social world. Languages, as cultural and social channels, are one source for placing ourselves as social and cultural agents. Specifi-cally, the collection of oral lessons, readings, and related activities is part of creating a place for its participants in their social world. Thus, the composer's reflection on the composition and the composition itself both refract back to the community.

LANGUAGE AS A CULTURAL SYSTEM

Each language of a bilingual, assisting in the formation of a cultural system, can be divided into many seemingly discrete elements. This may in-clude genre, discourse, and orthography. However, the differences among each of these factors are somehow related to the influence they have in de-fining a particular branch of a communicative practice. For example, *genre* seems a broader term than *discourse*. The former is popularly thought of as dealing with oral conversation and the conveying of ideas. Genre relates to the manner in which they are related. A critical contribution of the work presented in this book may be the view that bilingualism critically informs the development and maintenance of a cultural system. As the core of a cul-tural system, bilingualism is best perceived as a holistic, integral, and signifi-cant part of the lived experiences of its users.

These languages are culturally mediated, just as one other culturally defined practices. Therefore, what is bilingualism? A grammatical definition poses an interesting examination. As a noun, *bilingualism* is the state or quality, to some degree, of being able to understand, speak, read, and write two languages. The implication is that bilingualism exists at an individual level. In turn, as an adjective, a *bilingual* person shows extensive knowledge, learning, and culture related to the circumstances of language practices. Thus, life, bilingualism, and meaning-making are culturally driven and sustained.

A Web of Meanings

A web of meanings is reflected in any formal instructional setting. Cul-turally, the school becomes a place to acquire, diffuse, and transmit cultural values, beliefs, and customs through text, context, and graphics. The mean-ings in any schooling enterprise, however, are contextualized and reshaped through specific forms of interpretation and participation. There is alchemy in the curriculum, whether we like it or not. The meanings change with ex-posure to varying populations. Part of the changes in meaning relate to how languages function as a communicative act. Since culture is public because meaning is public, as Geertz (1973) states, the meaning-making function can only occur given the social competence of the community. Sociolinguists use Hymes's (1974) notion of communicative competence to refer to an individual's ability to express what he or she means socially. In turn, social competence connotes an individual's ability to express and recognize the culturally relevant meanings that certain symbols are intended to express.

CULTURE, LANGUAGE, AND SCHOOLING

Theoretically, languages and their practices are the most significant and meaningful way of being in the social world. Matisse concludes, "I am unable to distinguish between the feeling I have for life and my way of expressing it" (quoted in Geertz, 1973, p. 104). Bilingualism as a social entity provides varied ways of expressing life. These diverse modes of expression are evident in every piece of a curriculum as well.

The education of culturally and linguistically diverse students in the United States poses interesting challenges to educators. Garcia (2001b) challenges any perspective that accounts for educational inequity in terms of supposed intellectual and/or cultural shortcomings of children/families. An alternative explanation relates to the cultural mismatch that frequently occurs between language-minority students and the schools they attend. I have suggested in other publications (Garcia, 2001a) the need to build bridges between students' day-to-day lives and their learning in school. I have come to realize that the "bridge" metaphor is not appropriate. Instead, a student brings and takes from nonschool and school experiences in his or her effort to make meaning. This interaction includes a diversity of cultures, identities, and languages.

In my earlier research on effective schools for language-minority students (Garcia, 2002), I found that successful schools have several characteristics, including high expectations, a respect for students' lives, a clear sense of vision, and a dedicated staff. This research suggests that we should move away from superficial, tip-of-the-iceberg analysis and more fully understand the course of events through more comprehensive articulations. A sound educational policy must provide insights into the many subgroups and local communities that comprise the U.S. population (Garcia, 2001a).

Schools and curricula within schools contain contact zones. Too often texts stand in specific historical relationship to students, and few have a real stake in what they learn. Part of the answer appears to lie in engaging students in a number of different types of languages and literacies that begin with who they are but extend their opportunities to develop into new realms of who they are—a responsive/unification curriculum is needed.

I'm referring to schooling that honors traditional notions of school-based success while respecting assets of linguistic and cultural diversity. Too often, dialogic authenticity is missing in our classrooms. A pedagogy that is able to juxtapose and contrast students' multiple learning contexts is going to be a "winner." There is a crude but real distinction between school and nonschool social spaces. Yet, developing those "flows" seems critical at every schooling junction. Issues of race, ethnicity, linguistic differences, and educational background at times seem to be major distractions in the education of linguistic and culturally diverse students. In essence, schooling must reconsider the goals and values that each collaborator brings to a social setting in a new partnership. The teacher, as a lifelong learner, and all learners should be able to develop communicative skills where the means to develop and the reasons to develop them are responsive to an alternative multiplicity of language and literacy practices. This presumes a trusting and supportive relationship where each partner honors each other. The net consequence has to be that social spaces are created where official and unofficial, oral and written texts meet, clash, grapple, and ultimately converge.

The future is definitely not monocultural. People do indeed interpret themselves and others in a diversity of ways. Languages do intersect and interact with each other in many different ways. The same is true of cultures as people interpret others, and themselves, in what might be identified as bewildering diversity of idioms (Nieto, 1999). These idioms are not only linguistic but also cultural. These cultural idioms are unique forms of expression whose meanings are peculiar to a particular cultural setting. The implication for schools is that we, as educators, have a duty to acquire knowledge about diverse texts, contexts, and identities that will allow us to better serve bilingual students.

POLICY CONSIDERATIONS

Bilingual Education

Bilingual education often divides non-English-speaking immigrants, native people, and the general English-speaking population, exposing major ideological differences (Chavez, 1995; Crawford, 1999). Both proponents and opponents of bilingual education have found research to support their positions, although recent studies generally conclude that, over the long term, non-English-speaking children placed in bilingual programs in the early elementary grades perform as well as or better than children not placed in these programs (August & Hakutu, 1997; Garcia, 2001a; Garcia & Gonzalez, 1995).

Since 1 of 12 children entering U.S. public schools in 2000 had limited English proficiency, conflicts over bilingual programs have come to symbolize more than differences in educational philosophy. Rather, they represent fundamental differences in perspectives on cultural diversity and access to equal educational opportunities. Thus, as linguistic minorities increase in the U.S. population, the debate over bilingual education has the potential to exacerbate ethnic and racial tensions. In addition, the issue of bilingual programs versus English-immersion programs has become a lightning rod for groups that advocate declaring English the official language of the United States and eliminating all other languages—in the workplace, on election ballots, on consumer products, and on street signs. By 1995, 23 states had passed laws making English the official state language, but in April 1998, the Arizona Supreme Court struck down the state's law mandating that state and local government business be conducted in English.

In the November 1996 local elections, the voters of Orange County, California, approved an advisory measure supporting a school district decision to eliminate bilingual education in its schools. This measure was a forerunner of Proposition 227, an initiative outlawing most forms of bilingual education and mandating 1 year of English-language classes for the state's 1.6 million non-English-speaking students.

In a set of interesting developments, Arizona and Massachusetts have passed their own version of California's Proposition 227, while Colorado turned down a similar initiative and Texas and New Mexico are making policy efforts to maximize bilingualism for all students. The debate on bilingual education is likely to continue into the 21st century without any clear resolution. Such a debate will be carried out in national, state, and local forums and addressed at policy levels. That debate will continue to impact bilingual students.

Immigration Reform

National efforts to reform immigration policies, which traditionally have been under the exclusive jurisdiction of the federal government, are continuing at all policies levels and will continue to have a direct effect on Hispanics. With the passage of Proposition 187 in 1994, the voters of California overwhelmingly (59%) supported the denial of basic social services, health care, and public education to undocumented (illegal) immigrants as a way to discourage further influxes from Mexico and Central America. As Suarez-Orozco (1997) suggests, Proposition 187 symbolizes ambivalence about immigrants, who have become the scapegoats of the economic, demographic, and cultural anxieties created by the uncertainties of rapid technological and social changes in a global economy. Their participation in national and state educational efforts has been questioned: Why should illegals receive the benefit of a free U.S. education?

In March 1998, the U.S. District Court for the Central District of California overturned all but one provision of Proposition 187 because it unconstitutionally infringed on the federal government's right to set immigration policy. A week later, this decision was appealed but was upheld by the reviewing federal court.

Extrapolating from developments in these policy areas, one can predict several major implications for the formulation of future U.S. public policy initiatives addressing racial and ethnic issues that have a direct bearing on bilingual students.

Racial controversies in the 21st century will transcend the traditional Black–White polarity, with conflict continuing between Whites and people of color, and potential conflicts emerging among ethnic minority groups. To make the policy issues politically palatable, they will increasingly be framed as matters of cultural and class differences rather than racial differences.

Controversial public policy issues will heighten tensions between English-only speakers and bilingual populations and result in greater discord, but the tensions also may mobilize diverse ethnic, racial, and linguistic groups to form more effective coalitions to maximize social and economic resources.

EDUCATIONAL PRACTICE IMPLICATIONS

Concluding that the educational failure of bilingual students, particularly Hispanic immigrant and nonimmigrant students, in the United States was reaching crisis proportions, the U.S. Department of Education assembled a group of experts to assess the educational circumstances of those students, the reasons for these circumstances, and educational practices that were effective and/or promising. I was fortunate to serve on the Hispanic Dropout Project that guided the work of this endeavor and participated in developing its final report: *No More Excuses: The Final Report of the Hispanic Dropout Project* (U.S. Department of Education, 1998). The report concluded:

> We submit this report with a sense of urgency and impatience because of the slow pace of improvement. . . . There are dozens of proven programs, replicable programs capable of increasing Hispanic students' achievement, increasing high school completion, and increasing their college going rate . . . why, then, the persistent gap in Hispanic student achievement? Many explanations have been offered: student characteristics such as social class, language, and entering achievement levels, especially among recent immigrants; school-based forces

such as student retention, ability grouping, and tracking; and, non-school forces such as family and/or neighborhood violence and criminal activity, lack of community-based opportunity, and the historical and social and political op- pression of different ethnic and racial groups. Many of these "reasons" have assumed mythic proportions. They are used to explain a phenomenon that is portrayed as too large and too complex for schools to address. In short, these reasons have become little more than excuses for our schools and society's failure to act. We as a people, need to say: *No more excuses, the time to act is now.* (pp. 61–62)

This report recommended specific practices that needed attention. This and other reviews (August & Hakuta, 1997; Garcia, 2001b) identify com- prehensive educational practices for teachers and schools that will lead to bilingual student success.

As in other research, teachers were identified as crucial in the intellec- tual and academic development of Hispanic students. They were urged to do the following:

1. Teach content so that it interests and challenges bilingual students
2. Communicate high expectations, respect, and interest in each of their students
3. Understand the roles of language, race, culture, and gender in schooling
4. Engage parents and community in the education of their children
5. Become knowledgeable about and develop strategies to educate bi- lingual students and to communicate with their parents
6. Seek and obtain the professional development needed to engender these attitudes, knowledge bases, and specific instructional skills.

Schools serving bilingual students are similarly urged to adopt program- matic features and related attributes of effective programs that had been replicated in various school settings:

1. Schools should emphasize the prevention of academic problems. They need to become more aggressive in responding to early warning signs that a student may be doing poorly, losing interest, or in some other way becoming disengaged from school.
2. Schools, especially high schools, need to personalize programs and services that work with bilingual students.
3. Schools should be restructured to ensure that all students have ac- cess to high-quality curricula. They should recognize time, space, and staffing patterns that provide students with the support necessary to achieve.

4. Schools should replicate programs that have proven effective. In addition, new funding should be used to redeploy existing resources to run these programs.
5. Schools should carefully monitor the effectiveness of what they do for bilingual students, requiring the desegregation of student progress data and acting on that data to improve or replace failing strategies.

Such specific actions have been reinforced by more direct research addressed earlier in this book—in particular the research by Rossi (1995), Olsen (1997), Romo and Falbo (1996), Larson and Rumberger (1995), Zentella (1997), Rose (1995), Soto (1997), and Trueba (1998). These scholars are also echoed in other syntheses of research that have considered the linguistic and cultural character of the bilingual student and particular education practices: the report of the National Research Council regarding the education of language-minority students in 1997 (August & Hakuta, 1997); the report of the National Academy of Sciences regarding the teaching of reading, particularly to non-English-speaking students (National Research Council, 1997); the report of the University of California Task Force on Latino Student Eligibility (University of California, 1997); and the report of the National Task Force on Minority High Achievement (College Board, 1999). Over and over, a similar call to action resonates in these reports and directs educational institutions to implement specific practices that can enhance Hispanic student achievement.

Recommendations: Five *R*'s and a *T*

These summonses to change educational practices in the face of continued bilingual student underachievement are not to be ignored. I have often been called upon to translate such calls in ways that might be helpful to policy makers, educators, and the general public at large. In so doing, I have often presented a set of recommendations that use a particular mnemonic, "remember the five *R*'s and a *T*." Educational programs, initiatives, strategies, and policies that assist Hispanic students are *respectful, responsive, responsible, resourceful, reasonable,* and *theoretically* grounded. In short, attending to these five *R*'s and the *T* should serve as a shorthand guide for those concerned with practical translation of today's theory and research and their implication for the education of bilingual students.

Respect. Over and over, it is common to hear from parents of immigrant and bilingual children that they do not receive respect in schools. They are too often seen as the foreigner, the non-English speaker, the disadvantaged, someone who does not belong, is "less than"—and the school's mission is to change them so they can belong. This absence of respect actually begins the slippery slope of lowering expectations and academic standards, creating selection devices that separate the deserving from the nondeserving, the smart from the dumb, those with and those without a future. Bilingual students find themselves at the bottom end of this continuum through no fault of their own. Educational programs, teachers, and administrators that serve bilingual students well respect the students for what they bring—their language, culture, and worldview. They accept and respect all students and the families and the communities from which they come. They see these students as bringing assets to the schooling experience, not just exhibiting a set of needs.

Responsive. It is not enough just to have respect. Educational programs and those individuals who serve in them must be directly responsive to the students and families that they serve. This requires an active assessment of the learning tools that the student brings to the schooling process coupled with the use of those tools that optimize student learning. It is not enough to just to know your students well; you must take that knowledge and make it come alive in organizing and implementing teaching and learning environments for students. That is, we can come to know our students in various intellectual ways, but until we can translate that knowledge into the very specific ways in which we teach them, maximum benefits of the intellectual knowledge will go unrealized.

My own delineation of the responsive learning community "design" study presented in this book is a good example of using bilingual students' assets in ways that inform and enhance the instructional settings of the school. It is a real and productive example of educational *responsiveness* to bilingual students.

Responsibility. In constructing new federal legislation in the Improving America's School Act, U.S. Department of Education colleagues and I were continually confronted with the unequal achievement outcomes for selected students in U.S. schools (Garcia & Gonzales, 1995). It became evident that nationally we did not have a policy mechanism in place for holding educational institutions accountable for these disparate educational results. Moreover, general aggregation of achievement data did not reveal how subgroups of students were actually doing. For this reason, the federal legislation now requires schools receiving federal funds to report student achievement by race, ethnicity, native language/English proficiency status, gender, and socioeconomic status.

Unfortunately, local schools and states do not always adopt disaggregation practices for achievement data on the bases of relevant demographic categories.

For bilingual students, failure to make distinctions in this data for immigrants versus nonimmigrants, for non-English versus English speakers, and based on previous educational background makes interpreting this data confusing and unproductive. Most significantly, limited-English-speaking students are often out of the bounds of accountability simply because they were not assessed at all. In this case, educational entities have no knowledge regarding the academic effects of schooling for this population. The absence of such achievement data has often been defended on the basis that it is better not to take such measures than to do so with inappropriate (unreliable and invalid) assessments.

Some have observed that the tests may still not meet high standards of content and may even be suspect due to their questionable reliability and validity (Valenzuela, 1999). This type of *responsibility* is still the exception, not the rule. It must become commonplace as bilingual students grow in number throughout the United States so as inform practices that can hold educational agencies accountable for the educational progress of these and all students.

Resourcefulness. We are often admonished, particularly in education, that less is more and that throwing money at a problem is not the solution. For many bilingual students, these adages sound hollow in the face of the challenges they confront every day in school.

In the K–12 sector, we have learned that serving immigrant, non-English-proficient students *does* cost more—anywhere from $200 to $1,000 per student per year (Garcia, 2001a). The types of curriculum and assessment as well as the expertise of the instructor are critical resources in need of attention if Hispanic students are to do well. Teachers with bilingual and English-development instructional skills, reduction of class size, and resources (time and money) for professional development can enhance educational *responsiveness* in preschools and during the early grades. After-school programs, specifically targeted in-school reading programs, and community-based support programs are not free. They require public and private resourcefulness that is usually nonexistent.

Reasonableness. The antibilingual education movement—led by California's Proposition 227, but with extensions into other states and into federal initiatives aimed at immigrant students—seeks to unreasonably restrict the flexibility of states and local school districts to respond to bilingual students. These new policies mandate prescriptive instructional treatments, limit temporal access of students to these programs (from 1 to 3 years), and focus only on English-language development instead of high academic achievement without any concern for the accountability of the mandates they impose. Proposed new assessment practices in the U.S. Department of Education's "Reading-by-Third-Grade" initiative would require all students to be assessed in English reading, although the department presently funds programs whose direct goal is to teach children to read in their native language, with English reading competencies expected after the third grade. Does this incongruence seem reasonable? Similarly, in California, English tests in reading and mathematics for non-English-speaking students have been mandated by executive order of the governor with the support of the California State Board of Education. A "reasonable" judge found it of no use to test non-English-speaking students in an English achievement test that was not aligned with the student's language of instruction while placing the student in a very awkward and potentially harmful testing situation. In our urgency and goodwill, we need not act unreasonably.

Most often, as reasonable people attend these five *R*'s, they are often seen nodding their heads. In almost all cases, these general guidelines are relevant to all students. I have tried, however, to make the strongest case possible that for bilingual students and their present and future educational success, these guidelines are absolutely critical. Educational practices that respect who the students are, respond directly to what we have learned, hold themselves responsible for academic outcomes, and provide for and maximize new and existing resources organized in ways that are reasonable can make a significant difference in student learning.

Theory. Unfortunately, I cannot leave the educational treatment of bilingual students only within the domains of the five *R*'s. A fundamental and crucial aspect of addressing the education of bilingual students is the conceptual or theoretical approach to second-language learning. With the emergence of policy-driven English foci for instruction of bilingual students, like those in California's Proposition 227, educators were left to grapple with what should be done in their classrooms.

Stritikus (2002) points out in his research investigating the effect of Proposition 227 on instructional behavior that teachers were torn between following the new law in organizing their instruction or making quite different decisions based on their own judgments or "theories" of what was best for their bilingual students. In essence, some teachers decided to move from bilingual instructional strategies to English-only strategies, while others continued to use a broad array of bilingual strategies.

The deciding factor in doing one or the other was not the prevailing change in policy or even an overt resistance to the new policy—although some teachers did report doing just that (Stritikus & Garcia, 2000). Instead, it was the teacher's individual judgment regarding what was best for his or her particular students. These judgments were primarily based on a teacher's "theory" regarding the best ways for bilingual children to be "schooled." Therefore, teachers opting to rid themselves of bilingual education strategies that made use of the student's primary language during instruction indicated that this change would better promote academic success and related social success of students. Teachers opting to shun English-only instructional strategies continued and to some extent enhanced their use of bilingual strategies for the same reasons. In short, educational practices for bilingual students were radically different, yet the "reasons" for supporting those differences were exactly the same.

In light of the significance of these and related findings, any instructional decision for a student may very well rest primarily on the judgments, perspectives, and "theories" of those organizing and implementing the instruction. For bilingual students, where varying "theories" regarding what is best exist, it becomes important to ensure that those individuals making instructional decisions, particularly teachers, are well informed regarding the conceptual and practice consequences of their decisions.

FROM THE GENERAL TO THE SPECIFIC

It isn't often that a researcher is given the opportunity to grapple with education issues that he or she researches. I was given such an opportunity when the San Francisco School district asked me to serve on its Bilingual Task Force. The Bilingual Education Task Force was convened by Superintendent Arlene Ackerman to develop an improved Bilingual Education Master Plan for the district. The report and its findings and recommendations were adopted by the board of education at its meeting of May 15, 2002. It stands as my own and my colleagues' best recommendations for addressing the educational needs of bilingual students in the United States. The discussion of this report is my concluding attempt to move from the general to the specific regarding action needed by U.S. schools that wish to "reform" education for bilingual students.

This districtwide effort was based on a set of conditions that recognized that over 50% of its 60,000 students spoke a home language other than English, primarily Chinese (Cantonese, Mandarin, and various dialects) and Spanish. Moreover, the district was adopting a highly visible school reform agenda intended to guarantee equality of opportunity for all its children by undertaking a comprehensive restructuring of the system and accountability for student academic achievement.

The task force concluded that because of the lack of a systemic approach with a well-articulated accountability process, the district should move immediately to accomplish three tasks:

1. Hold all school and District office personnel accountable for full and successful implementation of educational programming that serves the academic development of English learners in the context of serving all students.

2. Initiate systemic programmatic attention to District wide efforts that build on the successes of its bilingual education history and further ensure the opportunity for all students to become bilingual and biliterate.
3. Require that every school provide an articulated academic English language development program. (San Francisco Bilingual Task Force Report, 2002, p. 2)

The task force and its working groups generated a set of action steps needed to fulfill its recommendations:

- Establish and support pre-K programs fully articulated with the K–5 programs that support maximum developmental growth for English-language learners in those programs.
- Establish fully articulated two-way immersion programs in high schools.
- Placed newly arrived immigrant students appropriately in newcomer programs that will prepare them to participate successfully in the SFUSD educational system.
- Establish procedures for monitoring and evaluating the implementation of programs.
- Have a fully functioning and effective oversight committee made up of administrative staff, teachers, and parents. Closely monitor all schools with 21 or more bilingual students.
- Ensure that all families and communities are knowledgeable about the school system and creative models of quality education, including language acquisition programs.
- Provide families with interpretation and translation services, as needed, for all home, community, and school activities.
- Form assessment committees to review existing bilingual assessments pre-K–12 and identify/obtain assessments that are lacking.
- Provide professional development necessary to adopt and adapt alternative performance-based assessments in English and other languages, including the Authentic Literacy Assessment System (ALAS).

These recommendations and actions recognize education reform efforts underway throughout the United States but attend particularly to the circumstances related to serving bilingual students.

CONCLUSION

This book has attempted to further problematize our understanding of education through the discussion of language, culture, and schooling. If the overviews and findings presented here are understood and acted upon, then one could predict that as more linguistically and culturally diverse students enter the "right" kind of schools and classrooms, barriers to their academic, social, and economic success and mobility will decrease. Likewise, as English-speaking majorities become more attuned to the linguistic and cultural diversity around them and the resources inherent in that diversity, distinctions will blend with other features of our society to create a more egualitarian, multicultural, and multilingual society. This is, of course, a highly optimistic scenario of the future for bilingual students and U.S. society in general. Yet it is most certainly a preferable alternative to having the United States become another Bosnian nightmare, where racial and ethnic conflicts could escalate into social unrest.

If the treatment of non-English-speaking and immigrant students in our educational institutions serves as an indicator of where we are in the process of achieving educational equity in this country, we clearly have much progress to make. How we react to making this progress is important. We now have the theory, knowledge base, and the educational tools with which progress can be made.

Simply put, our challenge is to help the United States become a multilingual society that embraces English while not denigrating other languages. We must both learn about and create new ways to do the following:

- Honor the linguistic diversity and social complexity in which we live
- Promote and ensure English competency in all its manifestations for all U.S. students
- Embrace and promote bilingualism at every opportunity for these students

References

Ahlgren, I., & Hyltenstam, K. (1994). *Bilingualism in deaf education*. Hamburg: Signum.

Anderson, J. (1983). *The architecture of cognition*. Cambridge, MA: Harvard University Press.

Aspira of New York, Inc. v. Board of Education of the City of New York, 394 F. Supp. 1161. (1975).

August, D., & Hakuta, K. (1997). *Improving schooling for language-minority children: A research, policy and practice*. Chicago: Thomas.

Baetens Beardsmore, H. (1982). *Bilingualism: Basic principles*. Clevedon, UK: Tieto Ltd.

Banks, J., & Banks, C. A. (1995). *Handbook of research on multicultural education*. New York: Macmillan.

Becijos, J. (1997). *SDAIE: Strategies for teachers of English learners*. Boston: Allyn & Bacon.

Benjamin, R., Pecos, R., & Romero, M. E. (1997). Language revitalization efforts in the Pueblo of Cochitie: Becoming "literate" in an oral society. In N. H. Hornberger (Ed.), *Indigenous literacies in the Americas: Language planning from the bottom up*. Berlin/New York: Mouton de Gruyter.

Bergmann, R. (1994). Teaching sign language as the mother tongue in the education of deaf children in Denmark. In I. Ahlgren & K. Hyltenstam (Eds.), *Bilingualism in deaf education* (pp. 83–90). Hamburg: Signum.

Berman, P. (1992). *Meeting the challenge of language diversity: An evaluation of California programs for pupils with limited proficiency in English*. San Francisco, CA: American Educational Research Association.

Berman, P. (1996). *The feasibility of statewide distance education* (Discussion Paper No. 5). Berkeley, CA: Commission on Innovation Policy.

Bernhardt, E. (1991). *Reading development in a second language: Theoretical, empirical, and classroom perspectives*. Norwood: Ablex.

Boggs, S. T. (1972). The meaning of questions and narratives to Hawaiian children. In C. Cazden, V. John, & D. Hymes (Eds.), *Foundations of language in the classroom* (pp. 146–163). New York: Teachers College Press.

Bowerman, M. (1975). Crosslinguistic similarities at two stages of syntactic development. In E. Lennenberg & E. Lennenberg (Eds.), *Foundations of language development* (pp. 267–282). London: UNESCO Press.

Brown, A. L. (1992). Design experiments: Theoretical and methodological challenges in creating complex interventions in classroom settings. *The Journal of the Learning Sciences, 2*, 141–178.

Brown, A. L. (1994). The advancement of learning. *Educational Research, 23*(8), 4–12.

Brown, R. A. (1973). *A first language: The early stages.* Cambridge, MA: Harvard University Press.

California Tomorrow. (1995). *The unfinished journey: Restructuring schools in a diverse society.* San Francisco: Author.

California Tomorrow (1997). *The schools we need now: How parents, families and communities can change schools.* San Francisco.

Camarota, A. (2001). *Immigrants and the schools.* Washington, DC: Urban Institute.

Canale, M. (1983). From communicative complete to communicative pedagogy. In J. Richards & R. Schmidt (Eds.), *Language and communication* (pp. 114–126). London: Longman.

Canale, M., & Swain, M. (1980). Theoretical bases of communicative approaches to second language teaching and testing. *Applied Linguistics, 1*(1), 1–47.

Carlisle, R. (1989). The writing of Anglo and Hispanic elementary school students in bilingual, submersion and regular programs. *Studies in Second Language Acquisition, 11,* 257–280.

Casanova, U. (1991). Bilingual education: Politics or pedagogy. In O. Garcia (Ed.), *Bilingual education* (Vol. 1; pp. 167–182). Amsterdam: John Benjamins.

Castañeda v. Pickard (1007 5th Cir.) (1981).

Cazabon, M., Lambert, W., & Hall, G. (1999). *Two-way bilingual education: A report on the Amigos program.* Washington, DC: Center for Applied Linguistics.

Cazden, C. (1988). *Classroom discourse: The language of teaching and learning.* Portsmouth, NH: Heinemann.

Chambers, J., & Parrish, T. (1992). *Meeting the challenge of diversity: An evaluation of programs serving LEP students: Vol. IV. Cost of programs and services.* Berkeley: BW Associates.

Chamot, A. U., & O'Malley, J. M. (1994). *Cognitive sensitive English instruction.* New York: Lindemann.

Chavez, L. (1991). *Out of the barrio: Toward a new politics of Hispanic assimilation.* New York: Basic Books.

Chavez, L. (1995, August). One nation, one common language. *Reader's Digest* (August), pp. 87–91.

Chomsky, N. (1959). Review of B. F. Skinner. *Verbal Behavior and Language, 35,* 116–128.

Christian, D. (1994). *Two-way bilingual education: Students learning through two languages.* Washington, DC: Center for Applied Linguistics.

Christian, D. (1997). *Directory of two-way bilingual education programs.* Washington, DC: Center for Applied Linguistics.

Christian, D. (1999). *Two-way bilingual education: Progress on many fronts.* Washington, DC: Center for Applied Linguistics.

Clare-Matsumura, L., Patthey-Chavez, G. G., Valdés, R., & Garnier, H. (2000). Teacher feedback, writing assignment quality, and third-grade students' revision in lower- and higher-achieving urban schools. *The Elementary School Journal.*

Cole, M., & Cole, S. R. (2001). *The development of children.* New York: Worth.

Cole, R. W. (1996). *Educating everybody's children: What research and practice say about improving achievement.* Alexandria, VA: Association for Supervision and Curriculum Development.

Coleman, J. (1966). *Equality of educational opportunity.* Washington, DC: United States Government Printing Office.

College Board. (1999). *Report of the national task force on minority high achievement.* New York: Author.

Collins, A. (1999). The changing infrastructure of education research. In E. C. Lagemann & L. S. Shulman (Eds.), *Issues in education research* (pp. 289–298). San Francisco: Jossey-Bass.

Colombi, C. (2000). En vias del desarrollo del lenguaje academico en espanol en hableantes nativos de espanol en los Estados Unidos. In A. Roca (Ed.), *Research on Spanish in the U.S.* New York, NY: Casacadilla Press.

Corder, S. P. (1976). The significance of learner's errors. *International Review of Applied Linguistics in Language Teaching, 5*, 161–170.

Council of Great City Schools. (2000). *Report of student characteristics of U.S. urban schools.* Washington, DC: Author.

Crandall, J., Dale, T., Rhodes, S., & Spanos, G. (1989). *English skills for algebra.* England Cliffs, NJ: CAL/Prentice-Hall Regents.

Crawford, J. (1995). Endangered Native American languages: What is to be done and why? *The Bilingual Research Journal, 19*(1), 17–38.

Crawford, J. (1998). *Ten common fallacies about bilingual education.* Washington, DC: ERIC Clearinghouse on Language and Linguistics, Center for Applied Linguistics.

Crawford, J. (1999). *Bilingual education: History, politics, theory, and practice* (4th ed.). Los Angeles: Bilingual Education Services.

Crawford, J. (2002). Comment: Bilingualism and schooling in the United States. *International Journal of the Sociology of Language, 155/156*, 93–99.

Cummins, J. (1979). Linguistic interdependence and the educational development of bilingual children. *Review of Educational Research, 19*, 222–251.

Cummins, J. (1981). The role of primary language development in promoting educational success for language minority students. In California Department of Education (Ed.), *Schooling and language minority students: A theoretical framework* (pp. 3–50). Los Angeles: Evaluation, Dissemination, and Assessment Center.

Cummins, J. (1984). *Bilingualism and special education.* San Diego: College Hill Press.

Cummins, J. (1986). Empowering minority students: A framework for intervention. *Harvard Educational Review, 56*(1), 18–35.

Cummins, J. (1991). The politics of paranoia: Reflections on the bilingual education debate. In O. Garcia (Ed.), *Bilingual Education* (Vol. 1; pp. 185–199). Amsterdam: John Benjamins.

Cummins, J. (1997). Minority status and schooling in Canada. *Anthropology and Education Quarterly, 28*(3), 411–436.

Darcy, N. T. (1953). A review of the literature of the effects of bilingualism upon the measurement of intelligence. *Journal of Genetic Psychology, 82*, 21–57.

Darcy, N. T. (1963). Bilingualism and the measurement of intelligence: Review of a decade of research. *Journal of Genetic Psychology, 7*(1), 259–282.

Davies, S. N. (1991). The transition of toward bilingual education of deaf children in Denmark and Sweden: Perspectives on language. *Sign Language Studies, 71,* 111–122.

DeHouwer, A. (1995). *Bilingual language acquisition.* Cambridge, MA: Blackwell.

DeKeyser, R. (1997). Beyond explicit rule learning: Automotizing second language morphosyntax. *Studies in Second Language Acquisition, 19*(2), 196–221.

Delgado-Gaitan, C. (1990). *Literacy for empowerment: The roles of parents in children's education.* Basingstoke, UK: Falmer.

Destefano, J. (1972). Social variation in language: Implications for teaching reading to Black ghetto children. In J. A. Figurel (Ed.), *Better Reading in Urban Schools* (pp. 18–24). Newark, DE: International Reading Association.

Development Associates. (1993). *Final report: Descriptive study phase of the national longitudinal evaluation of the effectiveness of services for language minority limited English proficient students.* Arlington, VA: Author.

Diaz, R. M. (1983). The impact of bilingualism on cognitive development. In E. W. Gordon (Ed.), *Review of research in education* (Vol. 10; pp. 23–54). Washington, DC: American Educational Research Association.

Diaz, R. (1985). Bilingual cognitive development: Addressing these gaps in current research. *Child Development, 56,* 1376–1388.

Diaz, R. M., & Klinger, C. (1991). Towards an exploratory model of the interaction between bilingualism and cognitive development. In E. Bialystock (Ed.), *Language processing in bilingual children* (pp. 140–185). New York: Cambridge University Press.

Diaz, S. L., Moll, C., & Mehan, H. (1986). Sociocultural resources in instruction: A context-specific approach. In B. E. Office (Ed.), *Beyond language: Social and cultural factors in schooling language minority students* (pp. 197–230). Los Angeles: Evaluation, Disseminations, and Assessment Center, California State University.

Dolson, D. (1984). *The influence of various home bilingual environments on the academic achievement, language development, and psychosocial adjustment of fifth and sixth grade Hispanic students.* Unpublished doctoral dissertation, University of San Francisco.

Drasgow, E. (1993). Bilingual/bicultural deaf education: An overview. *Sign Language Studies, 80,* 243–266.

Duff, P., & Early, M. (1999, March). *Language socialization in perspective: Classroom discourse in high school humanities courses.* Paper presented at the American Association for Applied Linguistics, Stamford, CT.

Dulay, H., & Burt, M. (1974). *Natural sequence in child second language acquisition.* Toronto, Ontario: Institute for Studies in Education.

Duquette, G. (1991). Cultural processing and minority language children with needs and special needs. In G. Duquette & L. Malve (Eds.), *Language, culture and cognition* (pp. 54–66). Philadelphia: Multilingual Matters.

Dwyer, C. (1991). *Language, culture and writing.* Unpublished manuscript, Center for the Study of Writing, University of California, Berkeley.

Dyson, A. H. (1993). *Writing children: Reinventing the development of childhood literacy.* Berkeley: Center for the Study of Writing, University of California.

Ebsworth, T., & Sanchez, C. (1997, November). *Providing an L2 intellectual challenge through L1 support.* Paper presented at the NYS TESOL annual conference, Rye Brook, New York.

Edelsky, C. (1986). *Writing in a bilingual program: Havia una vez.* Norwood: Ablex.

Edwards, J. (1981). *Ratings of Black, White and Acadian children's speech patterns.* Unpublished doctoral dissertation, Mount St. Vincent University, Halifax, Nova Scotia, Canada.

Eisenstein, E. M., Bodman, J., & Carpenter, M. (1995). Crosscultural realizations of greetings in American English. In S. Gass & J. Neu (Eds.), *Speech Acts Across Cultures.* Hillsdale, NJ: Erlbaum.

Ellis, R. (1993). The structural syllabus and SLA. *TESOL Quarterly, 27*(1), 91–113.

Erickson, F. (1987). Transformation and school success: The politics and culture of educational achievement. *Anthropology and Education Quarterly, 18,* 146–167.

Ervin-Tripp, S. M. (1974). Is second language learning like the first? *TESOL Quarterly, 8*(2), 111–127.

Fantini, A. E. (1985). *Language acquisition of a bilingual child.* Clevedon, Avon, UK: Multilingual Matters.

Fasold, R. (1984). *The sociolinguistics of society.* Oxford, UK: Blackwell.

Ferris, D. R. (1999). One size does not fit all: Response and revision issues for immigrant student writers. In L. Harklau, K. M. Losey, & M. Siegel (Eds.), *Generation 1.5 meets college composition.* Mahwah, NJ: Erlbaum.

Firth, A., & Wagner, J. (1997). On discourse, communication, and (some) fundamental concepts in SLA research. *The Modern Language Journal, 81,* 285–300.

Fishman, J. (1991). What do you lose when you lose a language? In G. Cantoni (Ed.), *Stabilizing indigenous languages* (pp. 147–173). Flagstaff: Northern Arizona University.

Fitzgerald, J. (1995). English-as-a-second-language reading instruction in the United States: A research review. *Journal of Reading Behavior, 27,* 115–152.

Fradd, S. (1997). School–university partnerships to promote science with students learning English. *TESOL Journal, 7*(1), 35–40.

Freeman, D. C. (1998). *Dual language analyses at Oyster School.* Unpublished doctoral dissertation, Georgetown University, Washington, DC.

Freire, P., & Macedo, D. (1987). *Literacy: Reading the word and the world.* South Hadley, MA: Bergin & Garvey.

Galambos, S. J., & Hakuta, K. (1988). Subject-specific and task-specific characteristics of metalinguistic awareness in bilingual children. *Applied Psycholinguistics, 9,* 141–162.

Gallimore, R., & Goldenberg, C. (2001). Analyzing cultural models and settings to connect minority achievement and school improvement research. *Educational Psychologist, 36,* 45–56.

García, E. (1983). *Bilingualism in early childhood.* Albuquerque: University of New Mexico Press.

García, E. (1991). Attributes of effective language minority teachers: An empirical study. *Journal of Education, 174,* 130–141.

García, E. E. (1994). Addressing the challenges of diversity. In S. L. Kagan & B. Weissbourd (Eds.), *Putting families first* (pp. 243–275). San Francisco: Jossey-Bass.

García, E. E. (1999). *Understanding and meeting the challenge of student cultural diversity* (2nd ed.). New York: Houghton Mifflin.

García, E. (2001a). *Hispanic education in the United States: Raices y alas.* Lanham, MD: Rowman & Littfield.

García, E. (2001b). *Understanding and meeting the challenge of student diversity* (3rd ed.). Boston: Houghton Mifflin.

García, E. (2002). Bilingualism and schooling in the United States. *International Journal of the Sociology of Language, 155*(156), 1–92.

García, E., & Carrasco, R. (1981). An analysis of bilingual mother-child discourse (pp. 46–61). In R. Duran (Ed.), *Latino Discourse.* Norwood, NJ: Ablex.

García, E., & Curry, J. E. (2000). The education of limited English proficient students in California schools: An assessment of the influence of Proposition 227 in selected districts and schools. *Bilingual Research Journal, 24*(1–2), 15–36.

García, E., & Gonzalez, G. (1995). Issues in systemic reform for culturally and linguistically diverse students. *College Record, 96*(3), 418–431.

García, E., Maez, L., & Gonzalez, G. (1983). Language switching in bilingual children: A national perspective. In E. Garcia (Ed.), *The Mexican-American child: Language, cognition and social development* (pp. 21–36). Tempe: Arizona State University.

Gardner, R. C., & Lambert, E. (1972). *Attitudes and motivation in second language learning.* Rowley, MA: Newbury House.

Gass, S., & Neu, J. (1995). *Speech acts across cultures.* Berlin: Mouton de Gruyter.

Geertz, F. (1973). *The intervention of culture: Selected essays.* New York: Basic Books.

Genesee, F. (1979). Acquisition of reading skill in immersion programs. *Foreign Language Annals, 12,* 71–77.

Genishi, C. (1984). Code switching in Chicano six-year olds. In R. Duran (Ed.), *Latino language and communicative behavior* (pp. 133–152). Norwood, NJ: Ablex.

Goals 2000. (1994). Educate America Act, Pub.L. No. 103–227, 108 stat. 125.

Goldenberg, C., Reese, L., & Gallimore, R. (1992). Effects of literacy materials from school on Latino children's home experiences and early reading achievement. *American Journal of Education, 100,* 497–536.

Goldman, S., & Trueba, H. (1987). *Becoming literate in English as a second language: Advances in research and theory.* Norwood, NJ: Ablex.

Gomez, R. J., Parker, R., & Lara-Alecio, R. (1996). Process vs. product writing with limited English proficient students. *The Bilingual Research Journal, 20,* 556–565.

Goncz, B., & Kodzepeljic, D. (1991). Cognition and bilingualism revisited. *Journal of Multicultural Development, 12,* 137–163.

Goodman, Y. (1980). The roots of literacy. In M. P. Douglass (Ed.), *Reading: A humanizing experience* (pp. 286–301). Claremont, CA: Claremont Graduate School.

Grabe, W., & Kaplan, R. B. (1996). *Theory and practice writing*. New York: Addison Wesley Longman.

Greenberg, J., Macias, R., Rhodes, S., & Chan, L. (2001). *Augmented analyses of the 1992 National Adult Literacy Survey*. Washington, DC: U.S. Department of Education.

Grosjean, F. (1982). *Life with two languages*. New York: Cambridge University Press.

Grosjean, F. (1996). Living with two languages and two cultures. In I. Parasnis (Ed.), *Cultural and language diversity and the deaf experience* (pp. 20–37). New York: Cambridge University Press.

Guadalupe v. Tempe Elementary Board of Education, 811 F. 2d1030. (1983).

Gutierrez, K. (1992). A comparison of instructional contexts in writing process classrooms with Latino children. *Education and Urban Society, 24*, 244–262.

Gutierrez, K. (1995). Unpacking academic discourses. *Discourse Processes, 19*, 21–37.

Gutierrez, K., Baquedano-Lopez, P., Alvarez, H., & Chiu, M. (1999). Building a culture of collaboration through hybrid language practices. *Theory into Practice, 38*, 87–93.

Gutierrez, K., Rymes, B., & Larson, J. (1995). Script, counterscript, and underlife in the classroom: Brown, James versus Brown v Board of Education. *Harvard Educational Review, 65*, 445–471.

Gutierrez, K., & Stone, L. (2000). Synchronic and diachronic dimensions of social practice: An emerging methodology for cultural-historical perspectives on literacy learning. In C. Lee & P. Smagorinsky (Eds.), *Vygotskian perspectives on literacy research: Constructing meaning through collaborative inquiry* (pp. 150–164). New York: Cambridge University Press.

Hakuta, K. (1974). *A preliminary report on the development of grammatical morphemes in a Japanese girl learning English as a second language*. Toronto: Ontario Institute for Studies in Education.

Hakuta, K. (1986). *Mirror of language: The debate on bilingualism*. New York: Basic Books.

Hakuta, K., & D'Andrea, D. (1992). Some properties of bilingual maintenance and loss. *Applied Linguistics, 13*, 72–99.

Hall, N. (1987). *The emergence of literacy*. Portsmouth, NH: Heinemann.

Halliday, M. (1975). *Learning how to mean: Explorations in the development of language*. London: Dover.

Halliday, M. A. K. (1989). *Spoken and written language*. Oxford, UK: Oxford University Press.

Hamers, J. F., & Blanc, M. (1989). *Bilinguality and bilingualism*. New York: Cambridge University Press.

Harrison, J. (1985). Functions of language attitudes in school settings. *Language in Society, 22*, 1–21.

Heath, S. B. (1983). *Ways with words: Language, life, and work in communities and classroom*. New York: Cambridge University Press.

Heath, S. B. (1986). Sociocultural contexts of language development. In California State Department of Education (Ed.), *Beyond language: Social and cultural factors in schooling language minority students* (pp. 143–186). Los Angeles: Evaluation, Dissemination, and Assessment Center, California State University.

Hinton, L. (1994). *Flutes of fire: Essays on California Indian languages.* Berkeley, CA: Heyday.

Hoffmeister, R. (1990). ASL and its implications for education. In H. Bornstein (Ed.), *Manual communication in America* (pp. 161–184). Washington, DC: Gallaudet University Press.

Hornberger, N. H. (1989). Continua of biliteracy. *Review of Educational Research, 59,* 271–296

Hornberger, N. H., & Skilton-Sylvester, E. (2000). Revisiting the continua of biliteracy: International and critical perspectives. *Language and Education: An International Journal, 142*(2), 96–122.

Huerta, A. (1977). The development of code-switching in a young bilingual. *Working Papers in Sociolinguistics, 21,* 1–16.

Hutton, E. R. (1942). Mexican children find themselves. In National Education Association (Eds)., *Americans all: Studies in intercultural education* (pp. 45–51). Washington, DC: National Education Association.

Hymes, D. (1974). *Foundations in sociolinguistics: An ethnographic approach.* Philadelphia: University of Pennsylvania Press.

Initiative on Educational Excellence for Hispanic Americans. (2003). *Fulfilling the educational needs of Hispanic Americans in the 21st century.* Washington, DC: United States Government Printing Office.

Irujo, S. (1988). An introduction to intercultural differences and similarities in non-verbal communication. In J. Wurzel (Ed.), *Toward multiculturalism* (pp. 114–138). Yarmouth, ME: Intercultural Press.

Jankowski, K. (1993). Reflections upon Milan with an eye to the future. In B. Snider (Ed.), *Post Milan ASL and English literacy: Issues, trends and research* (pp. 1–36). Washington, DC: Gallaudet University College for Continuing Education.

Just, M., & Carpenter, P. (1992). A capacity theory of comprehension: Individual differences in working memory. *Psychological Review, 99,* 122–149.

Kasper, G., & Blum-Kulka, S. (1993). *Intercultural Pragmatics.* New York: Oxford University Press.

Kendler, A. C. (2002). *Survey of the states' limited English proficient students 2000–2001.* Washington, DC: Office of English Acquisition, Language Enhancement and Academic Achievement for Limited English Proficient Students, U.S. Department of Education.

Kessler, C., & Quinn, M. E. (1985). Positive effects of bilingualism on science problem solving abilities. In J. E. Alatis & J. J. Staczek (Eds.), *Perspectives on bilingual education* (pp. 289–296). Washington, DC: Georgetown University Press.

Kessler, C., & Quinn, M. E. (1987). Language minority children's linguistic and cognitive creativity. *Journal of Multilingual and Multicultural Development, 8,* 173–185.

Keyes v. School District No. 1. (Keyes XIII 576F. Supp. 1503). (1983).

Krashen, S. D. (1981). Bilingual education and second language acquisition theory. In California State University, Los Angeles (Ed.), *Schooling and language mi-*

nority students (pp. 3–50). Los Angeles: Evaluation, Dissemination and Assessment Center, California State University.

Krashen, S. D. (1985). *The input hypothesis: Issues and implications.* New York: Longman.

Krashen, S. D. (1996). *Under attack: The case against bilingual education.* Culver City, CA: Language Education Associates.

Krashen, S. D. (1999). *Condemned without a trial: Bogus arguments against bilingual education.* Portsmouth, NH: Heinemann.

Kraus, M. (1992). The world's languages in crisis. *Language, 68,* 6–10.

Labov, W. (1972). The logic of nonstandard English. In W. Labov (Ed.), *Language in the inner city: Studies in Black English Vernacular* (pp. 201–240). Philadelphia: University of Pennsylvania Press.

Ladson-Billings, G., & Tate, W. F. (1995). Towards a critical race theory of education. *Teachers College Record, 97*(1), 47–68.

Lambert, W. (1990). Culture and language as factors in learning and education. In A. Wolfgang (Ed.), *Education of immigrant students* (pp. 138–153). Toronto: Ontario Institute for Studies in Education.

Laosa, L. (1998). *Research perspectives on constructs of change: Intercultural migration and developmental transitions.* Princeton, NJ: Educational Testing Service.

Larson, K., & Rumberger, R. (1995). Doubling school success in highest risk. Latino youth: Results from a middle school intervention study. In R. Marcus & R. G. Ramos (Eds.), *Changing schools for changing students* (pp. 154–179). Santa Barbara: University of California Linguistic Minority Research Institute.

Lau v. Nichols (414 US 563) (1974).

Lehrer, R., Carpenter, S., Schauble, L., & Putz, A. (2000). Designing classrooms that support inquiry. In J. Minstrell & E. van Zee (Eds.), *Teaching science in the inquiry-based classroom* (pp. 80–99). Washington, DC: American Association for the Advancement of Science.

Leopold, W. F. (1939). *Speech development of a bilingual child: A linguist's record. Vol. I: Vocabulary growth in the first two years.* Evanston, IL: Northwestern University Press.

Levin, H. M. (1986). *Education reform for disadvantaged students: An emerging crisis.* Washington, DC: National Education Association.

Lightbown, P. (1998). The importance of timing in focus on form in grammar. In C. Doughty & J. Williams (Eds.), *Focus on form in classroom second language acquisition* (pp. 177–196). Cambridge, UK: Cambridge University Press.

Lightbown, P., & Spada, N. (1990). Focus on form and corrective feedback on communicative teaching: Effects on second language learning. *Studies in Second Language Acquisition, 12*(4), 429–448.

Lindholm, K. (1999, April). *Two-way bilingual education: Past and future.* Paper presented at the American Education Research Association, Toronto.

Linguistic Society of America. (1997). *Linguistic society of America resolution on ebonics.* Chicago, IL: Author.

Lockwood, A. T. (1996). Caring, community and personalization: Strategies to combat the Hispanic dropout problem. In U.S. Department of Education (Ed.),

Advances in Hispanic Education (Vol. I) (pp. 96–118). Washington, DC: U.S. Department of Education.

Long, M., & Crookes, G. (1992). Three approaches to task-based syllabus design. *TESOL Quarterly, 26,* 27–56.

Long, M., & Robinson, P. (1998). Focus on form: Theory, research and practice. *Focus on Form in the Classroom, 1*(1), 15–41.

Lucas, T. (1997). *Into, through, and beyond secondary school: Critical transitions for immigrant youths.* New York: Teachers College Press.

MacNab, G. (1997). Cognition and bilingualism: A reanalysis of studies. *Linguistics, 17,* 231–255.

Mahshie, S. (1995). *Educating deaf children bilingually.* Washington, DC: Gallaudet University Pre-College Programs.

Mas, C. (1994). Bilingual education for the deaf in Paris. In I. Ahlgren & K. Hyltenstam (Eds.), *Bilingualism in deaf education, Stockholm, Sweden* (pp. 43–57). Hamburg: Signum.

McCarty, T. L. (2001). Bilingual/bicultural schooling and indigenous students. *International Journal of the Sociology of Language, 155/156,* 161–174.

McCarty, T. L. (2002). *A place to be Navaho—Rough Rock and the struggle for self-determination in indigenous schooling.* Wahwah, NJ: Erlbaum.

McCarty, T. L., & Watahomigie, L. J. (1999). Indigenous education and grassroots language planning in the USA. *Practicing Anthropology, 21,* 5–11.

McLaughlin, B. (1985). Second language acquisition in childhood. In *School age children* (Vol. 2). Hillsdale, NJ: Erlbaum.

McLaughlin, B. (1990). Restructuring. *Applied Linguistics, 11*(2), 113–128

McLeod, B. (1996). *School reform and student diversity: Exemplary schools for language minority students.* Washington, DC: Institute for the Study of Language and Education, George Washington University.

McNeil, L. M. (1988). *Contradictions of control: School structure and school knowledge.* New York: Rutledge.

McNeil, L. M. (2000). *Contradictions of reform: The educational costs of standardization.* New York: Rutledge.

McNeil, L. M., & Valenzuela, A. (2001). The harmful impact of the TAAS system of testing in Texas: Beneath the accountability rhetoric. In M. Kornhaber & G. Orfield (Eds.), *Raising standards or raising barriers? Inequity and high-stakes testing in public education* (pp. 167–182). New York: Century Foundations.

Melmed, P. J. (1971). *Black English phonology: The question of reading interference.* Philadelphia: Language-Behavior Research Laboratory.

Merino, B. J. (1992). Acquisition of syntactic and phonological features in Spanish. In H. Langdon & L. R. Lilly Cheng (Eds.), *Hispanic Children and Adults with Communication Disorders: Assessment and Intervention* (pp. 57–98). Gaithersburg, MD: Aspen.

Merino, B. J., & Hammond, L. (2001). *How do teachers facilitate writing for bilingual learners in "sheltered constructivist" science?* Retrieved from www.sweeneyhall.sjsu.edu/ejlts. (June, 2001)

Meyer, M. M., & Fienberg, S. E. (1992). *Assessing evaluation studies: The case of bilingual educational strategies.* Washington, DC: National Academy Press.

Montano-Harmon, M. (1991). Discourse features of written Mexican Spanish: Current research in contrastive rhetoric and its implications. *Hispania, 74*, 417–425.

National Association for the Education of Young Children. (1997). *Leadership in early age education.* Washington, DC: Author

National Center for Children in Poverty. (1990). *Five million children: A statistical profile of our poorest young citizens.* New York: Columbia University.

National Commission on Excellence in Education. (1983). *A nation at risk.* Washington, DC: United States Government Printing Office.

National Research Council. (1997). *The new Americans: Economic, demographic, and fiscal effects of immigration.* Washington, DC: National Academy Press.

Navarro, R. A. (1990). The problems of language, education, and society: Who decides. In E. E. Garcia & R. V. Padilla (Eds), *Advances in Bilingual Education Research* (pp. 289–313). Tucson: University of Arizona Press.

NCTE/IRA (1996). *Standards for the English Language Arts.* Urbana, IL and Newark, DE: Authors.

Nieto, S. (1999). *The light in their eyes.* New York: Teachers College Press.

Nine Curt, C. M. (1984). *Nonverbal communication.* Cambridge, MA: Evaluation, Dissemination and Assessment Center.

Noguera, P. (1999). Developing systems to drive student success. In C. P. D. Consortia (Ed.), *Systems for student success* (pp. 3–91). Berkeley, CA: California Professional Development Consortia.

Oakes, J. (1990). *Multiplying inequalities: The effects of race, social class, and tracking on opportunities to learn mathematics and science.* Santa Monica, CA: Rand Corporation.

Olsen, L. (1997). *Made in America: Immigrant students in our public schools.* New York: New York Press.

Olson, M. W., & Raffeld, P. (1987). The effects of written comments on the quality of student compositions and the learning of content. *Reading Psychology, 4*, 273–293.

Olson, V. P. B. (1990). The revising processes of sixth-grade writers with and without peer feedback. *Journal of Educational Research, 84*(1), 22–29.

Otero v. Mesa County School District No. 51, 408F. Supp. 162 (1975).

Ovando, C., & Collier, V. (1998). *Bilingual and ESL classrooms* (2nd ed.). New York: McGraw Hill.

Ovando, C., Collier, V., & Combs, M. C. (2002). *Bilingual and ESL classrooms* (3rd ed.). Boston: McGraw-Hill.

Padden, C. (1996). From the cultural to the bicultural: The modern Deaf community. In I. Parasnis (Ed.), *Cultural and language diversity and the Deaf experience* (pp. 79–98). New York: Cambridge University Press.

Padilla, A. M., & Liebman, E. (1975). Language acquisition in the bilingual child. *Bilingual Review, 2*, 34–55.

Palmer, D., & Garcia, E. E. (2000). Proposition 227: Bilingual educators speak. *Bilingual Research Journal, 24*, 169–178.

Peal, E., & Lambert, W. E. (1962). The relation of bilingualism to intelligence. *Psychological Monographs: General and Applied, 76*(546), 1–23.

Perry, J., & Delpit, L. (1998). Understanding Ebonics and schools. In C. B. Paulston & G. R. Tucker (Eds.), *Sociolinguistics: Essential readings* (pp. 41–56). Maldon, MA: Blackwell.

Phillips, D., & Cabrera, N. (1996). *Beyond the blueprint, directions for research on Head Start's families.* Washington, DC: National Academy Press.

Phillips, S. (1972). Participant structures and communicative competence: Warm Springs children in community and classroom. In C. Cazden, D. Hymes, & V. John (Eds.), *Functions of language in the classroom* (pp. 370–394). New York: Teachers College Press.

Poplack, S. (1981). Sometimes I'll start a sentence in Spanish y termino en espanol: Toward a typology of code switching. *Linguistics, 18,* 581–618.

Portes, A. (1996). *The new second generation.* New York: Russell Sage Foundation.

Portes, A., & Rumbaut, R. (1996). *Immigrant America: A portrait* (2nd ed.). Berkeley: University of California Press.

Ramirez, A. (1985). *Bilingualism through schooling.* Albany, NY: State University of New York Press

Ramirez, J. D., & Merino, B. J. (1990). Classroom talk in English immersion and bilingual education: First year results of a national study. In R. Jacobson & C. Faltis (Eds.), *Language distribution issues in bilingual schooling* (pp. 61–103). Clevedon, UK: Multilingual Matters.

Ramirez, J. D., Yuen, S. D., Ramey, D. R., & Pasta, D. J. (1991). *Final report: Longitudinal study of structured English immersion strategy, early-exit and late-exit transitional bilingual education programs for language-minority children.* San Mateo, CA: Aguirre International.

Ramsey, P. G. (1998). *Teaching and learning in a diverse world: Multicultural education for young children* (2nd ed.). New York: Teachers College Press.

Reppen, W., & Grabe, W. (1993). Spanish transfer effects in the English writing of elementary school students. *Lenguas Modernas, 20,* 113–128.

Reyes, I. (2001). *The development of grammatical and communicative competence in bilingual Spanish speaking children.* Unpublished doctoral dissertation, University of California, Berkeley.

Reyes, R. (1998). *A native perspective on the school reform movement: A hot topics paper.* Portland, OR: Northwest Regional Educational Laboratory, Comprehensive Center, Region X and Washington, DC: US Department of Education, Office of Educational Research and Improvement, Educational Resources Information Center.

Riessman, F. (1962). *The culturally deprived child.* New York: Harper.

Rivera, K. (1999). Popular research and social transformation: A community-based approach to critical pedagogy. *TESOL Quarterly, 33*(3), 485–500.

Rodriguez, R. (1985). *Hunger of memory: An autobiography.* Boston: Godine.

Rogoff, B. (1990). *Apprenticeship in thinking: Cognitive development in social context.* Oxford, UK: Oxford University Press.

Romo, H., & Falbo, T. (1996). *Latino high school graduation: Defying the odds.* Austin: University of Texas Press.

Roos, P. (1984, July). Legal guidelines for bilingual administrators. Austin, TX: Society of Research in Child Development.

Rose, M. (1995). Calexico: Portrait of an educational community. *Teachers & Writers, 26*(5), 1–15.

Rossi, R. J. (1995). *Education reform and students at risk. Volume III: Synthesis and evaluation of previous efforts to improve educational practice and development of strategies for achieving positive outcomes.* Washington, DC: American Institutes for Research.

Ruiz-de-Velasco, J., & Fix, M. (2000). *Immigration in the last decade.* Washington, DC: Urban Institute.

Rumbaut, R. (1994). The crucible within: Ethnic identity, self-esteem, and segmented assimilation among children of immigrants. *International Migration Review, 28,* 748–794.

Rumbaut, R. (1997). Ties that bind: Immigration and immigrant families in the United States. In A. Booth, C. Crouter, & N. Landale (Eds.), *Immigration and the family: Research and policy on U.S. immigrants* (pp. 3–45). Hillsdale, NJ: Erlbaum.

Rumberger, R., & Larson, K. A. (1998). Toward explaining differences in educational achievement among Mexican-American language minority students. *Sociology of Education, 71,* 69–93.

Rumberger, R. W., & Palardy, G. (2001). *Does segregation matter? The impact of student composition on academic achievement in high school.* Paper presented at the annual meeting of the American Educational Research Association, Seattle.

Sahakian, P. (1997). *An investigation of how writing in English develops for four Hmong high school boys.* Unpublished doctoral dissertation, California State University and University of California, Davis.

San Francisco Bilingual Education Task Force. (2002). *The past, present and future of bilingual education in the San Francisco unified school district.* San Francisco, CA: San Francisco Unified School District.

Scarcella, R. (2000). Some key factors affecting the English learners' development of advanced literacy. In M. Schleppegrell & C. Colombi (Eds.), *Developing advanced literacy in first and second languages* (pp. 218–246). Norwood, NJ: Erlbaum.

Scarcella, R. (2001). *Key issues in accelerating English language development.* Berkeley: University of California Press.

Scarcella, R. (2003). *Academic English: A conceptual framework.* Santa Barbara: University of California Language Minority Research Institute.

Schumann, J. H. (1976). Affective factors and the problem of age in second language acquisition. *Language Learning, 25,* 209–239.

Scribner, S., & Cole, M. (1981). Unpackaging literacy. In M. Farr-Whitman (Ed.), *Variation in writing: Functional and linguistic-cultural differences; Writing: The nature, development, and teaching of written communications* (Vol. 1; pp. 71–88). Hillsdale, NJ: Erlbaum.

Seliger, H. W. (1977). Does practice make perfect? A study of interactional patterns and L2 competence. *Language Learning, 27,* 263–278.

Sells Dick, G., & McCarty, T. L. (1998). Reclaiming Navajo: Language renewal in an American Indian school (pp. 118–137). In N. H. Hornberger (Ed.), *Indigenous literacies in the Americas.* Berlin/New York: Mouten de Gruyter.

Shamash, Y. (1990). Learning in translation: Beyond language experience in ESL. *Voices, 2*(2), 71–75.

Shavelson, R., & Towne, L. (2002). *Scientific research in education.* Washington, DC: National Academy Press.

Skinner, B. (1957). *Verbal behavior.* Englewood Cliffs, NJ: Prentice-Hall.

Skrabanek, R. L. (1970). Language maintenance among Mexican Americans. *International Journal of Comparative Sociology, 11,* 272–282.

Skutnabb-Kangas, T. (1997). *Language in the process of cultural assimilation and structural incorporation of linguistic minorities.* Rosslyn, VA: National Clearinghouse for Bilingual Education.

Skutnabb-Kangas, T. (2000). *Linguistic genocide in education—or worldwide diversity and human rights?* Mahwah, NJ: Erlbaum.

Skutnabb-Kangas, T. (2002). American ambiguities and paranoias. *International Journal of the Sociology of Language, 155/156,* 179–186.

Smith, T. W. (1971). *Understanding reading.* New York: Holt, Rinehart & Winston.

Snow, D. (1997). Children's acquisition of speech timing in English: A comparative study of voice onset time and final syllable vowel lengthening. *Journal of Child Language, 24*(1), 35–36.

Snow, C. E., Burns, S., & Griffin, P. (1998). *Preventing reading difficulties in young children.* Washington, DC: National Academy Press.

Sorenson, A. P. (1967). Multilingualism in the Northwest Amazon. *American Anthropologist, 69,* 67–68.

Soto, L. D. (1997). *Language, culture and power: Bilingual families and the struggle for quality education.* Albany: State University of New York Press.

Stern, H. H. (1992). *Issues and options in language teaching.* Oxford, UK: Oxford University Press

Stewart, D. (1993). Bi-BI to MCE? *American Annals of the Deaf, 138,* 331–337.

Stritikus, T. (2002). *Immigrant children and the politics of English-only: Views from the classroom.* New York: LFB Scholarly Publishing.

Stritikus, T., & Garcia, E. (2000). Education of Limited English proficient students in California: An assessment of Proposition 227 on selected teachers and classrooms. *Bilingual Research Journal, 24*(1&2), 75–86.

Suarez-Orozco, M. M. (1997). *Some thoughts on the "new" immigration.* Keynote speech. Spencer Foundation Symposium on Immigration and Education. Los Angeles, CA.

Swain, M. (1975). *Writing skills of grade three French immersion pupils.* Toronto: The Ontario Institute for Studies in Education.

Swain, M., & Lapkin, R. (1991). The influence of bilingualism on cognitive functioning. *Canadian Modern Language Review, 47,* 635–641.

Tharp, R. G., & Gallimore, R. (1988). *Rousing minds to life: Teaching, learning and schooling in social context.* Cambridge, UK: Cambridge University Press.

Thomas, W. P., & Collier, V. P. (1995). *A longitudinal analysis of programs serving language minority students.* Washington, DC: National Clearinghouse on Bilingual Education.

Thorton, S. (1981). *The issue of dialect in academic achievement.* Unpublished doctoral dissertation, University of California, Berkeley.

Trueba, H. T. (1998). *Latinos unidos.* Lanham, MD: Rowman & Littlefield.

Tyack, D. B., & Cuban, L. (1995). *Tinkering toward utopia: A century of public school reform.* Cambridge, MA: Harvard University Press.

University of California. (1997). *Latino student eligibility and participation in the University of California. YA BASTA!* (Latino Eligibility Task Force Report No. 5). Berkeley: University of California and the Chicano/Latino Policy Project.

U.S. Census Bureau (2000). *A profile of the nation's foreign-born population* (CENBR/00–2). Washington, DC: Author.

U.S. Census Bureau (2001). *Number and percent population speaking a language other than English.* Washington, DC: Author.

U.S. Department of Education. (1997). *National Assessment of Educational Progress, NAEP, in 1996 trends in academic progress.* Washington, DC: U.S. Government Printing Office.

U.S. Department of Education. (1998). *No more excuses: The final report of the U.S. Hispanic dropout project.* Washington, DC: U.S. Department of Education.

Valdes, G. (1996). *Con respeto: Bridging the difference between culturally diverse families and schools.* New York: Teachers College Press.

Valdes, G. (1998). The world outside and inside schools: Language and immigrant children. *Educational Research, 27*(6), 4–18.

Valencia, R. (1991). *Chicano school failure and success: Research and policy agendas for the 1990s.* New York: Falmer.

Valenzuela, A. (1997). Mexican American youth and the politics of caring. In E. Long (Ed.), *From sociology to cultural studies* (Vol. 2) (pp. 168–184). London: Blackwell.

Valenzuela, A. (1999). *Subtractive schooling: U.S. Mexican youth and the politics of caring.* Albany: State University of New York Press.

Van Patten, B., & Sanz, C. (1996). Explanation versus structured input in processing instruction. *Studies in Second Language Acquisition, 18*(4), 495–510.

Veltman, C. (1988). *The future of the Spanish language in the United States.* New York: Hispanic Policy Project.

Waggoner, D. (1984). The need for bilingual education: Estimates from the 1980 census. *NABE Journal, 8,* 1–14.

Waggoner, D. (1995). *Numbers and needs: Ethnic and linguistic minorities in the United States.* Washington, DC: Numbers and Needs, Inc.

Waldinger, R., & Bozorgmehr, M. (1996). *Ethnic Los Angeles.* New York: Russell Sage Foundation.

Walker, C. L. (1987). Hispanic achievements: Old views and new perspectives. In H. Trueba (Ed.), *Success or failure? Learning and the language minority student* (pp. 15–32). Cambridge, MA: Newbury House.

Wertsch, J. V. (1985). *Vygotsky and the social formation of the mind.* Cambridge, MA: Harvard University Press.

West, C. (1993). Learning to talk of race. In R. Gooding-Williams (Ed.), *Reading Rodney King, reading urban uprising.* New York: Rutledge.

White, J. (1998). Getting the learners' attention. In C. Doughty & J. Williams (Eds.), *Focus on form in classroom second language acquisition* (pp. 85–113). Cambridge, UK: Cambridge University Press.

Wiese, A., & García, E. (2001). The Bilingual Education Act: Language minority students and equal educational opportunity. *Bilingual Research Journal, 22*(1), 1–6.

Wilbur, R. B. (1987). Sign language acquisition. In R. B. Wilbur (Ed.), *American Sign Language: Linguistics and applied dimensions.* San Diego: Little, Brown.

Wilson, W. J. (1978). *The declining significance of race.* Chicago: University of Chicago Press.

Wolfram, W. (1994). Ethical considerations in language awareness programs. *Issues in Applied Linguistics, 4*(2), 225–255.

Wong Fillmore, L. (1976). *The second time around: Cognitive and social strategies in second language acquisition.* Unpublished doctoral dissertation, Stanford University, Palo Alto, CA.

Wong Fillmore, L. (1991). Second language learning in children: A model of language learning in a social context. In E. Bialystock (Ed.), *Language processing in bilingual children* (pp. 49–69). Cambridge, UK: Cambridge University Press.

Wong Fillmore, L., & Snow, C. E. (1999). *What educators—especially teachers—need to know about language: The bare minimum.* Santa Barbara: Language Minority Research Institute.

Wong Fillmore, L., & Valadez, C. (1986). Teaching bilingual learners. In M. C. Wittrock (Ed.), *Handbook of research on teaching* (3rd ed.) (pp. 648–685). New York: Macmillan.

Zentella, A. C. (1981). Ta bien you could answer me en cualquier idioma: Puerto Rican code switching in bilingual classrooms. In R. Duran (Ed.), *Latino language and communicative behavior* (pp. 109–112). Norwood, NJ: Ablex.

Zentella, A. C. (1997). *Growing up bilingual: Puerto Rican children in New York.* Malden, MA: Blackwell.

Index

Academic English development, 53–61
cognitive dimensions of, 57
conceptual and empirical studies of, 56
factors affecting, 60–61
high school qualifying examinations and, 55–56
linguistic dimensions of, 56–57
of trilingual students, 57–58
writing development in, 58–60
Academic Performance Index (API), 88
Accountability, 98–99
Acculturation, 75
Achievement. *See* Student achievement
Act psychology, 101–102
African Americans. *See* Blacks
Ahlgren, I., 71
ALAS. *See* Authentic Literacy Assessment System (ALAS)
Alaskan Natives, 64
Alvarez, H., 60
American Sign Language (ASL), 64, 71–75
Amigos Dual Immersion Program (Cambridge, Massachusetts), 49–50
Anderson, J., 53
Arizona
bilingual Spanish/English learners in, 25
English-only instruction and, xiii, 86–88, 161
English-only legislation, 161
immigrant population in, 12–13
program policy for language-minority students, 85–86
Aspira of New York, Inc. v. Board of Education, 79
Assessment. *See also* Authentic Literacy Assessment System (ALAS)
high school qualifying examinations, 55–56

of mathematics skills, 122
of reading skills, 167
standardized measures of intelligence, 29–30
Stanford Achievement Test 9 (SAT 9) in, 88, 91, 92, 136–139
of writing skills, 111–122, 127–136
Assimilationist agenda, ix
At-risk students, 1–2
August, D., xiii, 34, 40, 42, 44, 54, 59, 62–63, 64, 93, 104, 160, 163, 164
Authentic Literacy Assessment System (ALAS), 106–156
described, 106–107
design and implementation principles of, 111–112
development of, 109–114
frequency of administration, 113
linking to classroom instruction, 119–122
professional planning and development for, 108–109
Sierra Madre Elementary School site, 106–109, 112, 114, 115–116, 117–119, 121–122, 124–127, 136–139, 146–151
site descriptions, 107–108, 109, 110
teacher perceptions of student work, 139–143
Authentic Mathematics Assessment System (AMAS), 122

Baby-boom echo, 16
Baby boomers, 16
Baetens Beardsmore, H., 24
Bakhtin, Mikhail, 31
Banks, C. A. M., viii, 103
Banks, J. A., ix, viii, 103

Baquedaño-Lopez, P., 60
Becijos, J., 61
Bell, Alexander Graham, 72
Benjamin, R., 70, 71
Bergmann, R., 72, 73
Berman, P., 44–45, 103
Bernhardt, E., 57
Bilingual Education Act (1968), 92–99
Bilingual immersion. See Dual Language
Bilingualism. See also Bilingual students;
    Policy debate on bilingualism
  bilingual development and, 23–24
  code-switching and, 27–29
  cognition and, 29–34
  concept of, 158
  educational practice implications for,
    162–168
  linguistic development and, 24–27
  social/communicative aspects of, 34–35
  sociolinguistic conventions and, 35–38,
    159
Bilingual responsive learning community,
    145. See also Authentic Literacy
    Assessment System (ALAS);
    Responsive learning communities
Bilingual students. See also Bilingualism;
    Immigrants
  characteristics of, 4–7
  deaf and hard-of-hearing students, 64,
    71–75
  debate concerning education of, xiii,
    40–44
  defining, xiii
  dialects and, 64–69, 70
  distribution of U.S., 6
  English acquisition and, 20–21
  indigenous groups, ix, 35–36, 64,
    69–71
  number of U.S., 5
  terms for, xiii, 4, 7, 36, 51–52
Black English, 65–69
Blacks
  Black English/Ebonics and, 65–69
  communication patterns and, 36
  high school completion rates of, 2
Blanc, M., 32
Blum-Kulka, S., 51
Bodman, J., 51
Boggs, S. T., 36

Bowerman, M., 23
Boyson, B., 9
Bozorgmehr, M., 15
Brown, A. L., 105
Brown, R. A., 23
Brown v. Board of Education, 77
Bureau of Indian Affairs (BIA), 70
Burns, S., 54, 60
Burt, M., 25–26

Cabrera, N., 89
California. See also Authentic Literacy
    Assessment System (ALAS); San
    Francisco Unified School District
    (SFUSD)
  academic outcomes in, 45
  bilingual students in, xiii, 7, 8
  Ebonics recognition in, 67–68
  English-only instruction and, xiii, 42–43,
    48–50, 86–88, 90–92, 161
  immigrant population in, 12–14
  lack of native-language instruction in,
    42
  mandated reading assessment in, 167
  native languages spoken by immigrants,
    42
  program policy for language-minority
    students, 85–86, 88–92
  Proposition 187, 161–162
  Proposition 227, 88–90, 161, 166–167
  training for infant and toddler
    caregivers, 88
  waivers for primary-language use, 87
California English Language Development
    Test (CELDT), 7
California State Department of Education,
    vii, 8, 90
California Tomorrow, 44–45, 66
Camarota, A., 10–14, 19
Canale, M., 34, 55
Caribbean immigrants, 13
Carlisle, R., 58
Carnegie Corporation of New York, 97
Carpenter, M., 51
Carpenter, P., 57
Carpenter, S., 105–106
Carrasco, R., 37
Casanova, U., 93–95, 96
Castañeda v. Pickard, 79–81

Cazabon, M., 49
Cazden, C., 34, 38
Center for Immigration Studies, 10
Central American immigrants, 13
Ceppi, B., 9
Chambers, J., 43
Chamot, A. U., 52
Chan, L., 20–21
Chavez, Linda, xiii, 16, 40–41, 160
Chicanos. *See* Hispanics
Chinese. *See also* Authentic Literacy
    Assessment System (ALAS)
  federal rulings concerning education of,
    77–78, 80
Chiu, M., 60
Chomsky, N., 23
Christian, D., 9, 43, 47, 48, 49, 50
Citizenship rate, 13
Civil Rights Act (1964), 79, 93–94
  Title VI, 93
  Title VII, 78
Clare-Matsumura, L., 58, 60
Classroom discourse, 37–38
Code-switching, 27–29
Cognition, 29–34
  in academic English development, 57
  of deaf and hard-of-hearing children, 75
  development of, 33–34, 75
  individual learner and, 30–31
  meta-linguistic awareness in, 30
  model for human, 101–102
  nature of human, 32
  sociocultural theory and, 31–34
  standardized measures of intelligence,
    29–30
Cole, M., 31, 32, 34, 102
Cole, R. W., 122
Cole, S. R., 31, 32, 34, 102
Coleman, J., 93
College Board, 164
Collier, V. P., 1, 9, 39–40, 45, 52, 56–57,
    62–63, 64
Collins, A., 105
Colombi, C., 57
Colorado
  bilingual Spanish/English learners in, 25
  immigrant population in, 12–13
  program policy for language-minority
    students, 85–86

rejection of state referendum on English-
    only instruction, 87, 161
Combs, M. C., 1, 39–40, 52
Communication patterns, 35–38
Communicative competence (Hymes), 159
Compatibility theory, 100–101
Congress of Hispanic Educators (CHE), 81
Constructivist approach, 102–103, 106
Contact zones, in schools, 159
Continuum classes, 46
Conventions, in assessing writing
    development, 126–127, 128, 131
Coordination, in bilingual education
    programs, 44–45
Corder, S. P., 25
Council of Great City Schools (CGCS), 7
Crandall, J., 55
Crawford, J., 41, 70, 71, 73, 84, 95, 96,
    160
Crookes, G., 52
Cuban, L., 92–93
Cuban immigrants, 94–96
Culturally and linguistically diverse (CLD),
    xiii, 4, 159–160
Cultural validation, in bilingual education
    programs, 45
Culture. *See* Sociocultural knowledge
Culture of multiculturalism, 15–16
Cummins, J., 30, 41, 54, 56, 94, 102
Current Population Survey (CPS), 10–11
Curry, A. E., vii
Curry, J. E., 88, 89

Dale, T., 55
D'Andrea, D., 24
Darcy, N. T., 29–30
Davies, S. N., 73
Deaf students, 64, 71–75
DeHouwer, A., 24
DeKeyser, R., 53
Delgado-Gaitan, C., 59
Delpit, L., 65, 68
Demographic transformation, in the United
    States, 1
Design studies. *See also* Authentic Literacy
    Assessment System (ALAS)
  nature of, 104–106
Destefano, J., 66–67
Developmental Bilingual, 9

Development Associates, 39–40
Dewey, John, 31
Dialects, 64–69
  attitudes toward, 65
  Black English/Ebonics, 65–69
  Hispanic, 65, 66
  Native American, 70
  nature of language and, 64–65
Diaz, R. M., 23, 29–30, 33
Diaz, S. L., 102
Diversity. *See also* Language diversity;
  Sociocultural knowledge
  religious, vii
  in the United States, xv, 1, 16
Dolson, D., 36
Drasgow, E., 73
Dropout rates, 43, 77
Dual Language, 9, 47–50
  at Amigos Dual Immersion Program
    (Cambridge, Massachusetts), 49–50
  50:50 model, 47, 48–50
  goals of, 47–48
  at Key School (Arlington County,
    Virginia), 48–50
  90:10 model, 47, 49, 50
  at Oyster Bilingual School (Washington,
    D.C.), 51, 101
Duff, P., 50–51, 101
Dulay, H., 25–26
Duquette, Georges, 32–33
Dwyer, C., 66, 67
Dyson, A. H., 157

Early, M., 50–51, 101
Early childhood education, 88–89
East Asian immigrants, 13
Ebonics, 65–69
Ebsworth, T., 52
Echevarria, J., 9
Eck, Diana L., vii
Edelsky, C., 58
Educational attainment, 2, 17–18, 43, 77
Educational Excellence for Hispanic
  Americans, 89
Educational reform, 100–122. *See also*
  Student achievement
  compatibility theory in, 100–101
  constructivism and, 102–103, 106
  dual-immersion approach, 9, 47–50, 101
  integrated framework for, 100–103

responsive learning communities in, 103–
    156. *See also* Authentic Literacy
    Assessment System (ALAS)
Edwards, J., 66
Eisenstein, E. M., 51
Elementary and Secondary Education Act
    (1965)
  Title I, 97
  Title VII, 93–94, 96, 97, 98–99
Ellis, R., 53
El Nasser, H., vii
English-language development (ELD), 51–
    52
English-language development/English as a
    second language (ELD/ESL), 40
English-language learners (ELLs), xiii, 4
English-only instruction, xiii, 42–43, 48–
    50, 90–92, 161
Entitlement, 41
Equal Educational Opportunity Act (1974),
    79, 81–84, 93
Erickson, F., 94
Ervin-Tripp, S. M., 23, 26

Falbo, T., 164
Family. *See* Parents
Fantini, A. E., 23, 27, 28
Fasold, R., 64
Ferris, D. R., 58
Fienberg, S. E., 54
First-language acquisition, second-language
    acquisition versus, 26
Firth, A., 57
Fishman, J., 70, 71
Fitzgerald, J., 60, 95
Fix, M., 17, 24
Flexibility, of bilingual education
    programs, 44
Florida
  immigrant population in, 12–14
  native-language instruction in, 94–96
Fluent English proficient (FEP), 7
Formulaic expressions, 27
Fourteenth Amendment, 78
Fradd, S., 16
Freeman, D. C., 50, 101
Freire, P., 57

Galambos, S. J., 30
Gallimore, R., 59, 100, 122

García, Eugene E., ix–x, xiii, xiv, 4, 5, 10, 12, 14, 16, 18, 23, 25, 28, 31, 33, 37, 39–42, 54, 57, 59–61, 66, 82, 85, 88, 89, 93–96, 99, 100, 103, 122, 144, 157, 159, 160, 163, 165–167
Gardner, R. C., 34
Garnier, H., 58, 60
Gass, S., 51
Geertz, F., 158–159
Genesee, F., 57–58
Genishi, C., 28, 37
Glazer, Nathan, 16
Goals 2000, 88
Goldenberg, C., 9, 59
Goldman, S., 102
Gomez, R. J., 57, 58
Goncz, B., 30
Gonzalez, G., 25, 88, 93–96, 160, 165
Goodman, Y., 102
Grabe, W., 58
Greenberg, J., 20–21
Griffin, P., 54, 60
Grosjean, F., 24, 28, 29, 74
Guadalupe v. Tempe School District No. 3 (1978), 78
Gutierrez, K., 60

Hakuta, K., xiii, 23, 24, 26–27, 30, 33, 34, 40, 41, 42, 44, 54, 59, 62–64, 93, 95, 104, 160, 163, 164
Hall, G., 49
Halliday, M., 34
Hamers, J. F., 32
Hammond, L., 58, 59
Handbook of Research on Multicultural Education (Banks & Banks), viii
Haptics (touching), 36
Hard-of-hearing students, 64, 71–75
Harrison, J., 66
Hawaiian Natives, 36, 64, 100
Heath, S. B., 34, 36, 57, 102
High school completion rates, 2
High school qualifying examinations, 55–56
Hinton, L., 71
Hispanics. *See also* Authentic Literacy Assessment System (ALAS); *names of specific Hispanic groups*
  bilingual development of, 24–27
  code-switching by, 27–29

dropout rates of, 43, 77
English acquisition by, 20–21
family intervention programs for, 157
federal rulings concerning education of, 78–81
high school completion rates of, 2, 17–18
native-language instruction in Florida, 94–96
Hodgkinson, H., x
Hoffmeister, R., 71, 72
Hornberger, N. H., 50, 57, 59, 101, 157
Huerta, A., 25
Hunger of Memory (Rodriguez), 41
Hutton, Eddie Roth, 10
Hyltenstam, K., 71
Hymes, D., 23, 34, 159

Illinois
  academic outcomes in, 45
  immigrant population in, 12–14
  program policy for language-minority students, 85–86
Immersion
  Dual Language approach to, 47–50, 51, 101
  Sheltered English Immersion, 9, 40, 52
  total immersion approach to, xiii, 42
Immigrants. *See also* Bilingual students
  as agents of change, 15
  birth rate among, 12
  characteristics of, 10–11, 13–16, 17
  citizenship rate of, 13
  drop-out rates of, 43, 77
  economic landscape and, 15
  growth in number of, ix, vii, 12–13
  historical comparisons of, 11–12
  immigration reform efforts and, 161–162
  importance of understanding, 7–19
  native languages spoken by, 42
  poverty and, 13, 14, 19, 30
  rate of English acquisition, 41–42
  region and country of origin, 13
  state data on, 6, 12–13
  transnational phenomenon of, ix, 14–15
  undocumented, vii
  in U.S. schools, 6, 16–19
Improving America's Schools Act (1994), 100, 165–166
Indiana, program policy for language-minority students, 85–86

Indigenous groups, ix, 35–36, 64, 69–71, 100

Innate creative destruction (Krashan), 25–26

Innovation, of instruction, 46

Instructional time, 46

Instruction/program alternatives, 39–63. *See also* Authentic Literacy Assessment System (ALAS); Responsive learning communities

    academic English development in bilingual students, 53–61

    characteristics of effective approaches, 39–40, 44–47, 159–160

    costs of, 42–44

    debate concerning, 40–44

    Developmental Bilingual, 9

    Dual Language, 9, 47–50, 51, 101

    English-language development in bilingual programs, 51–53

    myths concerning, 40–44

    Newcomer Program, 9

    Sheltered Immersion in English (SEI), 9, 40, 45, 52

    sociocultural knowledge and, 50–51

    Specially Designed Academic Instruction in English (SDAIE), 61–62

    teacher perceptions of, 139–143

    total immersion approach, xiii, 42

    Transitional Bilingual, 9

    writing development, 58–60

Intelligence assessments, 29–30

Interference errors, 26

International law, on bilingualism, 84–85

International Reading Association (IRA), 89

Irujo, S., 36

James, William, 31

Jankowski, K., 72, 73, 74

Just, M., 57

Kaplan, R. B., 58

Kasper, G., 51

Kendler, A. C., 1

Kessler, C., 30

Keyes v. School District No. 1, 80–81

Key School (Arlington County, Virginia), 48–50

Kinesics (body movements), 36

Klinger, C., 23, 33

Kodzepeljic, D., 30

Krashen, S. D., 26, 61

Kraus, M., 69

Labov, W., 65

Ladson-Billings, G., 103

Lambert, E., 34

Lambert, W. E., 30, 48, 49

Language choice, 28, 64–65

Language diversity

    hard-of-hearing groups and, 64, 71–75

    indigenous groups and, ix, 35–36, 64, 69–71, 100

    in the U.S., ix–x, vii, 4–16

Language minority (LM), 4

Language through content (Chamot & O'Mally), 52

Laosa, L., 24

Lapkin, R., 30

Lara-Alecio, R., 57, 58

Larson, J., 60

Larson, K. A., 59, 164

LAS-O Oral English Proficiency measure, 48

Latin Americans. *See* Hispanics

Latinos. *See* Hispanics

Lau v. Nichols, 77–78, 80

Learner errors

    formulaic expressions and, 27

    importance of, 25

    interference errors, 26

    prefabricated patterns and, 26–27

Lehrer, R., 105–106

Leopold, W. F., 30

Levin, H. M., 94

Liebman, E., 24

Lightbown, P., 53

Limited English proficient (LEP), xiii, 4, 36

Lindholm, K., 43, 48–50

Linguistically and culturally diverse (LCD), 4

Linguistic codes, 34

Linguistic Society of America, 67–68

Local educational agencies (LEA), 94

Lockwood, A. T., 43

Long, M., 52, 53

Lucas, T., 10, 65, 66, 67

Macedo, D., 57

Macias, R., 20–21

MacNab, G., 30
Maez, L., 25
Mahshie, S., 71, 73, 74
Martin, P., vii
Martinez, G. M., vii
Mas, C., 72
Massachusetts
  academic outcomes in, 45
  English-only instruction and, xiii, 86–88,
    161
  program policy for language-minority
    students, 85–86
Mathematics, assessment tools for, 122
Matsch, Richard, 81
McCarty, T. L., 64, 69–71
McLaughlin, B., 27, 53
McLeod, B., 45–47
McNeil, L. M., 91, 92
Mehan, H., 102
Melmed, P. J., 67
Merino, B. J., 37, 58, 59
Meta-linguistic awareness, 30
Mexican American Legal Defense Fund, 97
Mexican immigrants, 10, 13, 17–18, 157
Meyer, M. M., 54
Midgley, E., vii
Milan Congress (1880), 72
Mixed-language utterances, 25
Moll, C., 102
Monitor hypothesis (Krashen), 26
Montano-Harmon, M., 58
Morphological development, 24
Multicultural education
  defined, viii
  dimensions of, viii–ix
  goal of, viii
  government support for, 73

National Academy of Sciences, 104, 164
National Adult Literacy Survey (1992), 20–
  21
National Assessment of Educational
  Progress (NAEP), 54
National Association for Bilingual
  Education, 97
National Association for the Education of
  Young Children (NAEYC), 89
National Center for Children in Poverty, 1
National Center for Educational Statistics,
  6

National Commission on Excellence in
  Education, 88, 100
National Council of Teachers of English
  (NCTE), 89
National Curve Equivalent (NCE), 143
National Research Council (NRC), 54, 77,
  164
  Roundtable on Head Start Research, 88–
    89
  study on responsive learning
    communities, 104–105
National Task Force on Minority High
  Achievement (College Board), 164
Nation at Risk, A, 88, 100
Native Americans, 35–36, 64, 69–71, 100
Natural order hypothesis (Krashen), 25–26
Navajo, 69–71
Navarro, R. A., 94
Neu, J., 51
Nevada, immigrant population in, 12–13
Newcomer Program, 9
New Jersey, immigrant population in, 12–
  14
New Mexico
  bilingual Spanish/English learners in, 25
  program policy for language-minority
    students, 161
New York, immigrant population in, 12–
  14
Nine Curt, S. M., 36
No Child Left Behind Act (2002), 88, 98–
  99, 100
Noguera, P., 103
No More Excuses (U.S. Department of
  Education), 162–168
North Carolina, immigrant population in,
  12–13

Oakes, J., 103
Oakland School District (California), 67–
  68
Occulisics (eye contact), 36
Office of Educational Survey of Equality of
  Educational Opportunity, 93
Office of English Language Acquisition,
  Language Enhancement, and Academic
  Achievement for Limited-English-
  Proficient Students (OELALEAALEPS
  or OELA), 98
Olsen, L., 18–19, 164

Olson, M. W., 58
Olson, V. P. B., 58
O'Malley, J. M., 52
Oralism, 72, 76
Organization, in assessing writing
　development, 125–126, 128, 131
*Otero v. Mesa County School District No.
　51*, 78
Out of the Barrio (Chavez), 40–41
Ovando, C., 1, 39–40, 52, 62–63, 64
Oyster Bilingual School (Washington,
　D.C.), 51, 101

Padden, C., 71
Padilla, A. M., 24
Palardy, G., 59
Palmer, D., 88
Parents
　deaf and hard-of-hearing communication
　　with, 74
　family intervention programs, 157
　involvement in education of children,
　　47
　language-minority, 36, 43–44
　respect and, 164–165
Parker, R., 57, 58
Parrish, T., 43
Pasta, D. J., 37, 38
Patthey-Chavez, G. G., 58, 60
Peal, E., 30
Pecos, R., 70, 71
Perry, J., 65, 68
Phillips, D., 89
Phillips, S., 34, 35
Phonological development, 24
Piaget, Jean, 31
Pierce, C. S., 31
Policy debate on bilingualism, 77–99
　Bilingual Education Act (1968), 92–99
　bilingual education and, 160–161
　educational practice implications of,
　　162–168
　EEOA requirements, 79, 81–84, 93
　federal court rulings, 77–81
　immigration reform and, 161–162
　international law, 84–85
　state and local, 85–92
Poplack, S., 28
Porter, Rosalie, xiii

Portes, A., 14, 15, 95
Poverty, 13, 14, 19, 30
Prefabricated patterns, 26–27
Proceduralization, of declarative
　knowledge, 53
Proxemics (personal space), 36
Pueblo, 70–71
Puerto Ricans
　areas of confusion for, 36
　code-switching by, 28–29
　dialects of, 65
Pull-out programs, 78
Putz, A., 105–106

Quinn, M. E., 30

Raffeld, P., 58
Ramey, D. R., 37, 38
Ramirez, A., 34
Ramirez, J. D., 37, 38
Ramsey, P. G., 74
Reading-by-Third-Grade initiative (U.S.
　Department of Education), 166–167
Reading skills, assessment of, 167
Reese, L., 59
Reform. *See* Educational reform
Religious diversity, vii
Reppen, W., 58
Respect, importance of, 164–165
Responsive learning communities,
　103–106
　design study for. *See* Authentic Literacy
　　Assessment System (ALAS)
　National Research Council report on,
　　104–105
　schoolwide practices in, 103–104
　teacher/instructional practices in, 104,
　　107
Reyes, I., 23
Reyes, R., 28
Rhode Island, program policy for
　language-minority students, 85–86
Rhodes, S., 20–21, 55
Riche, M. F., vii
Riessman, F., 94
Rivera, K., 52
Rivlin, A. M., ix
Robinson, P., 53
Rodriguez, Richard, xiii, 41

Rogoff, B., 31
Romero, M. E., 70, 71
Romo, H., 164
Roos, P., 79, 82
Rose, M., 164
Rossel, Christine, xiii
Rossi, R. J., 164
Roundtable on Head Start Research, National Research Council, 88–89
Rubrics, for assessing writing development, 114–119, 124–127
Ruiz-de-Velasco, J., 17, 24
Rumbaut, R., 17, 19, 59, 95
Rumberger, R., 59, 164
Rymes, B., 60

Sahakian, P., 57
Sanchez, C., 52
San Francisco Unified School District (SFUSD), 106–107. *See also* Authentic Literacy Assessment System (ALAS)
    Authentic Mathematics Assessment System (AMAS), 122
    Bilingual Education Language Academy, 109, 112
    Bilingual Education Task Force, 168–169
    Integrated Writing Assessment (IWA), 111–122
Sanz, C., 53
SAT-9 (Stanford Achievement Test 9), 88, 91, 92, 136–139
Scarcella, R., 54, 56, 58
Schauble, L., 105–106
Schools-within-schools approach, 46, 159
Schumann, J. H., 34–35
Scientific Research in Education, 104–105
Scribner, S., 102
Second International Congress on Education of the Deaf (Milan, 1880), 72
Second-language acquisition
    first-language acquisition versus, 26
    motivation and, 34–35
    relationship between cultures and, 34
Second-language acquisition/English as a second language (SLA/ESL), 51–53
Seliger, H. W., 35
Sells Dick, G., 69, 70

SFUSD. *See* San Francisco Unified School District (SFUSD)
Shamash, Y., 52
Shared vision, in bilingual education programs, 45
Shavelson, R., 104–105
Sheltered English immersion (SEI), 9, 40, 52
Skilton-Sylvester, E., 101, 157
Skinner, B., 23
Skrabanek, R. L., 24
Skutnabb-Kangas, T., 24, 84, 85
Smith, T. W., 102
Snow, C. E., 54, 55–56, 60
Snow, D., 16
Social engineering, 71
Socialization, of children, 22
Social justice, indigenous languages and, 71
Social mobility, 15
Sociocultural knowledge
    acquisition of, 75
    importance of, 46, 50–51
    language as cultural system and, 158–159
    monolithic culture and, 102–103
    theory of, 31–34
Sociolinguistic conventions, 35–38, 159
SOPR measure, 50
Sorenson, A. P., 24
Soto, L. D., 164
South American immigrants, 13
Spada, N., 53
Spanos, G., 55
Special alternative instructional programs (SAIP), 96–97
Specially Designed Academic Instruction in English (SDAIE), 61–62
Standard English, dialects versus, 64–69, 70
Stanford Achievement Test 9 (SAT 9), 88, 91, 92, 136–139
Stanford Working Group, 97
Stern, H. H., 51
Stewart, D., 72–73
Stone, L., 60
Stritikus, T., 89–90, 167
Student achievement, 123–156. *See also* Assessment
    at Chang Ching Elementary School (ALAS) site, 127–139, 141–143

Student achievement (*continued*)
  at Sierra Madre Elementary School
    (ALAS) site, 124–127, 136–141
  teacher perceptions of, 139–143
Style/voice, in assessing writing
  development, 126, 128, 131
Suarez-Orozco, M. M., 14, 15, 161
Swain, M., 30, 55, 58
Switched-language utterances, 25
Syntactic development, 24

Tate, W. F., 103
Teachability hypothesis (Lightbown &
  Spada), 53
Teachers. *See also* Authentic Literacy
  Assessment System (ALAS)
  expanding roles and responsibilities of,
    46
  federal rulings on qualifications of, 80–
    81
  perceptions of student work, 139–143
  professional development for responsive
    learning communities, 108
  in responsive learning communities, 104,
    107
  role in academic English development,
    60–61
  teachability hypothesis (Lightbown &
    Spada), 53
Texas
  academic outcomes in, 45
  bilingual Spanish/English learners in, 25
  immigrant population in, 12–14
  program policy for language-minority
    students, 85–86, 89, 91–92, 161
Texas Assessment of Academic Skills
  (TAAS), 91–92
Tharp, R. G., 100, 122
Thomas, W. P., 45, 56–57
Thorton, S., 65
Time-on-task theory of language learning,
  42
Topic, in assessing writing development,
  125, 128, 131
Total Communication, 72–73
Total immersion approach, xiii, 42
Towne, L., 104–105
Transitional Bilingual, 9
Trilingual students, 57–58
Trueba, H. T., 102, 164

Two-way bilingual approach. *See* Dual
  Language
Two-way immersion approach. *See* Dual
  Language
Tyack, D. B., 92–93

United Nations, on language rights of
  minority groups, 84–85
U.S. Census Bureau, vii, xiii, 5, 10–12, 19,
  69
U.S. Department of Education, 2, 5, 6, 16,
  20, 88–89, 162–168
U.S. Government Accounting Office, 39
University of California, Berkeley, 106–
  107
University of California Task Force on
  Latino Student Eligibility, 164
Unz, Ron, xiii

Valadez, C., 35
Valdés, G., x, 18, 48, 50, 57, 58, 157
Valdés, R., 58, 60
Valencia, R., 86
Valenzuela, A., 91, 92, 166
Van Patten, B., 53
Veltman, C., 24
Victim status, 41
Vygotsky, L. S., 31, 32

Waggoner, D., 24, 41–42
Wagner, J., 57
Waldinger, R., 15
Walker, C. L., 103
Walters, J. L., 2–4
Warm Springs Indian Reservation, 35–36
War on Poverty, 93–94
Washington, D.C.
  dialects of, 67
  Oyster Bilingual School, 51, 101
Watahomigie, L. J., 69, 70, 71
We Are All Multiculturalists Now (Glazer),
  16
Wertsch, J. V., 102
West, C., 99
White, J., 53
Wiese, A., 4
Wilbur, R. B., 73
Wilson, W. J., 99
Wolfram, W., 65, 66
Wong Fillmore, L., 27, 35, 54, 55–56, 59

Writing development, 124–136
  in academic English development,
    58–60
  assessment tools for, 111–122,
    127–136. *See also* Authentic
    Literacy Assessment System (ALAS)
  conventions in, 126–127, 128, 131
  of deaf and hard-of-hearing students, 71–
    75
  organization in, 125–126, 128, 131

  rubrics for assessing, 114–119, 124–
    127
  student writing samples and, 127–136
  style/voice in, 126, 128, 131
  topic in, 125, 128, 131

Yuen, S. D., 37, 38

Zentella, A. C., 24, 27–29, 37, 38, 57–58,
  164

About the Author

Dr. **Eugene E. García** is Vice President for University–School Partnerships and Dean of the College of Education at Arizona State University. Before joining Arizona State University in 2002, he served as Professor and Dean at the University of California, Berkeley from 1995–2001. He received his B.A. from the University of Utah in Psychology and his Ph.D. in Human Development from the University of Kansas. He has served previously as a national research center director, an academic department chair on two occasions, and as dean of a large Social Sciences Division in the University of California.

He has published extensively in the area of language teaching and bilingual development authoring and/or co-authoring over 150 articles and book chapters along with 17 books and monographs. He holds leadership positions in professional organizations and continues to serve in an editorial capacity for psychological, linguistic, and educational journals. He served as a Senior Officer in the U.S. Department of Education from 1993–1995. He is conducting research in the areas of effective schooling for linguistically and culturally diverse student populations.